INDIA'S N

INDIA'S MOMENT

CHANGING POWER EQUATIONS
AROUND THE WORLD

MOHAN KUMAR

HarperCollins *Publishers* India

First published in India by HarperCollins *Publishers* 2023
4th Floor, Tower A, Building No. 10, DLF Cyber City,
DLF Phase II, Gurugram, Haryana – 122002
www.harpercollins.co.in

2 4 6 8 10 9 7 5 3 1

P-ISBN: 978-93-5699-952-7
E-ISBN: 978-93-5699-879-7

Typeset in 10.5/15 Sabon LT Std at
Manipal Technologies Limited, Manipal

Printed and bound at
Replika Press Pvt. Ltd.

MIX
Paper from
responsible sources
FSC® C016779

This book is produced from independently certified FSC® paper to ensure
responsible forest management.

To

My late parents, Radha and S. V. Vaidyanath,
who taught me the most valuable lessons in life

The detailed notes pertaining to this book are available on the HarperCollins *Publishers* India website. Scan this QR code to access the same.

Contents

Introduction

India's interest and engagement with the world can be traced back to pre-Independence days. Indeed, India's representation and participation at the Paris Peace Conference in 1919 bears special mention. It may surprise many to know that the Maharaja of the Indian princely state of Bikaner was a signatory to the Treaty of Versailles, a multilateral treaty that was profoundly impactful in global affairs. The invitation and participation of the Maharaja of Bikaner was, of course, primarily due to the contribution of India to the Allied cause in World War I, which saw as many as a million Indian soldiers participating in the war and as many as 75,000 of them laying down their lives.

India's involvement in World War I and its independent representation at the Paris Peace Conference in Versailles, had implications for its subsequent entry into the League of Nations. Originally, the membership of the League of Nations was to be restricted to 'self-governing' countries, but clearly an exception was made in the case of India. Indeed, of the original thirty-one founding members of the League of Nations, all were 'self-governing' except India. It is worth noting that the decision to admit India as an original member of the League of Nations led to its subsequent admission to the International Labour Organization (ILO), the Permanent Court of International Justice (PCIJ) and other League organizations. This meant that India secured representation at almost every international conference, such as the Hague Reparations Conference and the World Disarmament Conference, to cite just two.

The San Francisco Conference in 1945, which followed the Dumbarton Oaks plan of 1944, had both British and Indian participation. The Indian delegation led by Sir Ramaswamy Mudaliar, while coordinating with the British delegation, certainly made a substantive contribution to the discussions on the UN Charter. At the third plenary session of the conference in April 1945, Sir Ramaswamy Mudaliar emphasized the need to think in terms of interdependence rather than independence of nations; to look at the causes of economic and social injustice that lead to aggression; and to the fundamental human rights of all living beings, without any distinction based on colour, creed, country or race. Subsequently, these were to become the mantra for independent India's participation in the United Nations (UN).

While only sovereign countries were expected to become members of the newly established UN in 1945, four countries were exceptions to this rule—Belarus, Philippines, Ukraine and of course, India. They were not independent at the time of their admission to the UN. Indeed, India signed the declaration of the UN on 1 January 1942, and since it was a good five years before its independence, it was signed by the Indian Agent-General, Sir Girija Shankar Bajpai. Subsequently, India also signed the UN Charter in San Francisco in June 1945. Strictly speaking, therefore, India was a founding member of the UN in 1945 even while it was a British colony.

In a similar vein, an Indian delegation had taken active part in the United Nations Monetary and Financial Conference held in Bretton Woods, New Hampshire, in 1944. The delegation comprised A.D. Shroff and Shanmukham Chetty. As with the UN above, India participated in the Bretton Woods Conference and articulated its concerns even before it became independent. Once again, the backdrop to India's participation in the Bretton Woods Conference was its contribution to World War II and its role in the global economy at the time. As for the General Agreement on Tariffs and Trade (GATT), the conference took place in October 1947 so independent India took part in it as a founding member. This is despite the fact that India was not a big trading power at the time, having just emerged from the colonial yoke.

One more factor that played a decisive part in India's commitment to multilateralism and international negotiations, was India's first Prime Minister (PM), Jawaharlal Nehru. Nehru had great respect for the ideals and principles of the UN. Indeed, he had so much faith in the UN that he often felt that without the UN, the world would be all the poorer for it and even dangerous. It is fair to say that no developing country leader at the time demonstrated greater faith and allegiance to the UN and multilateralism than Jawaharlal Nehru.

The Indian Constitution also enjoins the State to practice multilateralism through participation in international negotiations. Article 51 of the Indian Constitution states, 'The State shall endeavour to: (a) promote international peace and security;' and '(c) foster respect for international law and treaty obligations ... '. It adds for good measure that settlement of international disputes should be by arbitration. This too was the world view of independent India. It is therefore easy to understand India's commitment to multilateralism and international negotiations.

This book has five chapters, which are described below.

Chapter 1 deals with the establishment of an Integrated Framework for assessing India's actions in the realm of diplomatic negotiations. This framework is unique to India and it is important to understand this fully in order to make sense of how India deals with the world. For instance, acquiring policy space or the impact of domestic politics may be easy to comprehend, as is the case with geopolitical imperatives. But the 'Gandhi Litmus Test' is all too unique to India and is directly related to the vast number of people who live in abject poverty. And given the nature of demography and democracy in India, the Gandhi Litmus Test trumps every other consideration, almost all the time. The interesting hypothesis offered in this regard is that the more the number of people in poverty dipped post-1991 (onset of reforms), the more India became a stakeholder in international negotiations and a key strategic partner to the world.

The comparison between the Uruguay Round of trade negotiations in 1986 and the Doha Round in 2001 at the WTO, demonstrates this evolution. Even more dramatic is the evolution of India's position in climate change negotiations, which concluded in an Accord in Paris in 2015 and more recently, the negotiations at Sharm El-Sheikh in 2022 at the twenty-seventh Conference of the Parties (COP27) of the UN Framework Convention on Climate Change (UNFCCC). The book thus proposes an Integrated Assessment Framework of India's negotiating stand in international fora, outlining six criteria: the Gandhi Litmus Test, the need for policy space, influence of domestic politics, geopolitical imperatives at play, commitment to multilateralism/principles and finally, realpolitik/material gain. This framework is then applied to three different international negotiations in which India participated: WTO, Climate Change and the war in Ukraine.

Chapter 2 deals with India's stand in negotiations, first at GATT and subsequently at WTO over a period of time. It was at WTO that India developed the infamous reputation of being a naysayer. What tends to be overlooked is that India did make valiant attempts from time to time, to establish a positive negotiating agenda in WTO. This did not get the traction it deserved from the major players. Thus, three years after the entry into WTO in 1995, India and other like-minded countries conceived of a positive agenda that they termed 'Implementation'—referring to concrete problems that arose for developing and least-developed countries during the implementation of the results of the Uruguay Round.

Second, India singlehandedly set up a negotiating group for Mode 4 (Movement of Natural Persons) under the General Agreement on Trade in Services (GATS) and asked developed countries to engage in negotiations. Third, India along with the European Union (EU), wanted additional protection for Geographical Indications (GIs) for products other than wines and spirits, which again was a positive move to launch negotiations in this area. Last, but not least, India also wanted negotiations in the field of public stockholding (in agriculture), so that developing and least-developed countries could achieve legitimate goals related to their food security.

All of the above militates against the accusation that India was merely a naysayer at WTO; indeed, the above were serious attempts by India and some others to become responsible stakeholders in the multilateral trading system. Alas, all of it came to nought, primarily because developed countries simply showed no political will to engage in these negotiations. This book is an attempt to set the record straight on India's role in negotiations at WTO.

Chapter 2 also looks at why India has been averse to the launch of negotiations in certain new areas—such as investment, e-commerce, trade and public health—even though a majority of WTO members prefer to commence and conclude negotiations in these areas. While explaining the reasons behind India's reluctance to enter into these negotiations, the chapter raises questions as to whether this is necessarily the right approach. India has currently embarked on a series of free trade agreements (FTAs) with the EU, the United Kingdom (UK), Australia, the United Arab Emirates (UAE), Israel and Canada. Does this signal a weakening of India's commitment to the multilateral trading system? Or is it a case of following the herd? I have coined the term 'poverty veto' to describe the enormous impact—of some 500 million people living in poverty—on India's stand in trade and other negotiations. The WTO negotiations are a perfect example where the Gandhi Litmus Test and the need for policy space hold great sway in India's negotiating position.

Chapter 3 deals with the existentially important subject of climate change negotiations. If there is one area where the evolution of India—from being a passive onlooker to a strategic stakeholder—is clear beyond any reasonable doubt, it is with regard to climate change. Indira Gandhi's famously rhetorical question, 'Are not poverty and need the greatest polluters?', at the 1972 UN Conference on the Human Environment held in Stockholm, must be the starting point for anyone assessing India's position in climate change negotiations. Indeed, the statement left such a strong imprint that for a long time India's main objective in these negotiations was to preserve maximum policy space for its own economic development.

At Rio in 1992, India negotiated hard for the acceptance of the principle 'common but differentiated responsibilities' (CBDR) making it abundantly clear that developing countries were not expected to take on commitments inconsistent with their development needs. India argued then that it had no legal responsibility whatsoever to address climate change; in fact, it was for the developed countries to give additional financial resources and assured access to technology on preferential terms to developing countries so that they could deal with climate change caused primarily by developed countries.

Crucially, the UNFCC (agreed upon at Rio) recognized that the obligations and treatment of developed and developing countries were fundamentally different. The chapter goes on to trace the failed saga of the Kyoto Protocol following the decision by the United States (US) not to ratify it in 2001. In 2007, India made a remarkable show of flexibility when former PM Manmohan Singh said India's per capita greenhouse gas (GHG) emissions would never exceed those of developed countries.[1] The period post-2007 was a period of bitter contestation, when developed countries stated unambiguously that developing countries like China and India had to step up to the plate since they were on track to become huge emitters of GHGs in the future.

Chapter 3 also reveals how by 2012 the firewall of CBDR, assiduously built by India and others, was breached and a legal instrument was being thought of which would be applicable to all parties, both developed and developing. India, which was part of the Brazil, South Africa, India and China (BASIC) grouping, fought back on the issue of CBDR but the compromise in 2014 was that the CBDR would be 'in light of different national circumstances'. The role of India at the climate change negotiations in 2015 was critical, and in my view cemented India's transition from being seen as a naysayer to establishing itself as a strategic stakeholder and a solution provider. This was clearly evident in the lead role it assumed in the launch of the International Solar Alliance (ISA) at Paris in 2015. More recently at COP27 in Sharm El-Sheikh in November 2022, India again demonstrated leadership through its actions. This is perhaps the most definitive sign that India's transformation in the way it approaches international negotiations is well under way.

This is not to underestimate the challenges faced by India. For one thing, India is the only major country being asked to scrupulously follow a 'low carbon' pathway to development. The developed countries have all followed a pathway to development that involved burning coal and emitting huge amounts of GHGs. China has followed suit and presently accounts for more than 50 per cent of the world's coal consumption, but India alone is asked to follow a low-carbon pathway. It therefore becomes incumbent on the richer countries to not only assist India financially, but also to transfer green technology on favourable terms. India is absolutely right in making both its nationally determined contribution (NDC) and its net zero commitment (by 2070) contingent on availability of climate finance and accessibility to green technology.

Chapter 4 tackles another international hot potato—the case of the war in Ukraine—and offers an assessment of how well India's foreign policy has held up as of 2023 (as this book goes to print). The Russian intervention in Ukraine posed a huge strategic dilemma for India, as Russia is a close strategic partner and a nation that had stood by India in its most difficult moments in the past. Simultaneously, and to put it bluntly, there is no question that the sovereignty and territorial integrity of Ukraine has been violated. It is a tribute to the agility, nimbleness and ingenuity of India's foreign policy formulated and executed by the Prime Minister and the external affairs minister, that the country finds itself in a situation where: it can talk to all the sides in the conflict; its strategic partnership with all the major powers is intact; and its own national interests have not been compromised. The negotiations that India has conducted, not just with Russia but also with the US and others, have followed the basic criteria outlined in the Integrated Assessment Framework presented in this book, and tick most, if not all the boxes contained therein.

India's stand not to condemn Russia for its invasion of Ukraine came under a lot of fire from its partners in the West, especially the

US but also the EU and others. How India navigated this situation shrewdly through negotiations while subtly shifting its stand, is a stellar example of agility and firmness in the execution of foreign and security policy. It would be no exaggeration to say that this has turned out to be the crowning moment of India's foreign policy, based on multi-alignment and engagement with all while at the same time protecting its vital, national interests.

Chapter 5 provides a summary review of the subtle transformation of India in international negotiations, using the Integrated Assessment Framework crafted for the purpose. Obviously, this has occurred as India's own stock in the world has risen. It is also true that as India's gross domestic product (GDP) has risen and more crucially, as the percentage of Indians living in poverty has reduced (not the absolute number, which has risen), it has given more latitude to the government and the negotiators to approach the world of international negotiations differently. The 'poverty veto' continues to play a critical role, but hopefully this will matter less and less in future negotiations for India.

Quite simply, the stakes for India in future negotiations are enormous. The question really is whether India can make the full transition from being a rule-taker to a rule-shaper in international negotiations. It may be argued that what we are seeing—in the Quad (the Quadrilateral Security Dialogue comprising India, Japan, Australia and the US), the trilaterals and mini-laterals in the Indo-Pacific, the Coalition for Disaster Resilient Infrastructure (CDRI), the Global Green Hydrogen Coalition, etc.—are all incipient attempts by India to become a rule-shaper in developing regional/international architecture for achieving its own strategic objectives. There are a few related questions: Has the pandemic put a brake on the government's margin for manoeuvre to deal with the world? How has the war in Ukraine affected India's strategic autonomy? And finally, if the war continues indefinitely or ends in ways not conceivable, what adjustments should India make to its foreign and security policy?

The book concludes by arguing that India's ambitions, influence and margin for manoeuvre in negotiating with the rest of the world rests substantially, if not solely, on its economic and military clout. However, two factors above all will determine when India becomes a leading power with the ability to negotiate with the world from a position of strength: one, how soon it becomes, say, a $10 trillion economy; and, two how soon it brings down the number of people living in poverty to about 10 per cent of its total population (as opposed to 35 per cent now).

1

An Integrated Assessment Framework for India's Stand in International Negotiations

1.1 Background

At one level, the way India negotiates with the world is not substantially different from that of other countries. Simply put, the main purpose of international negotiations is to advance the national interest of a country through a process of give and take involving many players. The raison d'être for international negotiations is also obvious: there are global issues such as trade, climate change and matters of war and peace, which cannot be tackled by any one country alone, and hence require multilateral cooperation among all international stakeholders.

The real question, therefore, is how countries go about perceiving, understanding and defining their national interest. In India's case, this becomes devilishly complex since it is a rough-and-tumble

1

democracy with many stakeholders whose interests may not just differ from one another, but may also come into direct conflict. It then devolves on the government to reconcile these different viewpoints and arrive at a common negotiating position. This is no easy task and there have been occasions when the government has had to approach negotiations with a constantly evolving brief.

It is also worth noting in the Indian context that the outcome of negotiations must invariably be reported to the Parliament, especially if a domestic law must be enacted and/or amended to give effect to international obligations. Indeed, according to Article 253 of the Indian Constitution, the Parliament has the power to enact any law for implementing any international treaty, agreement or convention. However, the Parliament has not provided explicit guidance either in the matter of signing international treaties or agreements, or with regard to their implementation. This lacuna provides the executive in India almost unfettered power to sign an international treaty, agreement or convention by virtue of Article 73 of the Constitution, which authorizes the government to make decisions in matters where the Parliament has the power to make laws to give effect to international treaties.[1] This also explains why the Government of India does not seek prior authorization from the Parliament before signing international treaties, agreements or conventions; indeed, it is not even obliged to approach the Parliament after signing an international treaty unless it involves implementing/amending domestic law to give effect to the treaty so signed.

This is markedly different from the practice prevalent in the US where the President is empowered by and with the advice and consent of the Senate, to make international treaties. In the case of trade agreements, the US President therefore needs authority from the Senate; in other cases, the American Senate comes into the picture after the President has signed the treaty. It is evident that India has followed the British tradition, where the making of a treaty is an executive act, while the performance of its obligations, if they entail alteration/implementation of existing domestic law, requires legislative action.[2] While the government in India thus has enormous leeway in the matter of signing international treaties, the task of arriving at a basic, common negotiating brief is anything but simple. As the narrative below will show, various factors and different interests intersect to constitute a variable geometry, which makes the task of the Government of India exceptionally difficult.

1.2 The Gandhi Litmus Test

The most fundamental factor shaping India's position in negotiating with the world is what I choose to call the Gandhi Litmus Test. This is based on what Mahatma Gandhi conveyed by way of advice to policy and decision makers. Because this is crucial to the Integrated Assessment Framework, within which India's actions will be assessed in international negotiations, I quote the Mahatma in full:

> I will give you a talisman. Whenever you are in doubt or when the self becomes too much with you, apply the following test:
> Recall the face of the poorest and the weakest man whom you may have seen and ask yourself if the step you contemplate is going to be of any use to him. Will he gain anything by it? Will it restore him to a control over his own life and destiny? In other words, will it lead to Swaraj for the hungry and spiritually starving millions?
> Then you will find your doubts and your self melting away.[3]

It is thus axiomatic to assume that when India approaches international negotiations and deals with the outside world, the one fundamental factor it has uppermost in mind is the potential impact of the negotiating outcome on the millions of people who live in poverty. Since this is crucial in understanding India's negotiating stand, certain important questions must be addressed. What is definition of poverty and how many people in India can legitimately be considered as living in poverty? What are their existential interests, both economic and social? Since it is not always possible to implement the Gandhi Litmus Test in toto, is it possible to tweak it a little by making it akin to the Hippocratic Oath that medical doctors are required to take—first and foremost, do no harm to the patient? The patients in this case are the millions who live in poverty. Translated in the present context, it would mean that whatever obligations the government assumes through international negotiations, it cannot lead to a situation that leaves these millions living in poverty, worse-off than before. This then is the biggest determining factor for all governments in India when they approach international negotiations. I wish to term this the 'poverty veto', which comes into play in most, if not all, of India's international negotiations.

It may be useful to begin with an acceptable definition of extreme poverty. On the website of the World Bank, its former President Robert McNamara is quoted as describing extreme poverty as 'a condition so limited by malnutrition, illiteracy, disease, squalid surroundings, high infant mortality and low life expectancy as to be beneath any reasonable definition of human decency'.[4] In 1995, the UN Report of the World Summit for Social Development echoed the above definition of extreme poverty as a condition characterized by severe deprivation of basic human needs including food, safe drinking water, sanitation facilities, health, shelter, education and information. The World Bank subsequently monetized extreme poverty at $1.90 per person per day (at 2011 purchasing power parity),[5] and although this is not a perfect measure, it has stuck and is useful for assessing what is admittedly a complex issue. In September 2022, the World Bank revised this to $2.15 per person per day (at 2017 purchasing power parity). This then is the criterion for extreme poverty.

In 2010, the concept of the global Multidimensional Poverty Index (MPI) was developed through a collaboration between the

UN Development Programme (UNDP) and the Oxford Poverty and Human Development Initiative (OPHI). The global MPI is an international measure of acute multidimensional poverty covering over 100 developing countries. It complements traditional monetary poverty measures by capturing acute deprivations in health, education and living standards that a person faces simultaneously.[6] We will therefore be largely relying on one or more of the above for assessing the evolution of extreme poverty in India, from the early nineties till the present.

It is well recognized that extreme poverty levels really started declining in India only in the late nineties. This should come as no surprise since it was only in 1991 that India embarked on serious economic reforms by doing away with the 'licence raj'. The question as to how many Indians lived in extreme poverty in the early nineties is not easy to determine. But one way to look at the evolution is the chart taken from 'Poverty in India' (Wikipedia),[7] which is reproduced below.

Figure 1.1: Poverty Rates, India in 1993, 2004, 2009 and 2011

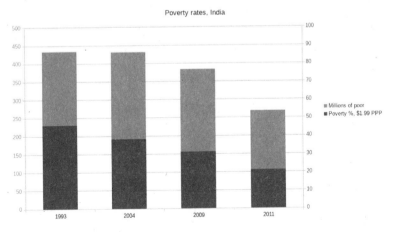

Source: 'Poverty in India' from Wikipedia.

The poverty chart for India since the nineties is revealing. The population of India in 1993 was 927 million and going by the chart there were as many as 440 million living in extreme poverty, i.e., 48 per cent of the population. In 2004, the population of India was 1.12 billion and roughly the same number as in 1993 (440 million) were living in extreme poverty. But then the percentage dropped marginally to a little under 40 per cent, because of the increase in the population. Under this measure (which is purely monetary), by 2011 the numbers living in extreme poverty were down to 275 million (population 1.2 billion) and the percentage also dropped to under 25 per cent, for the first time since Independence.

Beginning 2010, however, a consensus emerged that a monetary measure such as $1.90 per person, per day, simply did not do justice to the complex issue of measuring extreme poverty. Hence, it was the global MPI that complemented the $1.90 criterion with crucial factors such as Health, Education and Living Standards. In the context of India, this was a quantum jump in the criteria for measuring poverty. The MPI has detailed indicators under Health, Education and Living Standards.[8] Thus, under Health come sub-criteria such as nutrition and child mortality. Similarly, under Education, weightage is given to years of schooling and school attendance. Under Living Standards, are indicators such as cooking fuel, sanitation, drinking water, housing and household assets. It is immediately obvious that this is a much more credible measure of extreme poverty than the one that stops at just $1.90 per day, per person. It is by using the MPI as a measure that one can appreciate the progress made by India in reducing the incidence of extreme poverty.

Thus, the global MPI report 2018,[9] states categorically that between the period 2005/06–2015/16 India brought down the extreme poverty rate from something like 55 per cent of the population to 28 per cent. In other words, there were 635 million Indians living in extreme poverty in 2005–06 and this was brought down to 364 million Indians by 2015–16. Described as monumental progress, this achievement was arguably only second to that of China. By some estimates, China has been able to bring down the people living below extreme poverty from a whopping 60 per cent of the population (1990) to a figure as low as 16 per cent (2010).[10]

The fact remains that at this time the largest number of people living in poverty live in India—almost 35 per cent of the population. This was confirmed by the report from NITI Aayog prepared on the basis of National Family Health Survey (NFHS)-4 conducted in 2015–16.[11] This was the first ever report in India using the MPI, in line with the globally accepted and robust methodology developed by OPHI and the UNDP, who in fact were partners of the NITI Aayog in this effort. This first-ever report by NITI Aayog revealed that one in four persons were multidimensionally poor in India. Considering that this report was prepared on the basis of the 2015–16 figures (when India's population was estimated at 1.32 billion), the poor approximately number 330 million. It was further corroborated by the MPI for 2021, jointly launched by OPHI and UNDP, that 27.9 per cent of India's population was multidimensionally poor.[12] Given that the population of India in 2021 was estimated at 1.39 billion, this amounts to 392 million multidimensionally poor people. In May 2021, a report by the Azim Premji University stated that as many as 230 million Indians may have been pushed into poverty because of the Covid-19 pandemic.[13] So, at the time of writing, there could be several million people living in multidimensional poverty in India.

But the very latest report of the NITI Aayog on Multidimensional Poverty of July 2023[14] pegs the percentage of people in multidimensional poverty in India at 14.96 per cent for the period 2019–21 as opposed to 24.85 per cent for the period 2015–16. This would mean just 210 million Indians live in multidimensional poverty. But important caveats are in order. One is that it is not clear if the impact of COVID-19 has been fully considered in arriving at this figure. Second, how does one square this with so many other reports? Third, how does one square this with as many as 800 million people availing themselves of benefits from the Pradhan Mantri Garib Kalyan Yojana? As Bibek Debroy points out presciently[15], the above Yojana implementation means 75 per cent of rural India and 50 per cent of urban India gets subsidized food. In fact, he makes the point that the National Food Security Act needs amendment if we all agree that 800 million poor people in India is a gross overestimate. The bigger problem, though, is that there are no NSSO (National Sample Survey Office) head count figures on consumption expenditure after 2011–12. Indeed, a census due in 2021 is pending. This is a serious drawback. Besides, the Multidimensional Poverty Index includes not just living standards but also health and education. But as Bibek Debroy points out, it is living standards that reflect poverty much more accurately than the other two. The latest Multidimensional Poverty Index, therefore, has the unintended effect of diluting the physical and real poverty in which Indians may be living in. This may be the reason for the sharp reduction in poverty figures in the NITI Aayog report of July 2023. The report by Arvind Panagariya and Vishal More (2023) that 26.90 per cent of the population, or 372 million people, lived in poverty in India seems to have a more rational basis. This most recent exercise in poverty estimation was conducted by Columbia University economist Arvind Panagariya and Vishal More, an

economist and financial researcher with Intelink Advisors in New
Delhi, using consumption data gathered as part of the Periodic
Labour Force Survey (PLFS). They found that the number of
people below the Tendulkar poverty line fell in 2020–21 to 26.90
per cent. We will therefore take good note of the figure of 372
million (about 27 per cent of the population), knowing fully well
that this is an estimate in the absence of consumption expenditure
figures after 2001–12 and a pending census. The figure of 372
million is also based on the periodic labour force survey, which too
has some drawbacks. A survey, by definition, based on a sample
is less reliable than a census based on headcount. The World
Bank's India-Macro Poverty Outlook (MPO) 2021/22[16] states
that 40 per cent of the population still lives below the poverty
line, admittedly used in lower-middle income countries (India is
classified as the biggest lower-middle income country by the World
Bank), i.e., $3.65 per capita (2017 ppp).[17] It is my contention that
this is the criterion India should be using, since it is technically a
low-middle income country. This would lead to 560 million poor
people in India, which is then adjusted for 2023 to arrive at a
ballpark figure of 500 million poor people. This adjustment is
admittedly arbitrary but necessitated by the fact that the figure
of $2.15 relates to extreme poverty and will therefore be too low,
and the figure of $3.65 relates to moderate poverty and may be
on the higher side for a country like India. A figure of $3.00 per
person per head is broadly in line with MGNREGA wages, and if
taken as the yardstick, it would lead to a figure of approximately
500 million people in India living in poverty as of 2023. This will
then be the criterion used in this book, rather than people living in
extreme and/or multidimensional poverty.

For the purpose of examining India's role in international
negotiations, the point to note is that from about 2005 onwards

there has been a significant reduction in the rate of extreme poverty in India, a trend that continued till Covid-19 struck. My central contention is that it is precisely during this period that India attained enough flexibility to approach international negotiations as a responsible stakeholder. The crucial inference, therefore, is this: being a naysayer or a stakeholder in international negotiations is not a preconceived matter of policy choice, it is governed by the domestic economic and social situation and is linked substantially, if not wholly, to the application of the Gandhi Litmus Test in India. The poverty veto, therefore, is a real factor for India in international negotiations.

The situation is complicated by another factor. As opposed to other major players involved in international negotiations, India is perhaps the only major player that does not have a social safety net for its poor. This, combined with the fact that we still have large numbers living in multidimensional poverty, makes the task of the government difficult in approaching international negotiations. Since a comprehensive social safety net in India is next to impossible for the foreseeable future, the government has gradually introduced schemes to meet some of the most basic economic and social needs of the millions living in extreme poverty.

The first in this genre was the National Rural Employment Guarantee Act (NREGA) of 2005 (renamed as the Mahatma Gandhi National Rural Employment Guarantee Act or MGNREGA in 2009). Its main objective was to enhance livelihood security in rural areas by providing at least 100 days of guaranteed wage employment in a financial year to every household whose adult members volunteered to do unskilled manual work.[18] The goal was indeed to have a strong social safety net for the vulnerable groups.[19] As many as 111 million households benefited annually in 2022 from the scheme.[20]

In 2009, the government also enacted a legislation known as Right of Children to Free and Compulsory Education (RTE) Act. This Act empowers every Indian child's right to full-time elementary education of satisfactory and equitable quality in a formal school that satisfies certain essential norms and standards.[21] In 2013, the Government of India enacted the National Food Security Act. It marked a paradigm shift in the approach to food security, from welfare to a rights-based approach. The Act legally entitles 75 per cent of the rural population and 50 per cent of the urban population to receive subsidized food grains under the targeted public distribution system.[22] In 2017, the PM launched an initiative called 'Ayushman Bharat' or 'Healthy India' in order to achieve the vision of universal health coverage.[23] This ambitious scheme aims to cover as many as 500 million Indians, providing an insurance cover of up to Rs 500,000 per annum per family in a year.

The above list is not comprehensive, but illustrative. It may also be noted that the above programmes are all works in progress, but notice the timelines—they all fall between 2005 and the present (2023). This is no coincidence, since a comprehensive attempt was made by the government during this period to tackle multidimensional poverty in India. This period from 2005 till 2019 was also characterized by high GDP growth in India, falling below 5 per cent only in 2008 when the 'Great Recession', the global financial crisis of 2008, intervened. All in all, the environment was conducive for the government to play the role of a responsible partner in international negotiations.

The question of relying on an income pyramid in India is a difficult one, because of the size of the country, the diversity and the inherent difficulties of the sample size. Be that as it may, reproduced below is an income pyramid for 2010 drawn up by the

Centre for Macro Consumer Research (CMCR) which is part of the National Council of Applied Economic Research (NCAER).

Figure 1.2: Indian Income Pyramid (2010)

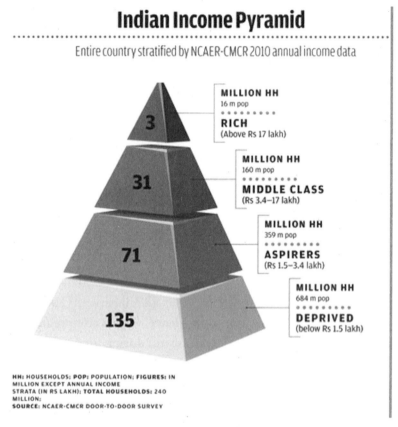

Source: NCAER-CMCR Door-to-Door Survey

For the sake of convenience and following the above pyramid, three broad income categories may be identified. (i) At the bottom of the pyramid are 684 million Indians who, in 2010, were in the 'deprived' category; in 2010 our population was 1.15 billion. Today, not just the global MPI but also the situation during and post-Covid has resulted in at least 500 million persons living in poverty (as we saw earlier). For the purposes of the Gandhi Litmus Test, the well-being and interest of these 500 million Indians trumps the rest in any international negotiations. (ii) Next, Figure 1.1 describes the 'aspirers'. The 359 million Indians who fell under this category in 2010 would be considered lower middle class in global parlance. (iii) Figure 1.1 places the rest of the population in the top two tiers of the pyramid, i.e., the middle class, and the rich, both of which comprised about 176 million people in 2010.

If the Government of India prepares a brief for multilateral trade negotiations at the WTO, it should be obvious the category that would have a veto power over the rest is the one that is at the bottom of the pyramid today, i.e., the 500 million who live in poverty without a safety net. It is only if the potential effect of the negotiating outcome on this category is positive or at the very least neutral, that the government can think of its possible impact on the next category above it, described in Figure 1.1 as 'aspirers'. It is only if the negotiating impact on both these categories is either positive or neutral, that one can look at whether international negotiations can be of some benefit to the categories at the top of the pyramid and therefore acceptable to India.

Let us consider two examples that we will examine in greater detail later in the book. One, the question of signing the Trade-Related Intellectual Property Rights (TRIPS) Agreement in the WTO, which was controversial particularly because of the anticipated increase in cost of non-generic and patented drugs, resulting in the 500 million people living in poverty having had no access at all to basic drugs. Two, commitments made by the government after the climate change negotiations in Paris on the other hand, would be beneficial for the country as a whole, even to the poorest citizens since they are often the most vulnerable to climate change.

The incontrovertible conclusion is this: India's naysaying or otherwise when dealing with the world in international negotiations has much more to do with the Gandhi Litmus Test than with any preconceived negotiating strategy to either accept or oppose an emerging international consensus. This poverty veto then is crucial in understanding India's negotiating stand. The more pertinent question is whether this development, namely a whopping number of 500 million who are poor, will constrain India in a post-Covid world.

1.3 Need for Policy Space

The role of national policies in economic development has been a subject of intense debate. The specific concept of 'policy space'— the second parameter of the Integrated Assessment Framework— focuses on the tension between international economic integration and the autonomy available to nation states, to pursue policies that effectively support their economic development.[20]

The best definition of policy space may be found in the *UNCTAD Trade and Development Report (2014)* with the theme: Global governance and policy space for development.[25] It defines policy space as the freedom and ability of governments to identify and pursue the most appropriate mix of economic and social policies to achieve equitable and sustainable development in their own national contexts, but as constituent parts of an interdependent global economy.[26] It also argues quite convincingly that States must decide on whether and how much of their own independence they are willing to barter for the advantages of having international rules and disciplines. In a world of unequal States, the UNCTAD report notes that the policy space required to pursue national economic and social development goals varies, as does the likely impact of an individual country's policy decisions on others.

The report also avers that the challenges of managing these trade-offs are particularly pronounced at the international, multilateral level, where the differences among States are significant—a fact particularly relevant for this book.[27]

Speaking of differences among States being significant, the only way to describe India is that it is unique and thus sui generis. There is no question that we are a developing and an emerging country, but parts of India could also be considered least developed. This should not come as a great surprise to anyone. After all, in the Human Development Index rankings (2022), India ranks a lowly 132, with Bhutan and Bangladesh, both characterized as Least-Developed Countries, coming ahead at 127 and 129[28]. It is no one's argument that India qualifies as a Least-Developed Country in the classic sense. But there is little doubt that given the vast disparities that exist in a continent-sized country, parts of India are so underdeveloped that they resemble a least-developed country. The fact that India displays features of a least developed, developing and emerging country all rolled into one makes the country sui generis and consequently the task of the government difficult, when dealing with the world in international negotiations.

Throughout the eighties it was de rigueur to let developing countries know about the unlimited virtues of the 'Washington Consensus'—a term coined by British economist John Williamson, referring to a set of free-market economic policies espoused by prominent institutions such as the IMF, the World Bank and the US Treasury.[29] Specifically prescribed for Latin American countries, and later recommended for others, it called on countries to selectively shrink the role of the State and simultaneously expand the role of market forces. More generally, it was also prescribed for those countries wishing to secure loans from the IMF. The policy measures comprised reducing fiscal deficits, tax reform, free-floating currency exchange rates, removing tariff barriers, liberalizing foreign investment and privatization of state enterprises. India did not subscribe to the Washington Consensus at the time, and for good reason. Nevertheless, some of the fundamental assumptions of the Uruguay Round of Trade Negotiations at GATT and later at WTO meetings, were based on the Washington Consensus.

The aspect of significantly shrinking the role of the State inherent in the Washington Consensus, and which constituted the basic tenet of the Uruguay Round, would have meant a significant erosion of policy space for countries like India. Hence India strongly opposed the inclusion of subjects such as 'Services' and 'Intellectual Property Rights' (IPR) in the mandate of the Uruguay Round at Punta del Este in 1986.[30] With more than 50 per cent of the population living in poverty, there was no way the Government of India in 1986 could have voluntarily given up policy space when negotiating in the multilateral trading system.

In a similar vein, the Earth Summit in 1992 saw India, along with other developing countries, insist on 'Common but Differentiated Responsibilities' as part of Principle 7 of the Rio Declaration on Environment and Development.[31] Simply put, CBDR is a principle of international law that means different countries have different capabilities and responsibilities to address cross-border environmental issues such as climate change. It recognizes the fact that not all countries are equally responsible for the problem of climate change, nor equally capable of resolving it. Strong espousal of this principle in the climate change negotiations was, again, an attempt by the Government of India to retain maximum policy space for pursuing its economic and social development goals, even while subscribing to the principle of sustainable development.

Indeed, it was this justified obsession with policy space that made India and other developing countries push, as far back as 1979 in GATT, for a 'Decision on Differential and More Favourable Treatment, Reciprocity and Fuller Participation of Developing Countries'.[32] The main outcome of this decision reaffirmed sufficient policy space for developing countries thus:

The developed countries do not expect reciprocity for commitments made by them in trade negotiations to reduce or remove tariffs and other barriers to the trade of developing countries, i.e., the developed countries do not expect the developing countries, in the course of trade negotiations, to make contributions inconsistent with their individual development, financial and trade needs.[33]

This became the famous 'Special and Differential Treatment' clause (S&D) in GATT and then in WTO. In GATT and WTO law, S&D Treatment is explicitly recognized as a legally acceptable waiver from the all-encompassing Article 1, which deals with the Most Favoured Nation (MFN) Treatment. One of the most important outcomes of this treatment for developing countries is that almost all WTO Agreements emanating from the Uruguay Round have accepted S&D Treatment, one way or the other.

In practical terms, this provides a longer transition period for developing countries for implementing WTO obligations. For instance, in the case of the TRIPS Agreement, developing countries have ten years as opposed to the five years available for developed countries to implement in full, the obligations arising out of this Agreement.[34] The extra time given may also be considered as policy space, for adjusting to the new and onerous obligations imposed by the WTO's TRIPS Agreement.

India's refusal to sign the Treaty on the Non-Proliferation of Nuclear Weapons (NPT), despite enormous pressure, may also be considered a means of retaining policy space to go nuclear at a

later date, which India subsequently did in 1998. As pointed out
by experts Jayita Sarkar and Sumit Ganguly, the grand bargain of
the NPT for non-nuclear weapon states, i.e., Article II (acquisition
of nuclear weapons) to be permanently forfeited for Article IV
(inalienable right to avail peaceful uses of nuclear energy), would
have severely constricted India's policy space and hence was
considered unacceptable by India.[35]

Again, when it came to the matter of customs tariffs, India is
consciously known to preserve a gap between bound tariffs (the
limit beyond which tariffs cannot be raised) and applied tariffs
(the level currently applied and in force). Thus, applied tariffs
may be much lower than the bound tariffs, which then provides
policy space to the government by way of flexibility to increase
the tariffs for either protection of domestic industry or for revenue
collection purposes, without violating WTO obligations that are
directly linked to bound tariffs. The WTO data for 2017 indicates
that while the average bound tariff of India for non-agricultural
products was 48.5 per cent, the average applied tariff for the same
was only 13.8 per cent. In the Central government's 2019 Budget,
the finance minister raised customs duties (tariffs) on at least
seventy-five items of imports.[36] This would have proved impossible
if India had not retained policy space for itself during the tariff
negotiations at the WTO. As we will see later in the book, India
also chose to exercise the option of buying discounted Russian oil
for the purpose of preserving policy space, since India is highly
dependent on crude oil imports and this commodity alone has
huge implications for the cost of living for poor people in India.

In a complex country such as India—where the government may
need to intervene for either tackling a crisis or an emergency—it
is imperative to retain policy space, which then becomes a mantra
when negotiating with the world.

1.4 Domestic Politics

Like many countries, especially in functioning and noisy democracies, domestic politics plays a crucial role when India negotiates with the world. We have seen earlier that the executive in India enjoys untrammelled power when it comes to signing international treaties or agreements. Be that as it may, there is a vigilant fourth estate and a boisterous Parliament, which eventually does catch up and takes the government to task. Over the last two decades, non-governmental organizations (NGOs) and civil society have become extremely vocal and play an important role in India's political landscape. As will be seen below, they exercise considerable influence in the way India negotiates with the world.

Perhaps the very first time NGOs and civil society in India mobilized themselves strongly was in the aftermath of the so-called 'Draft Dunkel Text' in the context of the Uruguay Round of trade negotiations. The 'Draft Dunkel Text' refers to a text put out by GATT Director General Arthur Dunkel, entirely on his own responsibility in December 1991, to bring the long-standing Uruguay Round negotiations to fruition. To say the text was controversial would be an understatement. India, in particular, had huge issues when it came to specific provisions in the Agreement on TRIPS, the Agreement on Agriculture and in the Agreement on Textiles and Clothing.

By 1993, it became clear that the Dunkel Draft, for the most part, would indeed be the final Uruguay Round Agreement. Indeed, Arthur Dunkel, through a stroke of genius, turned the principle of consensus on its head by saying that if a country wanted to see changes in his draft it would need a consensus from the entire membership to do so, which was next to impossible. The Dunkel Draft united all opposition parties in India and all of them accused the Government of India of a complete 'sell-out'. Although the government set up a committee in 1992 led by then Human Resource Development Minister Arjun Singh to look, inter alia, into it, almost all opposition parties decried the Dunkel Draft.[37]

The Bharatiya Janata Party (BJP), which was the main opposition party at the time, argued that the government did not have the mandate to agree to the draft and that agreeing to the text of the draft would be a total sell-out.[38] In a similar vein, the Communist Party of India (Marxist; CPI-M) said accepting the Dunkel Draft would mean that India would face developmental obstacles, while another opposition party, the Janata Dal (JD), said that if the government persisted in these kind of policies, it (JD) would bring down the government in the forthcoming budget session of the Parliament.[39]

The bastion of left intellectuals, represented by the reputed Indian magazine *Economic and Political Weekly* came up with a devastating critique entitled: 'GATT, the Dunkel Draft and India', dated 25 January 1992.[40] In 1993 there were huge protests by Indian farmers at Red Fort in Delhi against the TRIPS Agreement of the Dunkel Draft.[41] It will thus be seen that a wide coalition of political actors effectively aligned themselves against the government on the question of the famous Dunkel Draft. Arthur Dunkel himself had become a hated figure in India. Indeed, there were stray reports of his effigy being burnt and the Draft Dunkel Text, known by the acronym DDT, was often described as being as toxic as the pesticide by the same acronym!

In 1994, opposition parties once again ganged up on the government of the day to dissuade it from accepting the Dunkel Draft.[42] This tradition has continued since. In 2018, the Swadeshi Jagran Manch (an affiliate of the Rashtriya Swayamsevak Sangh or RSS), which is actually aligned with the ruling BJP, asked the government not to back the Investment Facilitation Agreement for which negotiations were on at the WTO.[43] Suffice it to say that even though the executive has unbridled power to sign international agreements or treaties, there are powerful domestic political interests that influence the government in international negotiations.

While domestic politics tends to be particularly virulent in the matter of international trade negotiations, climate change also invokes passions in India. While civil society in the developed West focuses primarily on conservation and preservation, environmental activism in India often takes the form of 'environmentalism of the poor'.[44] Protest in countries like India is an outcome of the existential crisis faced by the poor and the vulnerable, who are normally dependent on natural resources such as firewood and water. In the beginning, Indian activists were more concerned about challenges of development rather than climate change per se. Still, it is worth noting that unlike in the US, public discourse in India accepts climate change as real and anthropogenic. There are very few, if any, climate deniers in India. The oldest NGO that works in this area is of course The Energy and Resources Institute (TERI), but there are now others such as the Council on Energy, Environment and Water (CEEW) and the Center for Study of Science, Technology and Policy (CSTEP), that focus largely on climate science. There is also a group of NGOs that focus on climate justice.

Climate justice refers to a moral obligation to share the burden of negative impacts of climate change. It may be pointed out that the notion of climate justice is contested and approaches range from historical responsibility or legacy emissions, to per capita emission etc. From this perspective, the Center for Science and Environment (CSE) has worked a lot on climate justice issues. Sunita Narain, the indomitable leader of CSE, was among the first to make a distinction between the survival emissions of the poor and the luxury emissions of the rich. All these institutions, in their own ways, have influenced the government in international negotiations.[45] Indeed, it is as a result of all this that the Government of India has adopted climate justice as the leitmotif of its negotiating strategy.

This is not to say that political parties do not take an interest in how the government of the day approaches climate change negotiations under the auspices of the UN. In fact, domestic politics came into sharp focus prior to the December 2009 Copenhagen Summit on climate change. Ahead of the summit, India announced that it would voluntarily reduce carbon emission intensity by 20 to 25 per cent by 2020 on 2005 levels, through policy measures. This announcement generated fierce debate, with members of Parliament in the upper house, the Rajya Sabha, staging a walk-out.[46] Indeed, the then leader of the Opposition, the late Arun Jaitley, accused the government of unilaterally altering its negotiating stance without consulting the Opposition. Jaitley stated:

India's traditional position in climate change negotiations is that countries with low per capita emissions should have lower mitigation burdens compared with the rich nations that account for most of the stock of greenhouse gases in the atmosphere and should also get financial aid to adopt new low-carbon technologies.[47]

In a frank article much after he laid down office, India's environment minister Jairam Ramesh, says he was attacked by many politicians in India for having executed the mandate given to him by the then PM Manmohan Singh, who directed him to make India part of the solution at Copenhagen.[48] In his book, *Green Signals,* Jairam Ramesh describes the transformation of India's thinking on climate diplomacy and its entire approach to global warming and climate change.[49] So, domestic politics works both ways, it can be challenging on the one hand and on the other, it can lead to significant changes in negotiating positions.

If there is one domain in India where the civil society can be considered marginal and weak, it is in the field of Nuclear Disarmament and Non-Proliferation. Scholar Jayita Sarkar noted in an article in July 2011, that the anti-nuclear movement in India largely remained a marginal movement with sporadic spurts depending on the issue at hand, the nuclear site in question and the political parties involved.[50] India hopes to build thirty-odd nuclear reactors in order to derive a quarter of its electricity needs from nuclear energy by 2050. Following the Indo-US nuclear deal of 2008 allowing international civilian nuclear trade, protest movements had emerged in several sites chosen for the construction of new nuclear power plants. For instance, the biggest nuclear park was contemplated in Jaitapur (Maharashtra) with six nuclear reactors to be built with French technology and cooperation. And while there were protests in Jaitapur and elsewhere in India, most of the protests revolved around land acquisition.

In fact, the nuclear threat does not resonate so much with the public and we are yet to see the emergence of a strong and comprehensive anti-nuclear movement, similar to those seen in the West. Having said that, there is a nascent movement in the form of the Coalition for Nuclear Disarmament and Peace (CNDP).[51] The CNDP describes itself as India's national network of over 200 organizations, including grassroots groups, mass movements and advocacy organizations as well as individuals.[52] Established in 2000, CNDP demands that India and Pakistan roll back their nuclear weapons programmes. The CNDP also says 'no' to further nuclear testing, 'no' to deployment of nuclear weapons and 'yes' to global and regional nuclear disarmament. Apart from issuing statements, such as the one welcoming the adoption of the 'Treaty on the Prohibition of Nuclear Weapons' by the UN in July 2017, the CNDP does not appear to have the clout to force the government's hand in any significant manner.

Domestic politics played a big part in the Indo-US civilian nuclear agreement of 2008,[53] meeting stiff opposition from both political parties and activists in India. Then PM, Manmohan Singh, staked his reputation on the deal and after debate and discussion, the government survived by barely just nineteen votes in July 2008. While the deal was clearly in India's interest, the drama surrounding it demonstrated the complex interplay of domestic politics and national interest in a noisy democracy such as India. In my opinion, the left parties withdrew support not so much because of the contents of the nuclear deal but because they were viscerally opposed to the US. In the end, the principled position of PM Manmohan Singh saw the day through.

More recently, the decision by the Government of India to walk out of the Regional Comprehensive Economic Partnership Agreement (RCEP) again demonstrates the importance of domestic politics. When the decision not to join was made in November 2019, the Swadeshi Jagran Manch—which is affiliated with the RSS and is quite powerful—put out a statement that said it was a demonstration on how to protect national interest and the interests of our farmers, dairy workers and the manufacturing sector.[54] The Manch had earlier warned the government against signing on to the RCEP. The opposition Congress party also welcomed the decision saying it was in India's national interest not to join the RCEP. But it is the Swadeshi Jagran Manch that carried out a decisive campaign against India joining the RCEP.[55]

We will see later in the book that when hostilities broke out in Ukraine, domestic political parties put pressure on the Modi government to evacuate all Indian citizens (mainly students studying in various parts of Ukraine) as quickly as possible. Some voices were also heard about India not being on the right side of history because it did not condemn Russia for its invasion of Ukraine. Conversely, it is also public opinion that perhaps persuaded the government to not condemn Russia for its actions, since this was a sentiment shared by most Indians.

It is therefore fair to conclude that regardless of the political party in power, domestic politics in India always plays a big part in how the government of the day negotiates with the world, whether it is on the subject of trade, climate change, nuclear disarmament or indeed 'black swan' events like the war in Ukraine.

1.5 Geopolitical Imperatives

Negotiating with the world, by definition, entails geopolitics. All negotiations involve a detailed consideration of the geopolitical imperatives of the participating countries. Thus, governments carry out an assessment of how joining an international agreement serves certain geopolitical objectives. Equally, countries can also come under pressure from their strategic partners to join an international agreement or to take positions on landmark events like the war in Ukraine. India is certainly no exception to this. Previously, when India enjoyed less clout, it was customary for more powerful players such as the US or the EU to pressurize us to join international agreements or to take a certain position on international issues. At present though, it is not impossible for India to resist such pressure. The result is often a complex negotiation between India and its strategic partners, involving some give and take that may lead to a disagreement, a stalemate or mutually acceptable outcomes.

The Uruguay Round of trade negotiations, which lasted from 1986 to 1994 provides a perfect example of how India, a relatively weak player in those GATT days, had to face the mighty coalition of the US, EU and Japan when it came to accepting the results of the Uruguay Round. The most vivid example of India coming up against geopolitical compulsions is the one relating to TRIPS in the multilateral trading system. As is well known, India vehemently opposed the inclusion of IPRs in the negotiating mandate of the Uruguay Round. When that became impossible to resist, India continued to maintain till 1989, that the Uruguay Round mandate for IPRs was confined to trade in counterfeit goods and anti-competitive practices of the right holders and that the mandate did not extend to substantive norms and standards for the protection of IPRs. Indeed, the mandate was worded vaguely and was far from substantive.[56]

However, in April 1989 at the Trade Negotiations Committee meeting in Geneva, India made a volte-face and agreed to the inclusion of substantive norms and standards for the protection and enforcement of IPRs within the scope of the TRIPS mandate.[57] A.V. Ganesan, a key Indian negotiator for TRIPS and a member of the delegation at the Trade Negotiations Committee meeting in Geneva, gives reasons for this change of stand.[58] The tipping point, he admits candidly, was the 'pressure exerted by the United States through its unilateral actions under Section 301 of the US Trade Act 1974 and the Special 301 provisions of the US Omnibus Trade and Competitiveness Act 1988.'[59] This was important for the US because India was perhaps the last major developing country standing in opposition to the proposed TRIPS Agreement.

It may be worth noting that the Berlin Wall fell just months after April 1989, and the final disintegration of the Soviet Union also took place a couple of years after April 1989. So, it is fair to assume that in April 1989 the US was on the eve of becoming the sole superpower; it was the so-called unipolar moment if you like. India, on the other hand, was yet to embark on economic reforms and by 1991 was facing bankruptcy. The strategic disparity between a unipolar US and an economically weak India could not be starker. India could not have resisted the pressure from US in 1989 in the matter of TRIPS negotiations in the WTO. It was purely a matter of geopolitics.

Fast forward to November 2001 in Doha where the WTO negotiations were delicately poised. It was far from clear that the ministerial meeting would be successful in launching a new round of trade negotiations. This time around, the US had come to Doha with the clear intention to launch a new 'Round'.[60] Geopolitical factors, such as the profound impact of the events of 9/11 for instance, led quite a few to feel that the Doha ministerial meet must succeed or else the terrorists would have won.[61] The US did show some flexibility to conclude the declaration on TRIPS and Public Health to the general satisfaction of the African Group and key countries, such as India and Brazil. Nevertheless yet again we see geopolitical factors (such as 9/11) at play, which can profoundly impact the direction and outcome of multilateral trade negotiations.

The climate change negotiations, which culminated in a successful accord in Paris in 2015, were also a perfect demonstration of how geopolitical factors influence climate negotiations.

It is generally believed that India's position on climate change negotiations started changing just before Copenhagen (2009) and it subsequently became clear that India too was willing to make commitments and undertake obligations. There are of course several reasons for this shift and are examined in some detail in Chapter 3, which focuses on climate change. It is nevertheless interesting to note that some scholars felt geopolitical reasons were also behind the shift in India's position. In an article published by the Royal Swedish Academy of Sciences, the authors Himangana Gupta, Ravinder Kohli and Amrik Singh Ahluwalia argued that the shift in India's negotiating posture received international acclaim and quoted other experts to say that India became an emerging power in international climate negotiations because of a strategic reorientation.[62] The authors also argued that India thus disengaged from G77 on the issue of climate change and aligned its position with that of the US.

This is certainly questionable, but it is hard to deny that geopolitical considerations did play an important role in the evolution of India's negotiating position. For instance, well-known Indian climate change scholar Lavanya Rajamani argued that India's ratification of the Paris Climate Change Accords in 2015 would also strengthen Indo-American ties, given that climate change had been high on President Obama's agenda.[63] Other scholars such as D. Raghunandan were critical of India's shift in position, but nevertheless argued that India was seeking to advance a strategic alliance with the US.[64] Given this, it is cruelly ironic that the US under President Trump decided to pull out of the Paris Climate Change Accords. But this broad geopolitical orientation appears to have guided India at the COP26 meeting in Glasgow in 2021, when PM Modi announced that India would adhere to net zero emissions by 2070.[65] Geopolitics continued to guide India, which supported a 'loss and damage' fund at the COP27 meeting in Sharm El-Sheikh knowing full well it may not have access to this fund at all.

In a similar vein, geopolitical considerations also seem to have played an important role in India agreeing in 2015 to phase out Hydrofluorocarbons (HFCs) under the Montreal Protocol. Earlier, India was opposed to doing this under the Montreal Protocol and wished this to be done by developed countries under the aegis of the Kyoto Protocol. Indeed, during the visit by PM Modi to Washington in September 2014 it was clearly stated in a Joint Statement that the two leaders 'recognized the need to use the institutions and expertise of the Montreal Protocol to reduce the consumption and production of HFCs'.[66] And true enough in April 2015, India submitted a proposal to the Montreal Protocol for phasing out HFCs with a grace period of fifteen years.[67] Yet again, India appears to have had strategic imperatives to put itself in broad agreement with the US.

The Indo-US nuclear deal of 2008 was also arguably less about nuclear power and more about geopolitical calculus. Manpreet Sethi, a nuclear expert with the Center for Air Power Studies, argued in a recent article that two regional developments helped India's case: one, the irresponsible behaviour of Pakistan in the Kargil imbroglio; and two, the rise of China and the desire of the US to view India as a counterweight to China.[68] Again, we see profound geopolitical imperatives at work in an agreement, which though bilateral, had huge implications for India's prospects for membership with multilateral export control regimes such as the Missile Technology Control Regime, The Australia Group and The Wassenaar Arrangement. The membership of Nuclear Suppliers Group (NSG), on the other hand, has proved elusive for India primarily because of objections from China.

As will be seen later in the book, geopolitical imperatives loomed large for India while taking a stand on the war in Ukraine. India's principal security challenge is China, so it is in its interest to prevent a de facto alliance of China and Russia, to the extent it can. Similarly, India's strategic partnership with the US is critical as part of an external balancing act that India resorts to for coping with China, especially given the power differential between India and China. India also has a legacy relationship with Russia, given its dependence on Russian weapon platforms. All these geopolitical imperatives have eventually determined India's stand on the Ukraine issue.

1.6 Commitment to Multilateralism and Principles

We saw earlier that Article 51 of the Indian Constitution enjoins the State to promote international peace and security, to maintain just and honourable relations between nations and foster respect for international law and treaty obligations, and also encourages settlement of international disputes by arbitration. We also saw how India was involved in drafting the UN Charter and became a founding member even before it attained independence. For India therefore, multilateralism was and is an article of faith.

As early as 1947–48, India participated actively in the drafting of the Universal Declaration of Human Rights. Dr Hansa Mehta was representing India and she came across the draft Universal Human Rights Declaration that stated: 'All men are born free and equal'. She moved an amendment that was unanimously accepted and now read: 'All human beings are born free and equal!' Again, as early as 1953, Vijaya Lakshmi Pandit was elected the first woman President of the UN General Assembly (UNGA).

India took strong positions on two issues at the UN, very early on—decolonization and apartheid. India co-sponsored the landmark 1960 UN Declaration on granting independence to colonial countries, which inter alia proclaimed the need to unconditionally end colonialism in all its forms and manifestations. India was also the first country to raise the issue of apartheid and racial discrimination in South Africa at the UN, and was among the earliest signatories of the Convention on Elimination of all forms of Racial Discrimination adopted by the UN in 1965.

More recently in 2019, when France and Germany launched the 'Alliance for Multilateralism' aimed at supporting multilateralism and the UN, India was delighted to join it.[69] The Indian EAM made it a point to say that multilateralism really mattered and was under stress from both nationalism and mercantilism. Indeed, the EAM went on to say that the centrality of the UN to international relations and the WTO to international trade must be recognized, preserved and protected.[70]

One important index of India's commitment to multilateralism is its enormous contribution to UN peacekeeping operations. Not only is India one of the largest, if not the largest, contributor to UN peacekeeping efforts, but it has also suffered the most fatalities.

In fact, even before it became independent, India was part of the UN peacekeeping efforts in Palestine. Since the inception of the UN, India has contributed around 180,000 troops, has been involved in as many as 49 Missions and has lost 167 peacekeepers.[71] Indeed, the UN Under-Secretary General for peacekeeping, Jean-Pierre Lacroix, said as recently as August 2018 that UN peacekeeping operates in increasingly complex environments and the UN is grateful for steadfast partners like India, who have risen to new challenges and continue to participate meaningfully in UN efforts to protect vulnerable civilians.[72]

India's deployment of an all-women contingent to Liberia has also been praised by the UN. As of October 2022, there are over 5,887 Indian peacekeeping troops, the vast majority posted in Congo and South Sudan. It is not just peacekeeping that India contributes to, it also makes financial contributions to keep some of the UN institutions going. India has never defaulted in paying its membership dues to the UN—this, at a time when some developed countries owe millions in arrears to the UN. In January 2020, India was just one among four countries to pay its dues on time. In August 2020, India contributed $2 million to the UN Relief and Works Agency (UNRWA) for the welfare of Palestinian refugees. The UNRWA was in dire straits and acknowledged the assistance from India. The same month, India also contributed $15 million to the India-UN Development Partnership Fund, used for South-South cooperation. As of April 2023, India was the fourth largest contributor to the UN Democracy Fund after the US, Sweden and Germany.[73]

Apart from the financial contribution, India has a stellar record when it comes to acceptance of international law. For instance, in 2014 a tribunal of the Permanent Court of Arbitration in The Hague delivered a decision on a dispute between India and Bangladesh regarding the delimitation of the maritime boundary between them in the territorial sea, the exclusive economic zone and the continental shelf within and beyond 200 nautical miles in the Bay of Bengal.[74] Even though the general view was that India had 'lost' the case, India accepted the verdict. Contrast this with the dispute between China and Philippines, where the tribunal of the Permanent Court of Arbitration in The Hague had ruled against the so-called 'nine dash line' claim of China in the South China sea. Unlike India, China rejected the ruling describing it as unacceptable.

In multilateral negotiations, India is wary of making commitments that it cannot keep. This often results in India erring on the side of caution and being quite conservative when it comes to assuming international obligations. India would much rather do that than run the risk of being in flagrant violation of its obligations under international law. A good example of this is India's Nationally Determined Contribution, which was submitted to the UNFCC Secretariat in October 2015.[75] One part of the debate that took place at the time was whether India could signal a year when its GHG emissions would peak, commonly known as the peak year. After much debate and discussion, it was felt that we were so far behind China, the US and the EU, in terms of emissions and development parameters that it would not be possible for us to indicate a peak year with any degree of certainty or comfort. India was also concerned that once a peak year was agreed to, it would like to stick by it rather than ask for an extension. In the case of China, it was well-known that it would peak by 2025 so it obviously had no problem in indicating a peak year of 2030 in its NDC. Both India and China made their respective NDCs in 2015. Fast forward to December 2019 and it was observed that India had a much better track record of fulfilling its obligations, than China.

In an article in the *Washington Post* on 19 August 2022, Kevin Rudd, a Sinologist of some repute, stated unambiguously that China's thirst for coal was both economically short-sighted and environmentally reckless. Rudd said that China approved more coal plants in 2020, than in the two previous years combined. On the other hand, India seems well on its way to achieving its target of installing 175 gigawatt (GW) of renewable power capacity by 2022. India's renewable energy capacity reached 168.96 GW in February 2023.

A similar respect for international law and multilateral commitments may be observed when it comes to nuclear disarmament and non-proliferation. It is true that India decided to go completely nuclear in 1998, but that was not in violation of any international agreement since India had steadfastly refused to sign the NPT (chiefly on grounds that it discriminated arbitrarily against countries like India). Be that as it may, India has since then de facto followed all the export control regimes and has a stellar record on non-proliferation. In sharp contrast, one of the recognized nuclear powers under NPT, NPT-signatory China, has a dubious record of assisting countries like Pakistan, North Korea and some others in gross violation of its international commitments. As recently as 2017, the US State Department compliance report stated that Chinese entities continued to supply missile programmes of proliferation concern.[76]

India's commitment to the UN Charter and to the principle of territorial integrity and sovereignty has also come to the fore in the position taken by it on the Ukraine issue. In every single statement made by India after abstaining on resolutions, whether in the UN Security Council (UNSC) or in the UNGA, India has made it clear that the contemporary global order is built on the UN Charter, international law and respect for sovereignty and the territorial integrity of states. This commitment by India is unconditional and without any exception.

In the final analysis, the profile that emerges of India is this—it may be a difficult customer in international negotiations and does not fight shy of saying 'no', but once it has agreed to multilateral commitments and international obligations, it generally respects them even at great cost to itself.

1.7 Realpolitik and Material Gain

In any international negotiation and indeed in any dealing with the outside world, countries look for material gain and India is no exception. Even in the good old times of GATT, when India was relatively weak, it sought concrete market access for its products (textiles, tea and leather to name a few) in developed country markets. Indeed, even the Generalized System of Preferences (GSP) concession won by developing countries from developed countries, was about getting tariff advantages, increased market share and improved profit margins.[77]

Similarly, in the case of climate change negotiations, it is no secret that India stresses the important aspect of climate finance, partly, if not wholly, out of self-interest. It is a fact that India needs billions of dollars in green finance to execute its ambitious sustainable development goals (SDGs) pertaining to mitigation and adaptation.[78] The US too, subsequent to the Indo-US nuclear deal in 2008, wanted to sell Westinghouse nuclear reactors to India; evidence of material gain having played its part in the negotiations. The US signed the nuclear pact to open the way for nuclear commerce with India. It is another matter that the deal with Westinghouse never really took off and India turned to France and Russia following the Nuclear Suppliers Group waiver in September 2008. Reactors from France and Russia were available as a result of the NSG waiver.

In an article published by the Institute of Peace and Conflict Studies, S.R. Khan noted that India expected its nuclear industry to gain in terms of trade and employment.[79] the deal was expected to allow Indian nuclear industry to gain in terms of trade and employment. One of the most important objectives of India's dealings with the world is to keep foreign markets open for Indian goods and services. It is worth remembering that almost 50 per cent of India's current GDP of $2.8 trillion, comes from foreign trade. Without this, there is very little chance of India becoming a $5 trillion economy, much less a $10 trillion one. And without this happening, the imperative necessity of lifting the 500 million people living in poverty out of it will remain a pipe dream. It is also worth keeping in mind that emigration for the youth is a key strategic objective for India in negotiations. With a million job seekers entering the market every month, providing them opportunities to emigrate is critical. Indeed, India is on a signing spree for 'migration and mobility partnership' agreements with its key partners. Into this mix must also figure India's need for foreign direct investment (FDI) and access to state-of-the-art technology.

On the war in Ukraine, it is conventional wisdom to say there are no winners, but only losers. India, again, is no exception. The Indian economy—like many of the economies of developing and least-developed countries—has taken a huge hit and is reeling from inflation and rising unemployment, thanks to the war in Ukraine. India did try to cushion the terrible impact of the war in Ukraine on its poor, by buying discounted Russian oil. However, this was not nearly enough to compensate for the deleterious effects of the Ukraine war on the three Fs—food, fuel and fertilizer. There is evidence that poverty levels may have increased and inequalities may have widened because of the war in Ukraine. It is also becoming apparent that many developing and least-developed countries will simply not be able to meet the SDGs in the time frame in which they were originally intended.

The following six factors—Gandhi Litmus Test (poverty veto); policy space; domestic politics; geopolitical imperatives;

commitment to multilateralism/principles; and realpolitik/ material gain—constitute the Integrated Assessment Framework by which India's negotiations at some key international fora will be evaluated in the chapters that follow. These factors are not necessarily listed in order of priority. Depending on the subject matter being negotiated, the factors assume variable importance. But by crafting an Integrated Assessment Framework it is hoped that there will be a much better understanding of why India does what it does in international negotiations.

2

Trying to Set a Positive Agenda: The Case of WTO

2.1 Introduction

It is fair to say that of all the fora in which India has negotiated, the multilateral trading system, embodied first in GATT and then the WTO, presented the most difficult challenges. The substantive reasons for this are not hard to understand. First, this was a negotiating forum where national commitments, once made, were irrevocable. Second, the national commitments were tangible and concrete, quantifiable in terms of dollars and cents. Third, the dispute settlement mechanism, especially under the WTO, was binding. Last, but not the least, while India is a large and attractive market for outside powers, the Government of India has had to be constantly mindful of the vast number of its citizens living in poverty and protecting their interests. This last-mentioned point is what I had earlier described as the 'poverty veto' with regard to India's negotiating stand. Any objective assessment of India's actions must therefore bear this in mind.

As we saw earlier, India was fortunate to be a founding member of the GATT in 1947. But in the period between 1947 and 1967 there were several negotiating rounds in the GATT,[1] in which India took little or no part in and was a passive bystander. Indeed, this was true for most, if not all developing countries at the time. At that time, developing countries had neither a significant share of global trade nor constituted an important market for the products of developed countries. The negotiating outcome among developed countries was, in any case, made available to all (including developing and least-developed countries who were bystanders) on a Most Favoured Nation (MFN) basis, so it really did not matter one way or another.

However, even regarding this period, there are differing interpretations over the nature and extent of developing country participation in GATT negotiations. One widely prevalent interpretation is that developing countries were mere 'bystanders' in this phase. The second more interesting interpretation is that developing countries were keen not to take on any commitments and that they simply 'free rode'.

I, however, feel that both interpretations may be off the mark. Indeed, countries like India needed policy space and were therefore pragmatic in their approach to trade matters.[2] In an excellent article, Rorden Wilkinson and James Scott argue that while the energy of developing countries was often directed towards negotiations seeking more favourable treatment for themselves, this was a result more of the asymmetrical manner in which GATT was deployed and a consequence of their relative underdevelopment than of any desire to 'free-ride' on the favourable trading conditions created by the concession-exchanging activities of developed countries.[3]

This interpretation seems much closer to the truth, than the 'bystander' or the 'free-rider' explanation.

It is worth bearing in mind that the original text of the GATT did not allow for preferences in favour of developing countries. Indeed, the only exception to the MFN principle when GATT was conceived, was the Regional Trading Arrangements such as Free Trade Area (FTA) or Customs Union as contained in Article XXIV.[4] In a situation characterized by supreme irony, when GATT was established, it was simply illegal for other developed countries or by other developing countries to provide trade preferences to developing countries. The establishment of United Nations Conference on Trade and Development (UNCTAD) in 1964 changed things for developing countries. In 1964 UNCTAD had about 120 countries participating in the first Conference in Geneva, while GATT in 1964 had just 66 countries participating in the 'Kennedy Round' of tariff negotiations. These 66 countries belonging to GATT constituted 80 per cent of global trade at the time. While UNCTAD was more of an institution representing the point of view of developing and least-developed countries, GATT was a hardcore negotiating forum dominated by powerful, developed countries. This difference persisted until the entry into force of the WTO in 1995, when all countries made a beeline to join the new and powerful organization.

Be that as it may, the establishment of UNCTAD did have some impact on GATT. For instance, the introduction of Part IV of GATT titled 'Trade and Development' is directly attributed to the first Conference of UNCTAD in 1964.[5] There was political pressure on GATT to act and with the number of developing countries that were now contracting parties of GATT, it was important for GATT to demonstrate that it took cognizance of the interests of developing countries.

Thus, Part IV recalled the basic objectives of GATT, which included the raising standards of living and the progressive development of the economies of all contracting parties (as members of GATT were known) but especially for less-developed contracting parties (as developing countries were then known). It was also acknowledged that efforts were necessary for developing countries to secure a share in the growth of international trade commensurate with the needs of their economic development. But the most important outcome from a developing country perspective in Part IV is contained in paragraph 8 of Article XXXVI of Part IV in GATT which is quoted in full below:

> The developed contracting parties do not expect reciprocity for commitments made by them in trade negotiations to reduce or remove tariffs and other barriers to the trade of less-developed contracting parties.

This was hugely important since the developing countries in the sixties were in no position to offer reciprocal concessions to developed countries, given the weak trading position in which they generally found themselves. This principle of non-reciprocity was to guide developing countries right till the launch of the Doha Round and beyond. Article XXXVI para 8 in GATT further spells out what this principle of non-reciprocity means:

> It is understood that the phrase 'do not expect reciprocity' means, in accordance with the objectives set forth in this Article, that the less-developed contracting parties should not be expected, in the course of trade negotiations, to make contributions that are inconsistent with their individual development, financial and trade needs, taking into consideration past trade developments.

Part IV of GATT thus laid down a negotiating philosophy for developing countries based on non-reciprocity keeping in mind their trade vulnerabilities. That said, the developing countries wanted GATT Article I (MFN) itself to be amended so as to allow trade preferences for themselves. This was, however, not possible because the power differential between developing and developed countries in GATT at the time was considerable, and developing countries simply lacked clout. As the famous author John H. Jackson observed in his book, 'for the most part, the new GATT chapter in Part IV sets forth principles and objectives rather than legal obligations'.[6] Elsewhere, Jackson said the language of the legal obligation in Part IV was 'soft'.[7] The concrete outcome, apart from a reaffirmation of the principle of non-reciprocity, was the establishment of the permanent 'Committee on Trade and Development' first in GATT and then in WTO. Eventually, it also led to the establishment of the 'International Trade Center', an institution jointly run by GATT and UNCTAD, meant to promote the export marketing of developing countries.[8]

2.2 Special and Differential Treatment

It is important to note that India, along with other like-minded developing countries, played a crucial role in the inclusion of Part IV above in GATT. Thus, even though there was no level playing field in GATT at the time, developing countries including India tried hard and sometimes even succeeded in negotiating outcomes that were favourable to them. Part IV was certainly one such instance, but as we saw earlier it was not 'hard law' that one normally encounters in GATT. In this sense, the so-called 'enabling clause' ranks as a significant, legally-binding outcome favourable to the developing countries. The story of how the 'enabling clause' came about is therefore worth recounting.

At the first UNCTAD Conference held in Geneva in 1964, then Secretary General, Raúl Prebisch, presented the idea of granting developing countries preferential tariff rates in the markets of industrialized countries. By 1968 at the UNCTAD Conference in Delhi (where India obviously played a crucial role) the issue— preference for manufactures and semi-manufactures exported from developing countries to the markets of developed or industrialized countries—was considered mature for discussion and indeed was a key objective of the Conference itself. It was felt that the preference ought to be not only non-reciprocal but also non-discriminatory and that this should lead to an agreement on the main outlines of such a scheme of preferences.

India played a leading role in the establishment of the Generalized System of Preferences (GSP) so much so it became the symbol of the 1968 UNCTAD Conference.[9] The objectives of the generalized, non-reciprocal, non-discriminatory system of preferences in favour of the developing countries—including special measures in favour of the least advanced among the developing countries—were to increase their export earnings, promote their industrialization, and accelerate their rates of economic growth. This was formalized in 1971 as the GSP, at UNCTAD.

Though GATT was still not fully convinced about GSP, it did not want to be seen as opposing the interests of developing countries and so went for a 'waiver approach' towards GSP. In other words, every GSP scheme operated by developed countries had to request a GATT waiver (an approved exception) from MFN, prescribed in Article I. In 1971, the contracting parties approved a waiver to Article I of GATT for ten years authorizing the GSP scheme. Not satisfied with this waiver approach, the developing countries continued to look for a permanent and irreversible decision in this matter. The consequent result was the 'enabling clause' of the GATT.

There was enough evidence in the Tokyo Round (1973–79) of GATT trade negotiations that developing countries, including India, set out to win for themselves more favourable and preferential treatment. This can hardly be described as 'naysaying' and indeed the developing countries must be credited with astute negotiating strategy in a forum famed for mercantilist behaviour. The developing countries up until this point had to depend on GATT waiver for the GSP scheme. Even for exchange of tariff concessions amongst themselves, they were governed by Article I relating to MFN and so needed a waiver. After serious negotiations, the developing countries won their first legally binding outcome in the GATT through a decision on 'Differential and More Favourable Treatment, Reciprocity and Fuller Participation of Developing Countries', also known as the 'enabling clause' or quite simply as Special and Differential Treatment. Because it was such a landmark agreement, the provisions are relevant even today.[10]

Several features of the 'enabling clause' were noteworthy. First, the decision stated categorically that notwithstanding Article I relating to MFN, contracting parties may accord differential and more favourable treatment to developing countries without according such treatment to other contracting parties, which in normal circumstances would be violative of MFN. In other words, the act of developed countries providing more favourable treatment to developing countries was legally recognized as an exception to Article I. Second, GSP was covered and henceforth was deemed as possessing a permanent GATT waiver. Third, there was also more favourable treatment of non-tariff barriers faced by developing country exports. Fourth, agreements entered among developing country members (such as the Global System of Trade Preferences or GSTP, agreed to in Belgrade in 1988) would also be legally covered. Fifth, least-developed countries would obviously be entitled to special treatment.

The principle of non-reciprocity, already enshrined in Part IV of GATT, was reiterated for good measure. Thus, the 'enabling clause' reaffirmed that developed countries shall not seek and developing countries are therefore not required, to make concessions that are inconsistent with the latter's development, financial and trade needs. Considering the original GATT did not have any specific provision relating to developing (and least-developed) countries, the 'enabling clause' was nothing short of a masterstroke. It is worth bearing in mind that GATT was set up on the basis of two underlying principles: reciprocity and non-discrimination. The 'enabling clause', in direct contrast to this notion, was actually based on non-reciprocity and positive discrimination. In the original membership of GATT comprising twenty-three signatories, eleven were developing countries.[11] Of course, by the time Tokyo Round happened in 1979 the membership of GATT had risen to 102, the majority of which were developing countries. Still, GATT operated more based on trading clout and less on 'one country one vote'. In this sense, the amendment of GATT with the 'enabling clause' was quite a remarkable achievement by developing countries led by India and Brazil.

India's leadership role in mobilizing the support of other developing countries to get the 'enabling clause' legally incorporated in GATT, was proof that right from the beginning India did not fight shy of negotiations and sought concessions from its developed country partners based on its national interest. India's national interest at the time lay in protecting its domestic industry and its market, and in trying to get advantageous terms of trade for its exports. India also wanted to make clear that it could not be expected to make concessions to its developed country partners, which were inconsistent with its developmental priorities. The developmental priority at the time was linked to the Gandhi Litmus Test defined earlier. The 'enabling clause' also achieved the preservation of policy space, which again was a key negotiating objective for India. India, therefore, at this stage passed with flying colours at GATT and UNCTAD, if one were to view its actions in accordance with the Integrated Assessment Framework outlined in Chapter 1. India's commitment to multilateralism also comes through in this saga, as does its keen geopolitical sense of providing leadership to a bunch of developing countries to pursue its negotiating objectives and advance its national interest. Monetary gains were also not inconsiderable. The following is the evaluation of India's stand using the Integrated Assessment Framework when it comes to the way it negotiated Special and Differential Treatment in GATT:

Special and Differential Treatment (GATT)

Gandhi Litmus Test: Passes this test with flying colours.
Policy Space: Fully preserves policy space.
Domestic Politics: Not applicable in this case.
Geopolitical Imperatives: Leadership of developing countries.
Commitment to Multilateralism/Principles: Active in GATT, not a passive bystander.
Material Gain: GSP, tariff and monetary gains.

By 1979, it also became obvious that developing country exports to developed country markets faced significant non-tariff barriers. With this in mind, the 'enabling clause' also had a provision relating to this issue. It specified that there would also be 'differential and more favourable treatment' with respect to provisions of the General Agreement concerning non-tariff measures governed by the provisions of instruments multilaterally negotiated under the auspices of GATT. This issue was important, because for the first time in the Tokyo Round, non-tariff measures were also included in the negotiating agenda. This led to agreements like the Agreement on Technical Barriers to Trade and Agreement on Sanitary and Phytosanitary Measures, which were eventually concluded as part of the Tokyo Round.

Yet another 'victory' for developing countries in the Tokyo Round was the fact that a number of agreements concluded—such as the one on Anti-Dumping or the one on Subsides—were 'codes'. This meant that countries were free to either join these codes or not. This provided sufficient flexibility to developing countries in terms of policy space.

Of course, developing countries and least-developed countries, weak as they were, did not have it their way in all areas. In the final analysis, the 'enabling clause' could not become as legally watertight as the proponents wished. All things considered, GSP continued to be voluntary and the extent of preferences could be determined by the developed countries. It was perhaps for this reason that the UNCTAD V Conference stated that the results of the Tokyo Round were unsatisfactory from the standpoint of developing and least-developed countries.[12] But perhaps the biggest concession granted by the developing countries to the developed countries was that the seeds of 'graduation' were sown in the 'enabling clause' in paragraph 7, which is reproduced below:

Less-developed contracting parties expect that their capacity to make contributions or negotiated concessions or take other mutually agreed action under the provisions and procedures of the General Agreement would improve with the progressive development of their economies and improvement in their trade situation and they would accordingly expect to participate more fully in the framework of rights and obligations under the General Agreement.

The above concept of 'graduation' implies that countries will not be deemed as developing countries forever. When the developing countries grow over time and their GDP rises, they 'graduate' and cease to be developing countries. Ipso facto, they are also no longer entitled to special and differential treatment. Thus, developing countries would be fully integrated into the GATT system and would be subject to the same rights and obligations as the developed countries.

This idea of 'graduation' has assumed serious proportions in WTO, thanks to a move by the US and others to question the way developing countries are decided in the multilateral trading system. While the least-developed countries are decided by the UN and the list keeps evolving according to mutually-agreed upon criteria, the decision on developing countries in WTO has hitherto been based on 'self-election'. A country could deem itself a developing country and until recently there was no objection to it. Thus, even countries like Singapore and South Korea considered themselves as 'developing', despite having a high per capita GDP. This predictably led to a backlash.

One of the main reasons for this debate is of course the dramatic rise of China.

Despite a GDP of close to $18 trillion (2021), China vehemently insists that it is a developing country. The US has made it clear that countries which are high-income countries (the threshold being $12,000 per capita, as defined by the World Bank) or those with a share of world trade exceeding 0.5 per cent or those which are seeking membership of the Organization for Economic Cooperation and Development (OECD) or those which are members of G20 will henceforth not be eligible for GSP benefits based on developing country status. Using these criteria, the office of US Trade Representative (USTR) has come up with a list of developing countries,[13] which obviously excludes not just Republic of Korea, Singapore, China but also India. In other words, the US is seeking to 'graduate' countries like China and India out of the developing country category.

Thus, despite a very low GDP per capita, India has not been spared. The problem of course is that China is way more 'developed' than India, when viewed from China's GDP, GDP per capita or even the percentage of people living in poverty. This argument has fallen on deaf ears in the US, which went to the extent of depriving India of GSP benefits as of early 2020. The WTO Agreement on fisheries subsidies adopted at the twelfth Ministerial Conference on 17 June 2022 marks a major step forward for ocean sustainability by prohibiting harmful fisheries subsidies. The agreement represents an achievement for the WTO as the first SDG target met through a multilateral agreement and only the second agreement reached since the WTO's inception. Negotiations on some outstanding issues are continuing with a view to enhancing the disciplines of the agreement. India somehow must convince its WTO partners that it cannot be bracketed along with China on the issue of Special and Differential Treatment. From an Indian perspective the relevant criteria would be the World Bank classification, which places India in the lower middle-income category and places China as an upper-middle-income economy. Also, the large number of people living in extreme poverty should settle the issue beyond a shadow of a doubt and India should be conferred developing country status.

The above provides ample proof, if proof was needed, that the developing countries (at least till the completion of the Tokyo Round, i.e., 1979 in GATT) can scarcely be described as 'naysayers'. On the contrary even with limited trading clout, and even more limited negotiating resources, they engage seriously with developed country partners with a view to seeking a more favourable negotiating outcome for themselves.

2.3 The Naysaying Phase

Following the completion of the Tokyo Round by 1979, there were indications that a new round could be in the offing by 1982. Those days in GATT, impetus for a new round always gathered momentum whenever the global economy showed signs of slowing, and world trade had declined in 1982 for the first time since the 1930s. Arthur Dunkel, GATT Director General, had gone globetrotting as early as 1980 to get a sense from the leading countries as to the state of the global economy and what could be done about it. John Croome, who may be considered the official biographer of GATT, says in his book that although countries were busy implementing the Tokyo Round reforms, the momentum from the earlier rounds had been lost.[14] This line of reasoning is also based on the famous 'bicycle theory' which argues that the multilateral trading system is like a bicycle—one must keep on pedalling to move forward, else one will simply fall over! In other words, trade liberalization through successive rounds of negotiations is an endless process that needs to be pursued in a Sisyphean manner.

Fred Bergsten encapsulates this theory best when he says that whenever the GATT became 'largely comatose', major protectionist efforts were undertaken in the US and elsewhere, in the form of the Multi-Fibre Arrangement with regard to trade governing textiles and clothing, or the panoply of new Voluntary Export Restraints in autos etc., or indeed the US' dreaded 'Super 301' provision.[15] So it becomes even more imperative, according to this theory, to keep launching successive rounds of trade negotiations at frequent intervals to counter protectionist trends in the US and other developed countries.

There is, however, ample evidence to suggest that if there was one driving force behind the push to launch a new round of trade negotiations, it was the US. In an excellent article on the pre-negotiation phase of the Uruguay Round, Gilbert R. Winham makes it clear that in the eighties the US put enormous pressure on GATT to start thinking about a new round.[16] By doing so, the US was unabashedly pursuing its economic and trade interests. For one thing, the massive agricultural subsidies provided by the EU started bothering the US, because its export interest in third countries was beginning to be adversely impacted. The US also began pushing for inclusion of services in the GATT, since trade in goods was getting saturated in Western markets. The US was also seeking to prise open developing country markets for its goods and services.

Again, Winham, with remarkable lucidity, pointed to two developments: the first, that by 1985 China, Hong Kong, Korea and Saudi Arabia were among the world's top twenty exporters and importers. Brazil and Taiwan had joined the list as exporters, and Singapore joined the list as an importer. The second that developing countries had become an important market for developed countries, taking by 1987 approximately one-third of Japan's merchandise exports, one-fourth of North America's exports and one-eighth of Western Europe's exports.[17] Winham concluded with this valid observation: 'These circumstances motivated developed countries to seek a new negotiation to incorporate developing countries more firmly into GATT rules.'[18]

As for inclusion of services, it is worth noting that most countries of the world showed a decline in the agriculture workforce and a corresponding increase in labour in industry and services. However, the decline of agriculture and the movement into services was much greater in developed as opposed to developing countries. Developed countries realized that unless trade in services expanded there was little prospect of trade continuing to promote growth in their countries. A good example was the US economy—a major exporter of agricultural goods that over time had become more dependent on services than goods. Hence, the US's insistence on inclusion of services in a new round of trade negotiations made eminent sense. Developing countries such as India and Brazil of course saw through this and expressed strong opposition to inclusion of services in the Uruguay Round mandate at Punta del Este in 1986.

This 'naysaying' if you like, done by a group of developing countries led by India and Brazil, was based on self-preservation and self-interest. On services, they argued that they were not sufficiently advanced to negotiate on an equal footing with developed countries, which was undeniably true. Furthermore, they argued, with justification, that developed countries had not yet fully met their obligations in sectors such as agriculture and textiles (and clothing)—areas of vital interest to developing countries. The developing countries led by India and Brazil therefore demanded liberalization first in these areas by developed countries, before 'new issues' such as services could be taken up.

From 1982 to 1986, the developing countries led by India and Brazil stubbornly resisted expansion of GATT's negotiating agenda as demanded by the US and others. While both countries began with considerable support at first support diminished to twenty-four countries and by September 1986, when the Punta del Este meeting began, it had reduced to just ten countries.

It is important to understand how and why this happened, since this pattern was to repeat itself numerous times during the Uruguay Round negotiations. The question must also be posed as to why India has consistently failed to garner support from, say 100 developing countries in the WTO for its legitimate and principled negotiating positions. After all, in the UN, India does manage triple-figure support for its positions. For instance, India won 184 votes in the 193-member UNGA and was elected as a non-permanent member of the UNSC in June 2020. Again, on the issue of 'measures to prevent terrorists from acquiring weapons of mass destruction' India sponsored a resolution with seventy-five other countries, which was adopted by total consensus. Yet, when it comes to the WTO, India seems unable to secure the support of more than a handful of developing and least-developed countries.

There are substantive reasons behind this. First, India as pointed out earlier, is indeed sui generis on account of its size, the massive number of people still living in poverty and the rough-and-tumble nature of its vibrant democracy. The only other country which could compare with India is China, but the stark difference in the political system of the two and the phenomenal economic growth China has achieved since 1990 puts it in a different category altogether. Add to this the Indian government's legitimate interest in preserving 'policy space', in light of there being no safety net in India, and one begins to understand the reason for India's negotiating stand.

It is wrong to think of developing countries as a bloc, particularly in the context of WTO. Developing countries, as a whole, are at different levels of development and are at various stages of integration with the global economy. Thailand, for example, is an aggressive exporter of agricultural products and is very well-integrated with the global economy through regional/ global value chains. So, when it comes to agriculture negotiations in the WTO, one cannot expect Thailand to share India's negotiating position. It is far simpler for India and Thailand to co-sponsor a resolution in the UNCTAD on general economic objectives, such as South-South cooperation and inadequate official aid from developed countries to the developing countries. However, it is far more difficult to get Thailand and India to agree on specific issues, such as agriculture subsidies, in WTO since there is a world of difference between the challenges faced by Thai and Indian farmers.

It is undeniable that smaller developing countries are perhaps more vulnerable to pressure from the more powerful players in the WTO, namely the US or the EU. For instance, it is well known that the US, during the course of the TRIPS negotiations of the Uruguay Round, used the dreaded Section 301 of the Omnibus Trade and Competitiveness Act to arm-twist many developing countries and the latter simply succumbed. Similarly, the EU also has considerable leverage with respect to the seventy-nine African, Caribbean and Pacific (ACP) countries—forty-eight from Sub-Saharan Africa, sixteen from the Caribbean and fifteen from the Pacific and all of them (save one, Cuba) signatories to the Cotonou Agreement which binds them to the EU.

Last, but not the least, there are developing and even least-developed countries that seek effective market access from India and therefore wish India to open its market even more to their products and services. Thus, Malaysia may want more access for its palm-oil exports to India, while Bangladesh may want India to open up more to its garment exports. So, it would be unrealistic to expect them to support India on all occasions at WTO. It is for these reasons that India rarely gets the support of, say 100 developing countries, for its negotiating stand in WTO.

2.4 The Mother of All Rounds

Having decided to oppose the inclusion of services and IPRs at the GATT meeting in Punta del Este in 1986, India nevertheless fully participated in the Uruguay Round of trade negotiations once it was launched. The Uruguay Round has often been called the 'Mother of all Rounds' because of the vast scope of the negotiations, which included services and IPRs in addition to goods. Yet, not all developing and least-developed countries had the means and opportunity to participate fully in these negotiations. Indeed, it is fair to say that India along with Brazil, the Association of Southeast Asian Nations (ASEAN) and a handful of others, represented almost more than 100 other WTO members who were either developing countries or least-developed countries. This was more out of necessity rather than by design. Several developing countries and most certainly all the least-developed countries either did not have the negotiating resources (in terms of number of diplomats necessary to cover the sheer number of meetings in the Uruguay Round) or lacked the domain expertise to participate meaningfully in the complex negotiations that ensued in the Uruguay Round.

To critically analyse the 'naysaying' argument used against India, it is useful to look at the outcomes of the Uruguay Round negotiations in select areas and examine the eventual commitments made by India. Take the subject of non-agricultural market access, or NAMA as it is known as. By the time the Uruguay Round was launched in 1986, it was developing countries like India that had high tariffs and limited 'bound' tariffs in terms of coverage. By the end of the Uruguay Round in 1994, India's average bound tariff had come down from a high of 71 per cent (pre-Uruguay Round) to 32 per cent; equally, the coverage (a meagre 12 per cent pre-Uruguay Round) went up significantly to 65 per cent.[19] By any reckoning, this was a huge commitment towards liberalization by India.

It is true that the difference between the 'bound' tariff and the 'applied' tariff was large for India; but this may be explained by the strong Indian preference for policy space (explained in the introductory chapter). As a country used to triple-digit tariffs and an array of 'quantitative restrictions', India undertook deep commitments in this area in the Uruguay Round. More broadly, it is worth noting that the tariff cuts of developing countries in the Uruguay Round were deeper than those of the developed countries.[20]

One of the biggest conundrums of the multilateral trading system in the eighties was that issues fundamental to mankind, namely, food (agriculture) and clothing (textiles and clothing) were not fully subject to GATT disciplines. Developed countries always argued in favour of 'free trade' for products like chemicals, wristwatches or even automobiles, but when it came to food and clothing it was argued by them that these were somehow 'special' and therefore could not be subject to full GATT rules and disciplines. It may be that 'food' was 'politically sensitive' in Western countries, given aspects of food security and farmers livelihoods. But the case of textiles and clothing was an egregious example of protectionism, pure and simple.[21]

Ironically, it all began as the 'short-term arrangement regarding international trade in textiles' in 1961. The arrangement was intended to be short-term and temporary, so as to provide the cotton textile industry in developed countries some breathing space to adjust. It was not to last more than four years. However— as we would see happening repeatedly over time—after one year in operation it was converted into a long-term arrangement that lasted till 1973. Till 1973, protectionism may be said to have been confined to cotton textiles. But in 1973, the long-term arrangement gave way to the Multi-Fibre Arrangement, which covered not only cotton textiles but also textiles made of synthetic fibres. It is generally agreed that the MFA was a blatant violation of GATT rules. The above arrangements were supposed to give temporary breathing space to developed countries to allow competition from developing countries. But no one expected the temporary breathing space to last more than forty years running! For India, textiles and clothing offered one of the few areas of potential benefits in the Uruguay Round of trade negotiations.

One of the clearest negotiating objectives of India in the Uruguay Round was the complete integration of the textiles and clothing sector into the GATT framework. In other words, India's overriding objective was to get rid of prevailing quotas and allow free trade to rule in this sector. This was easier said than done. As seen above, protectionism in textiles had a long history and it was also politically difficult for developed countries to get rid of quotas at one go, since vested interests were well entrenched owing to distortions caused by the quotas. So in this sense, inclusion of this subject in the Uruguay Round itself was an achievement for countries like India. The only reason this was accepted by developed countries was because, in exchange, they got to bulldoze developing countries like India to agree to the inclusion of services and TRIPS in the negotiating mandate.

In negotiating proposals submitted to GATT at the time, India wanted the product coverage to be confined to items under restrictions. India, after arguing against any transition period for developed countries (after all they'd had more than forty years of 'breathing space' to adjust), suggested a maximum five-year-long transition period and sought a front-loaded integration of items and substantial growth rates during the early part of the transition period. It is fair to say that India failed in achieving both these objectives. The Agreement on Textiles and Clothing as it finally emerged, was characterized by a few features. For one, product coverage was inflated to include all items, including those that were not under any restrictions; and second, the transition period under pressure from US, supported by other developed countries, was set at ten years. Third, the integration percentages were arbitrarily decided at 16, 17 and 18 per cent, for the ten-year transition period, leaving a whopping 49 per cent to be integrated on 1 January 2005. In other words, the agreement was so back-loaded as to be commercially meaningless in the short to medium term. Again, India found itself in a minority and reluctantly accepted the Uruguay Round deal on textiles and clothing despite it not meeting its original negotiating objectives.[22]

Perhaps the strongest 'naysaying' was reserved by India for the TRIPS Agreement in the Dunkel Draft, which subsequently became the basis for the Uruguay Round Final Act establishing the WTO.[23] The case of the inclusion of IPR in the negotiating mandate of the Uruguay Round was a curious one. There was already a forum, the World Intellectual Property Organization (WIPO), based in Geneva. Its explicit purpose was to promote the protection of intellectual property worldwide and to ensure administrative cooperation among the intellectual property unions established by treaties that the WIPO administers. In other words, WIPO was *the* global forum for intellectual property services, policy, information and cooperation.[24] Indeed, it is worth looking at the 'Convention Establishing the World Intellectual Property Organization',[25] signed in 1967 and amended in 1979, well before the launch of the Uruguay Round in 1986. Article 4 of the aforesaid convention clearly states that the functions of the WIPO include: 'Encouraging the conclusion of international agreements designed to promote the protection of intellectual property and participating or administering any other international agreement designed to promote the protection of intellectual property.' Here was a forum readily available for negotiating IPR. Countries like India therefore asked why then did the US push for inclusion of the TRIPS Agreement as part of the GATT Uruguay Round?

The GATT multilateral trading system is based on the principle of free trade, i.e., trade must be made as free as possible from barriers so that its benefits can trickle down to all. It is therefore ironical that IPRs, which actually restrict trade in favour of the rights-holders, were sought to be included in the GATT system. Indeed, countries like India stated upfront that IPR was not a trade issue at all! It was clear why the industrialized countries led by the US were interested in this issue. After all, they were, at the time, the owners of nearly 99 per cent of all global patents and other forms of IPRs. It was clear from the beginning that inclusion of IPRs would severely constrain domestic policy space for developing countries.

Despite all these valid objections, the final Uruguay Round mandate agreed to in Punta del Este in 1986 stated, ominously, that the negotiations shall aim to clarify GATT provisions and elaborate as appropriate new rules and disciplines. But it also stated that there was a need to reduce the distortions and impediments to international trade, a phrase that gave some comfort to developing countries. The mandate was not entirely clear about whether new norms and standards would be part of the negotiations. It thus took another two years until April 1989, when India was forced to accept the mandate for the TRIPS Agreement in the Uruguay Round. The best explanation for this volte-face is provided by a former Indian negotiator for TRIPS, A.V. Ganesan, in his article 'Negotiating for India'.[26] He says persuasively:

> When the scope of the mandate was finally settled in April 1989 in favour of norms and standards, it was not so much because the developing countries came to see clarity or conviction in the mandate as because of other factors, including, in particular, the pressures exerted on them by the United States through unilateral action under its Trade Acts, changes in the internal policies and negotiating approach of some developing countries, the trade-off perceived by some developing countries from the inclusion of agriculture in the negotiations and the hope that sufficient flexibilities could be negotiated to balance protection with their own policy objectives.[27]

The question as to why more than 100 nations that were large, net importers of IPRs, signed a TRIPS Agreement that basically benefitted a tiny number of countries led by the US, is perhaps the most unfair feature of the Uruguay Round.[28] India fought valiantly in the TRIPS negotiations, it must be said. One of the other reasons why India objected to the TRIPS Agreement was also the character of the Indian Patents Act of 1970, which provided only for process patents, for liberal granting of compulsory licences and for 'licences of right' in the food, pharmaceuticals and chemicals sectors, among other things. A.V. Ganesan explains why and how India fundamentally changed its position in the TRIPS negotiations after opposing it so stridently in the beginning. He frankly admits that the main reason was the pressure exerted by the US through its unilateral actions under Section 301 of the US Trade Act 1974 and the Special 301 provisions of the US Omnibus Trade and Competitiveness Act 1988.[29]

The American proclivity for unilateralism was so strong that even the name of the new institution has an interesting story to it. Initially, the name for the new institution was supposed to be MTO, i.e. Multilateral Trade Organization. This made ample sense since we were after all talking about the multilateral trading system. The idea of an MTO was not without allure for countries like India and Brazil, which were often the target of US Special 301 actions under the US Omnibus Trade Act. In fact, one unwritten understanding of countries accepting the WTO dispute settlement mechanism was that the US would eschew all unilateral trade measures after the entry into force of the WTO and its binding dispute settlement mechanism. At the last minute however, the US objected to the name and said it preferred 'World Trade Organization' instead of the already agreed upon MTO.

The story of why the US sought such a change at the last minute has been explained in my book, *Negotiation Dynamics of the WTO*.[30] The official reason given was that American Senator Daniel Patrick Moynihan reportedly expressed reservation

about the nomenclature, MTO. The fact of the matter is that
there was a visceral objection to the word 'multilateral' and
there was concern that the US Congress would not approve of
it, since that may be construed to mean that their ability to take
unilateral trade measures would be constrained. Not wanting
to make a big deal out of this, all the countries humoured the
US by agreeing to the amended name, i.e., the anodyne 'World
Trade Organization'.

How then was the outcome of the Uruguay Round trade
negotiations from India's perspective? India's original negotiating
objective of keeping out services and IPRs from the multilateral
trading system, obviously, did not succeed. The TRIPS Agreement
cast an onerous burden on India, since it had to completely
overhaul its domestic law, especially on patents. Full integration
of textiles and clothing into GATT must be considered a major
achievement for India, even if the backloading of the benefits
in the agreement was disappointing. How fair was the Uruguay
Round outcome, from the perspective of developing countries
such as India? The best response may be found in the article by
Sylvia Ostry, 'The Uruguay Round North-South Grand Bargain:
Implications for Future Negotiations'.[31] She makes it categorically
clear that it was not a balanced outcome and ergo, not fair. In fact,
Ostry calls it a 'bum deal'. The unbalanced nature of the outcome
of the Uruguay Round is also the subject of much literature.[32]

Continuing with our Integrated Assessment Framework, the
following is the performance chart of India when it comes to
the Uruguay Round:

Uruguay Round Negotiations

Gandhi Litmus Test: Tried hard but had limited success
owing to lack of international support.

Policy Space: Serious erosion of policy space, eg., TRIPS Agreement.

Domestic Politics: Played a key role, with government being accused of a sell-out to US and others.

Geopolitical Imperatives: US pressure all too obvious. No sympathy from EU and others. India isolated.

Commitment to Multilateralism and Principles: Could not afford not to be part of WTO and the multilateral trading system.

Realpolitik and Material Gain: Textiles Agreement perhaps the only tangible gain along with an impartial dispute settlement mechanism.

The Uruguay Round resulted in the establishment of the WTO, which replaced the erstwhile GATT. As is well known, the WTO hardly bore any resemblance to GATT. While GATT dealt with just goods, the WTO included services and IPRs in its ambit. The dispute settlement mechanism in the WTO was rigorously enforceable, unlike the one in GATT, which was based on best endeavour by the parties to the dispute. From the integrated assessment above, it is clear that while India tried hard, it did not entirely succeed in achieving its initial negotiating objectives. The obligations assumed by India were onerous and binding, while the benefits were limited and not commensurate with the obligations undertaken. This led to what I call 'negotiation resentment', explained in my book as being caused by:[33]

- Negotiating outcomes being unfair and unbalanced;
- Use of brute force by powerful nations to achieve their negotiating objectives at the expense of others;
- Lack of accommodation or sensitivity to others' national interests or negotiating concerns;

- Use of disproportionate negotiating effort by developing countries with no corresponding results to show for in negotiations; and
- There being a skewed outcome for some in terms of benefits and obligations in the negotiations.

This negotiation resentment was all too obvious for India, which had fought so hard only to find itself isolated and most of its efforts torpedoed. As we will see below, this had a huge impact on how India approached further negotiations in the newly minted institution, namely, the WTO.

One of the distinct features of the newly formed WTO was that the top decision-making organ was the Ministerial Conference, which had the authority to take decisions on all matters under any of the multilateral trade agreements.[34] This Ministerial Conference was expected to meet at least once every two years.[35] Soon after the WTO came into force in 1995, Singapore began throwing broad hints that it would be keen to host the very first Ministerial Conference of the new organization, the WTO. For Singapore, it was meant as a validation of the fact that it was a 'good pupil' of the WTO and also a reflection of its soft power. In discussions prior to WTO's coming into force, the view of most WTO members was that the Ministerial Conference ought to be held in a business-like manner in Geneva, which housed the WTO headquarters. This would save considerable time, money and effort, since having a conference outside Geneva would entail flying out the WTO Secretariat and delegates, putting them up in hotels etc. But since Singapore was extremely keen, no one wanted to refuse their kind offer. Another big problem was that the host wished it to be a success at any cost. The first Ministerial Conference was not just about showcasing the WTO, but also showcasing Singapore as an ardent 'free trader'. So, it was important for Singapore to demonstrate at all costs that the first meeting was a successful one. Preparations for the first Ministerial Conference to be held towards the end of 1996, began in right earnest in 1995 itself. Two things deserved attention—as noted earlier, there was negotiation resentment among a few countries like India; yet others were busy implementing the onerous commitments undertaken by them during the Uruguay Round. In the case of India, domestic law had to be amended to be compliant with WTO in the case of TRIPS, Anti-Dumping, Subsidies and Technical Barriers to Trade, to name a few. Yes, there was a transition period for developing countries like India, but amending domestic law meant taking it to a rambunctious Parliament, no easy task in a country like India. In fact, most developing countries merely sought technical assistance to fully implement the Uruguay Round Agreements. Countries like India were certainly smarting and licking their wounds but had reconciled themselves to the Uruguay Round negotiating outcome, keeping the greater good of the multilateral trading system in mind.

This was a perfect moment for the more powerful WTO members, such as the US and the EU, to be sympathetic to the concerns of the developing and least-developed countries and to do a bit of handholding. Instead, what happened was hardly believable. The developed countries led by the QUAD (a grouping in the GATT that carried over to the WTO and comprised the US, EU, Japan and Canada and constituted an overwhelming proportion of global trade at the time) started pushing for a vastly expanded negotiating agenda at the first Ministerial Conference.[36] In effect, they sought the inclusion of new subjects such as investment, competition policy, and transparency in government procurement and trade facilitation. These came to be known as 'Singapore Issues' in the WTO, since they found mention there for the first time.[37] Adding insult to injury, the Quad also sought the inclusion of 'labour standards' in the negotiating agenda.

Labour standards—always a highly controversial topic in the GATT/WTO system—was unanimously opposed by almost all developing and least-developed countries, as either a non-trade issue, or worse, as a thinly disguised protectionist move by the powerful countries against the weaker countries. When this was conveyed to the US delegation, they merely shrugged, saying the American Congress wanted this to be on the agenda for the Ministerial Conference. Either way, this was a serious error of judgment by the powerful countries. Instead of helping the weaker members of the WTO, they preferred to rub salt into the latter's wounds. It resulted in increasing the trust deficit between the developed and developing countries in the new organization, the WTO. Nevertheless, the developing countries and the least-developed countries agreed to the final ministerial declaration, establishing working groups for 'studying' the so-called Singapore Issues. On labour standards, given the strident opposition by countries, the Singapore Ministerial Declaration merely reiterated that the International Labour Organization (ILO) was the competent body to set and deal with Core Labour Standards.

The next WTO Ministerial Conference in 1998 in Geneva had a landmark moment when US President Bill Clinton made a seemingly impetuous statement, that the US would be happy to host the next Ministerial Conference. The Geneva conference also became famous for the ugly protests in Geneva against WTO, which marred what should have been a joyous occasion celebrating fifty years of GATT's existence. While the US hinted it could live with a limited round of trade negotiations, the EU stuck to its guns calling for a comprehensive 'Millennium Round' of trade negotiations. With the US and the EU not seeing eye-to-eye on even the negotiating agenda, the signs for the Ministerial Conference to be hosted by the US did not look too hopeful.[38]

India is often accused of being a naysayer at WTO. Superficially, that may seem like a valid observation. There is, however, a need to dig deeper to understand India's negotiating motives. India's objection to the TRIPS Agreement in the Uruguay Round for instance, may be understood against the background of: there being no universal health coverage in India; a pharmaceutical industry that thrived on generic (not patented) drugs; and the impact of patented seeds on mostly subsistence farmers. India's opposition to the inclusion of the Singapore Issues (investment, competition policy, transparency in government procurement and trade facilitation) at the very first Ministerial Conference in Singapore (1996) was mainly because of the unfinished business from the Uruguay Round not receiving attention, and for fear of overloading the negotiating agenda.

Be that as it may, Indian negotiators started chafing at being criticized as naysayers and efforts began to draw up an India-led 'positive agenda'. The result was a set of issues simply known as 'Implementation Issues', and these were put forward for negotiations by a handful of countries led by India.[39] The like-minded group of nations comprised countries such as Cuba, the Dominican Republic, Egypt, El Salvador, Honduras, Indonesia, Malaysia, Pakistan, Nigeria, Sri Lanka and Uganda, and of course India. The Indian ambassador to the WTO invariably chaired these open-ended meetings. The Implementation Issues were so-called because they arose while countries were faithfully trying to implement the Uruguay Round Agreements and comprised: non-realization of anticipated benefits from some Uruguay Round agreements; imbalances and asymmetries in some agreements; and last, but not the least, non-operational and non-binding nature of Special and Differential Treatment provisions in the Agreements.[40] Here was India, often accused of being a naysayer, putting forward a positive negotiating agenda in the WTO for consideration by developed countries. The negotiating logic behind the Implementation Issues was morally persuasive, even if politically difficult.[41]

In classic WTO fashion, the demand for resolution of Implementation Issues fell on deaf ears and were at times met with derision by more powerful WTO Members. The point to be noted is this: India often did say no to proposals made by developed countries, but these objections were grounded in national interest, such as the Gandhi Litmus Test or the imperative need to preserve domestic policy space. But when India did put forward negotiating proposals—such as the Implementation Issues, the Negotiating Group on Movement of Natural Persons, or asked for Additional Protection of Geographical Indications for products other than wines and spirits (Basmati rice for instance)—these did not get traction, often being rejected out of hand by the powerful WTO members led by the US. It is important to note this since the customary accusation that India blocked everything in WTO, is simply untrue.

When WTO members started arriving in Seattle by end-November 1999 for the third Ministerial Conference, there was no broad agreement among members on virtually anything. Efforts to resolve issues failed miserably and the trade envoys based in Geneva simply passed on all the unresolved issues to their respective ministers to tackle in Seattle. To make matters worse, Seattle itself was under siege by NGOs of all hues, most of them protesting against WTO. The negotiating method in WTO was often driven by the 'green-room process'. A small, drab room in the WTO headquarters in Geneva, the 'green room' could not accommodate more than about a dozen or so people. So, on difficult issues, the Director General as the Chair of the Trade Negotiating Committee, would convene representatives from a dozen delegations to discuss the issue first. India was almost always lucky to be among them, but it is true that the vast majority of developing countries and an overwhelming majority of least-developed countries were simply out of the negotiating loop, at least at the beginning of the green-room process.

It was incumbent on the director general, WTO, and others to at least keep those outside the green room briefed on the progress made. In Seattle, the WTO Secretariat and key delegations failed miserably in this regard. With no consensus in sight and lack of transparency in negotiations (made worse by rampaging protesters outside), the 1999 Ministerial Conference was doomed to fail. And fail it did, in a spectacular fashion with not even a statement issued at the end of the conference. A bunch of ministers belonging to the least-developed countries walked out of the conference in protest even before it formally ended.

To say that this was WTO's nadir would be an understatement. Within three years of its establishment, WTO, which had been riding high, had experienced utter failure. While there were reasons why the Ministerial Conference failed in Seattle, one thing was clear—a few developing countries led by India but most importantly, the least-developed countries, were getting increasingly disenchanted with WTO. Their negotiating positions were ignored at best, and disrespected at worst. So when WTO reconvened in Geneva in 2000 after the failure in Seattle, the mood was sombre. Negotiators simply had no choice but to go back to the drawing board.

It was not that WTO Ministerial Conferences had not failed before. But the spectacular manner in which the meeting in Seattle failed was unprecedented. No WTO meeting had witnessed protester violence and police tear gas at the scale that Seattle had. I was an Indian delegate to the Seattle conference and had to run for cover when the police tear-gassed the NGO protesters menacingly approaching the meeting venue. Once back in Geneva in 2000, the negotiators sat down to discuss what really went wrong in Seattle. While the list of what went wrong was long, the negotiators began by focusing on transparency, effective participation in negotiations, especially by least-developed countries (since some of them had walked out of the Seattle meeting even before it finished), improving the way WTO dealt with NGOs and trying to address the disenchantment among some developing countries. After months of consultations among WTO members it was finally agreed that no fundamental changes were necessary, but that more information would be made available to NGOs, the least-developed countries would be kept in the negotiating loop and perhaps most importantly, an attempt would be made to accommodate the demands of the least-developed countries.[42]

2.5 The Development Round

Once these issues were addressed, efforts began anew for the launch of a new round of trade negotiations. The developed countries shrewdly started laying the groundwork by stating rhetorically that any new round must take into account the needs of developing countries. It was the UK Minister for International Development Clare Short, who first coined the term 'Development Round' of multilateral trade negotiations.[43] The WTO Director General, Mike Moore, also made a shrewd calculation that after the failure in Seattle, the only way to launch a new round ostensibly was to have a development agenda that addressed developing country needs.[44] On the whole, it made eminent sense to call the new round a 'Development Round', since the main criticism against past rounds was that the negotiating outcome had not helped in achieving developmental goals of the developing and least-developed countries, a point made repeatedly by India and others.

The choice of Doha as the venue for the 2001 WTO Ministerial Conference was not without controversy. As we saw, both the 1998 and the 1999 ministerial conferences in Geneva and Seattle had evoked street protests by NGOs and assorted activists. The 1998 protests were limited and the Swiss police with their ruthless efficiency managed it well. On the other hand, there is no gainsaying the fact that the 1999 street protests in Seattle went out of hand despite massive police presence and action. The net result of these two events was that the Swiss authorities made it known that they would henceforth be reluctant to host WTO ministerial meetings in Geneva. Furthermore, after the experience at Seattle, no Western country was overly keen to host WTO ministerial meetings for fear of creating law and order problems for itself.

It was against this backdrop that the Qatari authorities in early 2000 put forward their offer to host the next ministerial meeting in Doha. Instead of grabbing the offer, some key WTO members and the WTO Secretariat began to drag their feet, saying neither yes nor no to the Qatari offer. By January 2001, the Qataris issued an ultimatum to the WTO membership reminding them about their offer and seeking a response by 26 January 2001 at the latest.[45] The issue threatened to divide the WTO membership with developing countries (such as India, which had good bilateral ties with Qatar) taking the side of Qatar, and the developed countries led by the US expressing reluctance in the matter. By February 2001, the WTO General Council formally decided to accept Qatar's offer.[46] Despite this however, when a mini-ministerial meeting was held in Singapore in October 2001, there were attempts to change the venue from Doha to Singapore.

The most reliable account of how Qatar prevailed over US objections is found in Paul Blustein's book.[47] The Emir of Qatar phoned then US Vice President Dick Cheney and apparently told him that if Qatar was safe enough to host a US airbase then surely it was safe enough for a WTO Ministerial Conference. The US had no choice but to agree. With the 9/11 attacks having taken place by September 2001, it would have been politically difficult for the US and others to turn down the candidacy of an Islamic nation to host the WTO Ministerial Conference.

India played a pivotal role in negotiations leading to the launch of a new round of trade negotiations at Doha in November 2001. The Doha Round itself is the subject of several books and articles and it is not the purpose of this book to look at that.[48] There is no gainsaying, however, that India negotiated against all odds to try and preserve its national interests. Given below are the main areas that will indicate broadly to the reader how India made certain concrete negotiating gains in the WTO Ministerial Conference in Doha:

(a) **Central importance of developing countries:** Paragraph 2 of the Doha Ministerial Declaration states: 'The majority of WTO Members are developing countries. We seek to place their needs and interests at the heart of the Work Programme adopted in this Declaration.'[49] This is the very first time that a WTO ministerial declaration explicitly acknowledged that developing countries' needs and interests would be at the very core of the negotiations in WTO. This was no mean achievement and was in no small measure due to efforts of countries like India to push this.

(b) **Special and Differential Treatment:** Paragraph 44 of the Doha Ministerial Declaration states: 'We reaffirm that provisions for special and differential treatment are an integral part of the WTO Agreements.'[50] Using the formulation suggested by India it goes on to say that:

We therefore agree that all special and differential treatment provisions shall be reviewed with a view to strengthening and making them more precise, effective and operational. In this connection, we endorse the work programme on special and differential treatment set out in the Decision on Implementation-Related Issues and Concerns.

The US and some others wanted dilution of the concept of Special and Differential Treatment and to get a cross-cutting statement like this was a significant achievement.

(c) **Implementation-Related Issues and Concerns:** When a handful of like-minded countries led by India had raised 'Implementation Issues' for inclusion in negotiations, it evoked derision among many others. No one gave this like-minded group led by India, a chance of succeeding. To therefore get special mention in the Work Programme[51] and for the ministers to say that they attached utmost importance to implementation-related issues and concerns and that they were determined to find appropriate solutions to them, was nothing short of a miracle. If nothing else, getting these issues on to the negotiating agenda gave the proponents valuable leverage.

(d) **Declaration on TRIPS Agreement and Public Health:** Among all the substantive issues, this was the most significant achievement by India, working alongside Brazil and the Africa Group. A detailed account of this saga may be found in my book *Negotiation Dynamics of the WTO*.[52] Suffice it to say that this was the first issue to be resolved at the Doha Ministerial Conference and the Americans realized that without a resolution on this important issue, India and the African Group would not agree to anything else. Negotiating success was achieved through a combination of skills, tenacity and expertise possessed by India and Brazil on the one hand, and geopolitical clout possessed by the Africa Group on the other. The fact that developing country negotiators worked with Western NGOs like OXFAM and Doctors without Borders, was a novel feature and this made a big difference as well. This negotiating example should provide a counterfactual to those who argue that India is not enough of a stakeholder in WTO.

(e) **Agriculture:** Although India had a defensive negotiating posture in agriculture, this was an important negotiating area for several developing and least-developed countries. The following sentence was heavily negotiated till the last day in Doha in 2001:

> Building on the work carried out to date and without prejudging the outcome of the negotiations we commit ourselves to comprehensive negotiations aimed at: substantial improvements in market access; reductions of, with a view to phasing out, all forms of export subsidies; and substantial reductions in trade-distorting domestic support. We agree that special and differential treatment for developing countries shall be an integral part of all elements of the negotiations and shall be embodied in the Schedules of concessions and commitments and as appropriate in the rules and disciplines to be negotiated, so as to be operationally effective and to enable developing countries to effectively take account of their development needs, including food security and rural development.[53]

Again, Indian negotiators ensured that the mandate for negotiations in agriculture took fully into account the needs with regard to food security and farmer welfare.

(f) **Singapore Issues:** The real drama in Doha (2001) occurred with regard to the so-called Singapore Issues— investment, competition policy, transparency in government procurement and trade facilitation. India was determined not to allow negotiations in these areas to commence, unless its 'Implementation-Related Issues and Concerns' were properly addressed. This was, above all, a point of principle. After all, Implementation-Related Issues were a spillover from the Uruguay Round and deserved immediate attention from the perspective of developing countries. India was also acutely aware that if it said yes straightaway to the 'new' Singapore issues, there was zero possibility of Implementation-Related Issues being addressed by developed countries.

So, for India there was no question of expanding the WTO negotiating agenda without at least some of the Implementation-Related Issues being resolved. This resulted in India single-handedly blocking the Ministerial Conference, and proceedings were suspended for some hours.[54] India ensured that there would be no automatic launch of negotiations on the Singapore Issues at the following ministerial conference. Again, this was no mean achievement since it was virtually India alone versus the vast majority of the WTO membership.

India's role in the launch of the Doha Round came in for a lot of scrutiny. Leading British newspaper *Financial Times* on 15 November 2001 described India as the 'worst villain'. The weekly magazine *Economist* on 17 November 2001 alleged that India 'almost scuttled' the launch of the new trade round at Doha. The *Corporate Europe Observer* newsletter issue dated 10 December 2001 argued that India's position was more a shrewd negotiating tactic than a serious attempt to block the launch of a new round. The truth of the matter was much more complex. With meagre results in Implementation-Related Issues and Concerns, India could not have agreed to further expansion of WTO's negotiating agenda.

On TRIPS, India's efforts proved to be remarkably clairvoyant, since the WTO had to grapple with a TRIPS waiver for dealing with the Covid pandemic. India's stance in Doha was subsequently fully vindicated. Two other points merit attention. One, the Indian commerce and industries minister addressed the Parliament to brief members of Parliament (MPs) on the Doha meeting and won plaudits for standing up for India at the conference, even if he was alone. Second, the 9/11 events played a significant role in the negotiating position of the Western countries who wanted the Doha Round to be launched, lest an impression gain ground that the terrorists had 'won'.

The negotiating performance of India based on the Integrated Assessment Framework at the Doha Round is summarized below:

DOHA ROUND

Gandhi Litmus Test: Fully met by focusing on the needs of developing countries.

Policy Space: By ensuring postponement of negotiations in Singapore Issues and ensuring Special and Differential Treatment, this was fully safeguarded.

Domestic Politics: This was taken care of by resisting external pressure till the very end, evoking the admiration of the Indian Parliament.

Geopolitical Imperatives: Withstood pressure from the US, EU and others.

Commitment to Multilateralism and Principles: Tried to shape the system by getting it to focus on developing countries. Alliance-building with Africa was a key feature.

Realpolitik and Material Gain: Limited gains in TRIPS and Implementation Issues.

It is fair to conclude that the final negotiating agenda of the Doha Round was balanced and broad enough to have something in it for everyone. It was a litmus test for the WTO, which for the first time undertook to put 'development' at the heart of all trade negotiations. In the author's view, it was a golden opportunity for developed countries to win the confidence of the developing and least-developed countries, especially after what transpired in the Uruguay Round. It is therefore regrettable that the more powerful members of WTO allowed the Doha Development Agenda to first atrophy and then eventually allowed it to perish.

It is important to examine the failure of WTO to conclude the Doha Round (i.e., come to a common consensus on all issues raised in this round) despite more than twenty years having passed.[55] The first warning signs for WTO appeared at the Cancun Ministerial Conference in 2003, when a powerful coalition of developing countries called G20 appeared on the scene demanding ambitious reforms in agriculture from developed countries and sufficient flexibility for developing countries.[56] The G20 comprised not just India, China and Brazil but also other heavyweights like South Africa, Thailand and Nigeria. The G20 had clout because it accounted for 60 per cent of the world's population, comprised 70 per cent of all its farmers, and 26 per cent of all its agricultural exports, giving the grouping enormous heft in negotiations.

One can already see the evolution in India's negotiating strategy from the Uruguay Round—where it had led Venezuela, Cuba, Dominican Republic and some other countries in the like-minded group—to the G20 now, the membership of which was described above. So when the US and EU tried to push for a deal in Cancun (2003) with weak outcomes in agriculture, even while wishing to launch negotiations on the Singapore Issues, the G20 coalition simply said 'no' and the Cancun meeting failed.

Perhaps the closest the WTO members came to concluding the Doha Round was in July 2008 in Geneva. Agriculture has always been the biggest bugbear for WTO and it is impossible to conclude any Round without reaching a consensus on this delicate subject. Then Director General of the WTO, Pascal Lamy, tried to get a consensus among seven important members first, i.e., the US, EU, Brazil, China, India, Japan and Australia. Although not a bad idea, the Africans were miffed, since they were unrepresented in this group of seven.[57] When the deal in agriculture fell through leading to the eventual collapse of the Doha Round in July 2008, the common misperception was that a difference between India and the US on the issue of the Special Safeguards Mechanism (SSM) had caused it to fall through. However this was contested by the reputed journalist Paul Blustein in a blow-by-blow account of the negotiations conducted by Director General Pascal Lamy.[58] Blustein demonstrated beyond any reasonable doubt that the powerful American farm lobby was dissatisfied with the deal on offer and finally walked away from the negotiations.

In many quarters in WTO, it was simply convenient to blame India for being obstinate and torpedoing a deal. One must therefore thank Blustein for revealing the truth. India's reasons for wanting a strong SSM, which is about curbing import surges to protect domestic farmers, was based on the precarious nature of Indian agriculture, which is highly dependent on rainfall, whereas American insistence on a weak SSM was about getting significant

‌‌

market access for its own farmers in the huge Indian market. Again India was guided largely by the Gandhi Litmus Test and the need to preserve policy space, in the tough negotiations on agriculture in the context of the Doha Round.

2.6 The Public Stockholding Conundrum

By the time a WTO Ministerial Conference was scheduled in Bali in 2013, India had drawn attention to its unique problem regarding public stockholding of food grains. In the Uruguay Round Agreement on Agriculture this was fixed at subsides (difference between administered price, i.e., Minimum Support Price or MSP, and the market price) being no more than 10 per cent of the value of production of the commodity in question. Worse, the fixed external reference price was based on 1986–88 rates and there was no provision for inflation. India in 2013 made the strategic decision to belong to the G33,[59] a coalition of developing countries that pressed for flexibility to undertake limited market opening in agriculture. This was a grouping that had a much more defensive interest in agriculture, compared to the G20 grouping in Cancun described earlier.

While China was part of the G33 grouping, there was no Brazil, Thailand or South Africa, all of whom had offensive export interests in agriculture. On the other hand, Indonesia, South Korea and a number of African and Caribbean countries were part of the G33 grouping. India, a key player in the G33 grouping succeeded in linking the public stockholding issue with the conclusion of the first multilateral agreement in the WTO, namely, the Trade Facilitation Agreement. In the event, the Bali Ministerial Conference in 2013 effectively concluded the Agreement on Trade Facilitation and agreed to put in place an interim mechanism for the issue of public stockholding for food security purposes and a promise to negotiate a permanent solution to this issue.

Initially, the interim mechanism was to be in place till the eleventh Ministerial Conference (Bali was the ninth such conference).

For India, public stockholding was critical for food security purposes and for farmers' livelihood. So, an interim mechanism may have provided temporary relief, but a permanent solution was necessary. So, when the issue of final adoption of the Agreement on Trade Facilitation was to come up in the General Council in November 2014, India shrewdly linked this to making the interim mechanism more permanent. In other words, India wanted language to the effect that until a permanent solution was found to the issue of public stockholding, WTO Members would not challenge, through the dispute settlement mechanism, the compliance of a developing member country in relation to support provided for traditional staple food crops in pursuance of public stockholding programmes for food security purposes. Finally, this linkage paid off and the WTO General Council confirmed that the interim mechanism would continue until a permanent solution was found.

India continues to be seen actively negotiating in WTO and using trade-offs to achieve its negotiating objectives. After all, developed countries do so all the time and no one raises an eyebrow. But when India linked these two issues cited above, the Western press cast India as the villain. In a statement to the Indian Parliament in 2017, the commerce minister stated that after the WTO General Council decision in 2014, India's public stockholding programmes were to be protected by the interim mechanism which was available in perpetuity.[60]

The problem faced by India when it comes to its public stockholding for food security purposes is a legacy issue from the iniquitous Agreement on Agriculture concluded by WTO as part of the Uruguay Round negotiations. While the massive agriculture subsidies of the EU and the US were 'adjusted' through convenient 'amber and green' subsides, developing countries were not expected to exceed 10 per cent of the value of a particular commodity (say rice, wheat or sugar) through price support. Given the fact that

India has MSPs for a range of commodities, the calculation of subsidies (based on outdated 1986–88 prices without allowing for inflation) is such that India is in danger of exceeding the 10 per cent threshold, and has since done so for rice and sugar. Hence, the issue of public stockholding is actually a make-or-break issue for India. Not only is it important for food security purposes (it passes the Gandhi Litmus Test) and for the PM's Garib Kalyan Yojana catering to some 800 million poor people, but it is also terribly important for the farmers—and for the government therefore to preserve policy space in this regard.

The 2020–21 farmer protests were proof, if proof was needed, that farmers are an important electoral constituency and are totally wedded to the MSP regardless of whether India is in compliance with its WTO obligations or not. It is in situations like this that WTO must try and be sensitive to the concerns of its weaker members. It is not just enough to allow the powerful members to set the agenda. It must go the extra mile to accommodate the needs of developing and least-developed countries. After all, that is what the Doha Round had promised to the developing and least-developed countries.

The evaluation on this issue using the Integrated Assessment Framework is given below:

PUBLIC STOCKHOLDING

Gandhi Litmus Test: Full safeguards for the poor and for subsistence farmers.

Policy Space: Fully preserved for government with regard to MSP.

Domestic Politics: Important consideration as seen from farmer protests and withdrawal of farm bills by the government in 2021.

Geopolitical Imperatives: Ironically, the same Western countries who opposed a permanent public stockholding solution for India supported the farmer protests demanding unlimited procurement by government, in ostensible violation of WTO disciplines.

Commitment to Multilateralism and Principles: Preference for a multilateral solution.

Realpolitik and Material Gain: WTO members wary of India indulging in subsidized exports.

2.7 The Current WTO Challenge

The current negotiating climate in the WTO, as of 2023, is challenging for India. For one thing, Brazil and China have broken ranks with India, each for very different reasons. Brazil, under President Bolsonaro, had accepted the American diktat and given up its developing country status. It has applied to join the rich countries club, namely, the OECD. It remains to be seen whether Brazil will change tack under President Lula.

China, on the other hand, has wrecked bilateral ties with India, thanks to Ladakh (2020) and this has inevitably had an impact on Sino-Indian cooperation in the WTO. China has also selectively relinquished developing country status. India has now questioned developing country status for China (something India had never done before, for the sake of not offending China) since the latter's per capita GDP is now over $10,000. By its own admission, China has managed to abolish extreme poverty. That leaves India, pretty much by itself with the only negotiating option available being, to join forces with the Africa Group. But the Africa Group has a fair number of least-developed countries whose interests in the WTO may not always be fully aligned with those of India.

The principal challenge for India now is to keep its developing country status and hence the Special and Differential Treatment that it is entitled to under the WTO. The US (and EU implicitly) has openly questioned developing country status for India, thereby lumping India and China together on this issue. It must be hoped that India's foremost strategic partner, namely the US, will see reason in India's demand to be treated as a developing country partner.

I have proposed a two-tier solution for this issue in WTO.[61] One category could comprise all least-developed countries plus all countries belonging to South Asia and Sub-Saharan Africa. The rationale for including countries in South Asia and Sub-Saharan Africa is that these are now the only two regions with significantly large numbers of people who live in extreme poverty. The Oxford Multidimensional Poverty Index (now used by NITI Aayog in India), as well as other relevant indices, may be utilized for this purpose.

As for other countries like China, they can be addressed by case-to-case approach, where the WTO Membership may decide after looking at the specificities of the country concerned. Either way, the present approach in the WTO, whereby countries like Singapore, South Korea or China get to self-elect themselves as developing countries, is completely untenable.

The other challenge that India faces is that future negotiations in WTO are likely to be plurilateral rather than multilateral in nature. Seeing that there is no consensus in the WTO on launching multilateral negotiations on a range of 'new issues' (which is opposed to by a handful of countries, including India), a fairly large number of WTO members have embarked on what is called 'Joint Initiatives', also known as Joint Statement Initiatives.[62] These aim at initiating in WTO, forward-looking, result-oriented negotiations or discussions on issues of increasing relevance to the world trading system. The main feature of these initiatives is that they are not part of a multilaterally agreed-to process in

WTO. So, it has been initiated by those who constitute a coalition of willing and, in some instances, there are as many as 100 WTO members participating in these Joint Initiatives. However, because it is not strictly multilateral, India has preferred to steer clear of these negotiations. Nevertheless, these negotiations, informal as they are, deal with subjects that are critical for the future of international trade. Thus, there are Joint Initiatives on Electronic Commerce, Investment Facilitation, Micro/Small & Medium Enterprises, Services Domestic Regulation and Trade & Environmental Sustainability.

My contention is that India is adopting a high-risk strategy by staying away altogether from these Joint Initiatives. India's explanation is that all negotiations in the WTO must be multilateral in character and even plurilateral Joint Initiatives need the consensus of all members to be housed in WTO. In a strictly legal sense and in a perfect world, the Indian position is of course valid, but having thwarted the launch of multilateral negotiations in the WTO several times on, say, the subject of Investment, India cannot legitimately prevent over 100 WTO members from negotiating on this subject. More importantly, India is the only major country not participating in some of these negotiations. All of India's major investors, namely, the EU, UK, Japan, South Korea, China, UAE, Qatar, Mauritius, and Singapore are participants. The US has a special reason for not participating. It genuinely believes the investment regime it has is vastly superior to the rest of the world and therefore it stands to lose by joining in these negotiations. It is a fair guess that the US will join eventually though. In the author's view, India as a major investment destination and as a country which bids fair to be the largest recipient of FDI, cannot afford not to be part of these negotiations.

India staying away from the plurilateral negotiations is borne from a defensive mindset and is coloured by the experience of 'negotiation resentment' it experienced in the Uruguay Round of trade negotiations. But the India of 2023 is certainly not the India of 1986 when the Uruguay Round was launched. It is not even the India of 1994, when the Uruguay Round was concluded. If, after participating in several rounds of negotiations in RCEP, India in 2019 could walk out of it at the last minute, there is no reason why India should not participate in the Joint Initiatives discussions at the WTO with the clear understanding that it will not join the final negotiating outcome if it finds it against its vital national interests. At least this way, India would have had the opportunity to shape the negotiations from within. India not joining the Joint Initiatives at WTO militates against its stated ambition to be a rule-shaper rather than a rule-taker.

The twelfth WTO Ministerial Conference, postponed due to Covid-19, was finally held in June 2022. The backdrop was sombre. All three functions of the WTO—the negotiating function, the dispute settlement function and the trade monitoring function—were moribund. In its more than twenty-five years of existence (since 1995), the WTO had concluded just two agreements: The Trade Facilitation Agreement in Bali in 2013, and the decision to end Agriculture Export Subsidies in Nairobi in 2015. The dispute settlement mechanism, often referred to as the jewel in WTO's crown, was run aground by its most powerful member, the US, and the trade monitoring function was paralysed by the unwillingness of players such as China to share basic information on subsidies etc., with the WTO Secretariat. All in all, on the eve of the twelfth Ministerial Conference, the WTO faced an uncertain future. Those actively involved with WTO knew that the powerful countries had invested way too much to allow it to wither away.

In the event, the Ministerial Conference was an exercise to save the WTO from extinction. In an article in the *Economic Times*, I had asked rhetorically: 'Swim or sink in Geneva?', but the answer should have been known in advance.[63] What the Ministerial Conference did was to essentially paper over the cracks and opt for self-preservation.[64] It kept alive the fiction of negotiation with a half-baked multilateral agreement on fisheries subsidies, which is yet to clarify exactly the contours of the Special and Differential Treatment for developing and least-developed countries. The other hot-button issue—TRIPS waiver—was also dealt with only partially, leaving negotiations on diagnostics and therapeutics for a later date. Negotiations on the crucial issue of a dispute settlement mechanism were put off till 2024. What the Ministerial Conference did therefore, was to keep WTO alive while kicking several cans down the road.[65] Its biggest failure was that members were not even able to agree on a roadmap for future work in agriculture, let alone find a permanent solution for public stockholding for food security.[66]

So, how did India fare at the twelfth Ministerial Conference? The most charitable interpretation is that India decided in favour of supporting the multilateral trading system, rather than pushing its own narrow agenda, which could have complicated the outcome of the conference. That said, important battles lie ahead for India in the WTO—Agriculture, Special and Differential Treatment, TRIPS Waiver, Plurilateral Negotiations and Dispute Settlement. All these will require tough negotiations and shrewd alliance-building with the crucial Africa Group that has gained enormous clout compared to the Uruguay Round in the late eighties.

2.8 The Rush for FTAs

The WTO generally operates on the principle of non-discrimination, enshrined in the famous 'Most Favoured Nation' clause. The MFN prescribes that any trade concession granted by one WTO member to another, must be immediately and unconditionally granted to all other members.[67] This subscribes mainly to the philosophy that free trade—the removal of trade barriers and promotion of trade based on comparative advantage—is a win-win scenario for all concerned. This philosophy made sense in the aftermath of World War II when economic reconstruction was deemed necessary to avert another war, and continued to hold sway till about 1991 when MFN-based trade was considered the best way to achieve collective prosperity. Indeed, the zenith of this philosophy was reached with the conclusion of the Uruguay Round and the entry of the new institution called WTO.

Around this time, the concept of Free Trade Area (or Agreement) also started to take hold. Although GATT was based largely on MFN, there were important exceptions, one such being the FTA or the Customs Union, explicitly provided for in GATT.[68] The FTA is a departure from being treated as an MFN, since it is an arrangement between two or more countries in which customs duties and other restrictive regulations of commerce are eliminated in substantially all the trade between them.[69] It is obvious that an FTA can be both trade-creating and trade-diverting. Generally speaking, an FTA that is more trade-creating than trade-diverting is considered kosher and may even be a building block for a more effective multilateral trading system.

In actual practice though, WTO has failed to reject even one FTA and has blessed all FTAs regardless of whether they strictly adhere to the provisions of Article XXIV or not. One of the earliest FTAs was the North American Free Trade Agreement (NAFTA) in 1993 and since the most powerful player, the US, was behind it there was no way WTO could have said no to it. The EU, the other major player, also has a number of FTAs.[70] The bottom line is that while in 1991 there were barely six FTAs in the world, by 1999 there were some forty-two FTAs. By 2016, there were as many as 350 preferential trade agreements according to WTO.[71]

The trend, therefore, is unmistakeable—MFN-based trade is on its way out, preferential trade is in and is growing. India, one of the strongest defenders of MFN and WTO's multilateral trading system, could not have remained immune to this phenomenon. One of the earliest FTAs that India signed was with Sri Lanka in 1998. But from then on till about 2011, India signed as many as forty-two FTAs.[72] But from 2011 onwards till about 2020 there was a lull with India eschewing FTAs altogether. It is important to ask why. The main reason was that the FTAs signed by India with Thailand (2004), Singapore (2005), Korea (2009), ASEAN (2010) and Japan (2011) all led to increased imports and exports for India, but our imports were much higher than our exports to them, leading to a significant trade deficit for India.

There were substantive reasons for this. First, Indian industry's manufacturing competitiveness was no match for the industry in Southeast Asia. Second, the utilization rate of all the FTAs was low to moderate, indicating the need to make Indian entrepreneurs aware of the opportunities available due to the FTAs. Third, Indian products and services faced several non-tariff barriers in these countries, a field not normally covered by the FTAs. Last, but not the least, domestic economic reforms must proceed in tandem if benefits from FTAs have to accrue to India. For all these reasons and more, India between 2011 and 2020 did not sign any FTA nor was any announcement made about entering into new FTAs. In November 2019, India walked out of RCEP. There has been considerable literature as to why India walked out.[73] By 2020, the general feeling in the government was that India should not sign FTAs indiscriminately, but should only do so after careful consideration and attention to detail.

Yet by 2021, India had started contemplating a flurry of FTAs, most of which were to the west and north of India, while the past FTAs, without exception, had all been signed with countries to the east. The reasons for this volte-face[74] are not far to seek: The end of the MFN era, the advent of resilient supply chains and the fact that some of our major trading partners lie in these directions were all factors in India's change of heart. So, it is not surprising that we have now embarked on FTAs with the UAE and Israel to the west, UK, the EU, and Canada up north, and Australia, down south.

It is one thing, however, to announce our intention to enter FTAs, and another to implement it successfully. It must be noted that FTAs with the UAE and Australia have been concluded. But India must draw on lessons learnt and must seek comprehensive economic partnership with these countries that will include services, investment, tackling non-tariff barriers, visas for professionals etc. Other factors such as a good transition period, regulatory framework for digital trade and corresponding domestic reforms must be executed thoroughly and in a timely fashion.[75] These alone will provide a level playing field where India can benefit significantly from the FTAs it is embarking upon.

There is also another imponderable with the FTAs that India is negotiating with the EU and UK, relating to issues such as environment and labour standards. Until recently, these were not even considered 'trade issues' by India, but the concept of 'fair trade' as opposed to 'free trade' has taken deep roots and is here to stay. Indeed, the EU is seriously contemplating introduction of Carbon Border Adjustment Mechanism (CBAM),[76] defined as the landmark tool to put a fair price on the carbon emitted during the production of carbon-intensive goods entering EU, and to encourage cleaner industrial production in non-EU countries.

Similarly, FTAs—such as the United States-Mexico-Canada Agreement (USMCA), which came into force in 2020 and has substituted NAFTA[77]—have clear provisions on labour standards about wages etc. Seeing the writing on the wall, India has already embarked on discussions on these issues under the relevant pillar of the Indo-Pacific Economic Framework (IPEF) Agreement for prosperity that the US has floated as part of its Indo-Pacific strategy, though it is yet to make up its mind on joining the trade pillar. This is an area that will involve tough negotiations for India with its chosen FTA partners. It is interesting that India has chosen to go the bilateral route on these 'non-trade' issues, rather than participate in the WTO's plurilateral negotiations. The strategy seems to be that it will negotiate with some of its key partners bilaterally and then decide if it wants to be part of the WTO plurilateral negotiating landscape.

An interesting question arises. By choosing to enter FTAs, is India diluting its much-vaunted commitment to multilateralism? The rational explanation is that India really did not have much choice in the matter. The WTO is pursuing plurilateral agreements and with no imminent prospect of meaningful multilateral negotiations at the WTO, India cannot afford to stand still when all its trading partners and competitors are signing FTAs right, left and centre. If Indian exports have to remain competitive and if India is to be an integral part of the emerging, new, resilient supply chains, then it has to be part of the evolving international trade architecture, which is now characterized by FTAs.

The evaluation of FTAs using the Integrated Assessment Framework is given below:

Free Trade Agreements

Gandhi Litmus Test: Indirect relevance, hopefully will attract investment and create manufacturing jobs.
Policy Space: FTAs offer flexibility that multilateral agreements may not. But, issues like environment and labour standards are red flags and may constrict policy space.
Domestic Politics: Easier to justify FTAs than big multilateral trade agreements.
Geopolitical Imperatives: If China is the reason why we left RCEP, then FTAs with EU, UK, Australia, Canada etc., make

sense. It also makes sense for us to eventually join the trade pillar of the Indo-Pacific Economic Framework Agreement put forward by the US, our most important, strategic and biggest trading partner.

Commitment to Multilateralism and Principles: A breakdown in the Multilateral Trading System is much too obvious and India lacks the clout to fix it. So, no choice but to join FTAs.

Realpolitik and Material Gain: FTAs are necessary for maintaining competitiveness in exports and to achieve the dream goal of a $10 trillion economy.

In conclusion, India is not yet a major trade player in the world. With just over 2 per cent of the share in global trade, it still has a lot of catching up to do.[78] India does negotiate with the world at all levels, multilateral, plurilateral and bilateral. But it is hard to ignore the fact that it is heavily constrained at present by the 500 million people who live in property resulting in the 'poverty veto' we talked about. While it is true that the domestic market is big, it can be even bigger if these 500 million can be lifted out of poverty and put to productive work. This then is the central challenge for Indian policymakers.

3

Becoming Part of the Solution: The Case of Climate Change

3.1 Introduction

The very first UN document on the global environment was the Declaration of the UN Conference on the Human Environment in 1972, also known as the Stockholm Declaration.[1] In many ways, it contained the seeds of the politics of climate change that has continued to grow to this day. The idea that the natural resources of the earth must be safeguarded for the benefit of present and future generations, figures prominently in Principle 2 of the said declaration.[2] The idea of emissions is also referred to, by calling them the discharge of 'toxic substances' (Principle 6). Most importantly, the idea of Common but Differentiated Responsibilities, while not referred to in such terminology, along with technical and financial assistance to developing countries as well as their sovereign right to development actually figures very

90

prominently in Principles 11, 12 and 21. Late PM Indira Gandhi gave a stirring speech at the Stockholm Conference, noteworthy for the question she rhetorically posed: 'Are not poverty and need the greatest polluters?'[3] She also pointed out the plight of poor countries by noting that 'the environmental problems of developing countries are not the side effects of excessive industrialization but reflect the inadequacy of development.'[4]

India's approach on how to negotiate with the world in the field of environment/climate change was thus determined from the time of the Stockholm Conference. While the politics of climate change may have changed since 1972, the basic underpinnings of India's negotiating position have remained constant. It is therefore worth recalling the fundamental parameters of India's negotiating stand on the subject of climate change:

(a) The right to fight poverty is unconditional and India sees this as a moral duty to defend. This cannot be sacrificed at the altar of other goals, even those that are as noble as protection of the environment. In many ways, this is the 'poverty veto' that is a key driver in the way India negotiates with the world. Thus, the Gandhi Litmus Test referred to in our Integrated Assessment Framework is a constant in the way India deals with the world. Principle 8 of the Stockholm Declaration reads thus: 'Economic and social development is essential for ensuring a favourable living and working environment for man and for creating conditions on earth that are necessary for the improvement of the quality of life.' This is also couched in terms of the 'right to development' debate in the UN, which rightly culminated in the adoption by the UNGA of a Declaration on the Right to Development in 1986. Among other things, this Declaration asserts that the right to development is a human right on par with all other human rights. This was a hard-fought victory for developing countries in the UN system.

(b)   The need for policy space is something the government obsesses about, precisely because of the large number of people living in poverty. In an earlier chapter, we saw that this figure at present in India could be as high as 500 million. Besides, India does not have the economic and social safety net that developed countries do. Principle 12 of the Stockholm declaration, for instance, talks of taking into account the circumstances and particular requirements of developing countries. India's circumstances make it a unique case in climate change.

(c)   Considering that in 1972 the developed countries were exclusively responsible for climate change, it is interesting that the Stockholm Declaration has nothing explicit that puts the onus of historical responsibility for emissions and climate change on them. Both China and India were yet to emerge on the scene as big emitters of GHG, but the preamble of the Stockholm Declaration states that environmental problems were caused by underdevelopment in developing countries. Late PM Indira Gandhi, however, stated clearly in her speech:

> Countries with but a small fraction of the world population consume the bulk of the world's production of minerals, fossil fuels and so on. Thus, we see that when it comes to the depletion of natural resources and environmental pollution, the increase of one inhabitant in an affluent country, at his level of living, is equivalent to an increase of many Asians, Africans or Latin Americans at their current material levels of living.[5]

(d) India's position has always been that if poor countries are to adapt to better environmental standards, then they need both technology transfer and financial assistance. Principle 9 of the Stockholm Declaration recognized this and clarified the need for transfer of substantial quantities of financial and technological assistance as a supplement to the domestic effort of developing countries. So, India's mantra of climate finance and technology transfer goes right back to the Stockholm Declaration.

(e) The motto of '*Vasudhaiva Kutumbakam*' has been a guiding motto for India's approach to the world on a whole range of matters and climate change is no exception. Late Indira Gandhi did say in her speech that: 'Life is one and the world is one.' She concluded by emphasizing that global cooperation was the way forward. This too has remained an article of faith for India. As the current president of the influential G20 grouping, India's logo and theme for its presidency is 'One Earth, One Family and One Future', with the words 'Vasudhaiva Kutumbakam' inscribed beneath the logo. The emphasis on climate change could not be any clearer.

In many ways, India's basic approach to climate change negotiations is still based on the above arguments. The right to development continues to be a major driver even today. Indeed, the Pradhan Mantri Garib Kalyan Yojana, wherein 800 million people receive 1 kg of lentils and 5 kg of food grains, has now been extended till December 2024. That should serve as a sober reminder to those who underestimate the poverty challenge in India. It is simply impossible for India to overlook the problem of providing access to basic needs such as health, education, energy, water and sanitation for millions of its citizens. The corollary to this is also true, in India economic poverty is closely linked to energy poverty. And one way to lift people out of economic poverty is to first provide them with some source of energy. It is therefore hard to see how you can lift people out of economic poverty in India without alleviating energy poverty for the poor.

The second strand of the argument, as to why India believes it is not primarily responsible for historical emissions, is also based on incontrovertible evidence. The chart below from 'Carbon Brief' [Figure 3.1] is a stark demonstration of India's argument. Since cumulative historical carbon emissions lead to global warming, the historical responsibility of various emitters can be seen. India comes in last with a historical responsibility that is next to negligible. It is only from 1990 onwards, after India accelerated its economic growth, that it started to become a major emitter. Even so, in the ranking of GHG Emissions by Country,[6] India ranks third, after China and the US (for 2019 data); its emissions are actually one-half of that of US, and one-fourth of China's.

This brings us to the issue of per capita emissions—an important argument that India uses in climate change negotiations and which goes to the heart of what is known as 'climate justice'. Is an Indian entitled to some carbon space and if so, should it be the same as for an American or a Chinese? In a 2020 report the World Bank it was clear that India has one of the lowest per capita emissions in the world, a mere 1.8 as opposed to China's 7.6 and the US' whopping 15.6.[7]

The argument that India ought to have an entitled carbon space for fulfilling its fundamental right to development, over the claims of already developed countries, is far from rhetorical and goes to the heart of the matter. Much as India has convincingly made this argument, it is sad to note that the developed countries have taken no note of it, blithely ignoring this argument during climate negotiations.

Figure 3.1: Cumulative Carbon Emissions per Capita 1850–2021 (CO2)

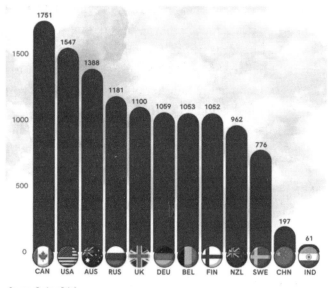

Source: Carbon Brief

Source: Carbon Brief: Clear on Climate

3.2 Negotiating the UN Framework Convention on Climate Change

Perhaps the first thing to be noted is that few international agreements were concluded as quickly as the UNFCCC. From the UNGA meeting in 1989 to the conclusion of UNFCCC in May 1992, it was a mere three years or so. Compare this with the Uruguay Round of trade negotiations, which took eight long years, and the UN Convention on the Law of the Seas (UNCLOS), which took a little under ten years! Given this, it is quite remarkable how India was able to leave an indelible imprint on the Framework Convention.

India was actually quite well prepared in terms of arguments when UNGA passed a resolution in 1989 calling on member states to urgently prepare a 'framework convention' to address the global problem of climate change. One interesting fact is that the early negotiations on climate change were led by IFS mandarins. Thus, the leader of the Indian climate change negotiating team was the late Ambassador Chandrashekhar Dasgupta, an outstanding IFS officer from the Ministry of External Affairs (MEA). This was also necessitated by the fact that the Ministry of Environment and Forests (MoEF) was established in India only in 1985. But by the time Paris happened in 2015, it was the MoEF that had the lead role in climate change negotiations, with the MEA playing a secondary role. This may not have made a material difference to negotiating outcomes, but it might have served India better in terms of its alliances with its partners had MEA continued with the lead role.

In terms of negotiating strategy, India first and foremost relied on being the voice of the developing countries and sought their support for the positions it took. Soon after UNGA decided in 1989 that a Framework Convention was to be negotiated, India convened a 'Conference of Select Developing Countries on Global Environmental Issues' in New Delhi in April 1990. This was a smart move to garner support from developing countries and proved to be extremely useful in the negotiations leading up to Rio in 1992 when UNFCCC was concluded.

India pushed hard for its points: the main responsibility for climate change lay with the developed countries; the emissions of developing countries were low and their right to development was both fundamental and non-negotiable; and technology transfer and financial assistance was necessary from developed countries, to enable developing countries to address the challenge of climate change.

One trick that India and other developing countries may have missed (in hindsight of course) is the absence of any reference at this stage in their statements and negotiating strategies to the 'polluter-pays principle (PPP)'. After all, the PPP was adopted as far back as 1972 by the Paris-based OECD that comprised the richest countries of the world, as an economic principle for allocating the costs of pollution control. In fact, the OECD Environment Directorate in 1992 termed PPP not just an economic principle but a legal one. Since the developing countries had made it a point to dwell on technology transfer and financial assistance in their negotiating strategy, it would have been useful to buttress it with the PPP, which incidentally was a Western construct. Interestingly, there is little or no reference to PPP even in later negotiation strategies formulated by India or indeed by other major developing countries such as Brazil.

In the run-up to the UNFCCC negotiations in Rio, the main actors were: the G77 plus China; OECD countries; Organization of Petroleum Exporting Countries (OPEC); and the Alliance of Small Island States (AOSIS). However, even within each grouping, there were significant differences in country positions, as we will see shortly.

The one thing to remember though, is that economic and trade considerations loomed large in climate change negotiations. These negotiations were not just about the politics but also the economics of climate change. The first leader of the Indian negotiating team, the late Ambassador Chandrashekhar Dasgupta, rightly said at the time that climate change agreements were essentially economic agreements. This also explains why India, with its monumental developmental challenges, is still paranoid about taking on too many climate change commitments, which may then be an encumbrance in its fight against poverty.

China has always played its cards smartly in climate change negotiations. When it did not have enough clout to swing the climate change negotiations in its own direction, it attached itself to the G77, but still allowed itself some wiggle room. It therefore 'free-rode on India and G77 positions in the run-up to the Rio Earth Summit. China's negotiating strategy in climate change negotiations can be divided into three phases: the first till 2009, when it was happy to tag along with the G77 in a loosely defined fashion; the second from 2009–14, when it was part of the BASIC grouping, comprising Brazil, South Africa, India and China; and third, from 2014 onwards, when it has essentially done bilateral deals with the US, often at the expense of BASIC. Indeed, as we will see later, China pretty much wrecked the BASIC coalition before the COP21 meeting in Paris in 2015.

The US has perhaps been the most recalcitrant player for the better part of all climate change negotiations. It denied, outright, that it or other developed countries had any historical responsibility for climate change, even as it opposed calls for time-bound reduction targets for GHG emissions. Europe sounded more reasonable, but only just. Germany, for instance recognized the 'special responsibility' of developed countries, but also called on the developing countries to do their part.

It would also be wrong to say that the G77 was completely united. There were the oil exporting countries led by Saudi Arabia, which did not want strong commitments to be undertaken by developed countries for fear of losing markets for their oil. The AOSIS, on the other hand, was facing an existential threat from rising sea-levels and so pushed for very ambitious climate goals by all concerned.

Given the above negotiating scenario, the framework agreement that emerged from Rio was a success for India and other developing countries for the reasons discussed next.

3.2.1 Common but Differentiated Responsibilities

The story behind 'common but differentiated responsibilities' (CBDR) and how it came to be incorporated in the Rio Declaration and the UNFCCC is both interesting and intriguing. As recounted earlier, India and other developing countries held that the 'main' or 'primary' responsibility for climate change lay with developed countries. In fact, China too in its non-paper (an informal discussion paper) prior to the Rio summit called upon developed countries to assume the 'main responsibility' in addressing climate change. So, how did the CBDR idea come about?

The idea of differentiation itself was not new. As we saw in the chapter on trade negotiations, Special & Differential Treatment became part of GATT law in 1979. The question about CBDR is whether this was a better formulation, than the 'main' or 'primary' responsibility lying with developed countries. It could be argued that the word 'common' in CBDR imposes some obligation on all countries, including developing ones. And the word 'differential' only gives cover to the extent that the responsibility of developing countries will be different (not the same) as that of developed countries.

It is also interesting to hear from various Indian negotiators as to how this was introduced in the text. There is no clear or authentic account in this regard. But it would appear that it was the US that drove the Western group to introduce the term CBDR in the UNFCCC negotiations. The term first appears in the record of the second Climate Conference held in Geneva in 1990 organized by the World Meteorological Organization. The relevant record is quoted below:

Participants recognized a number of principles that had emerged in international climate discussions, including the concept of climate change as a common concern of humankind, the principle of equity and the common but differentiated responsibility of countries at different levels of development, the concept of sustainable development, and the precautionary principle.[8]

So, ironically enough, the CBDR concept was actually imported into UNFCC negotiations by the Western group to perhaps duck the 'main' or 'primary' responsibility being laid at its doorstep. Some Indian negotiators do believe this was a climb-down and it is possible the mandarins at the MoEF may not have fully grasped the significance of this. On the other hand, even if the words 'main responsibility' had been inserted, the question of clarifying what 'main' responsibility was and what 'residual' responsibility entailed, would have remained.

Be that as it may, US lawyers who traditionally accompany their negotiators would have found CBDR a far more preferable formulation than say 'main' or 'primary' responsibility. In the UNFCC itself, the 'historic responsibility' for emissions is mentioned in the preamble but not in the body of the text. A further addition to this tortuous phrase may be found in paragraph 1 of Article 3 of the UNFCC titled 'Principles.': 'The Parties should protect the climate system for the benefit of present and future generations of humankind, on the basis of equity and in accordance with their common but differentiated responsibilities and respective capabilities.'

Again, it is possible that the US lawyers thought through this issue better than others. Respective capabilities can be interpreted as a way to distinguish India's commitments from say, Mali or Chad. And this did come to haunt us down the road. All this should not detract from the excellent achievement of our negotiators but this is to merely set the record straight on what is customarily thought to be an Indian or at least a developing country formulation. The CBDR figures in Principle 7 of the Rio Declaration on Environment and Development (Rio Declaration), in Article 3 of the UNFCCC as CBDR-RC and in the chapeau of Article 4 of the UNFCC Agreement thus: 'All Parties, taking into account their common but differentiated responsibilities and their specific national and regional development priorities, objectives and circumstances'.

The word 'circumstances' may also be noted, since it appears for the first time, only to be picked up later in an India-US Joint Statement (2009) and then in a US-China Joint Statement (2015).

3.2.2 Commitments by Developing Countries

A key negotiating objective of developing countries in the UNFCCC negotiations was that they should not be obligated to do anything that would clash with their development priorities or did not overtly benefit from technology transfer or financial assistance from developed countries. The late Ambassador Chandrashekhar Dasgupta in an excellent article says that this was the most difficult thing for India and developing countries to achieve.[9] In the event, Article 4, paragraph 7 of the UNFCC quoted below must rank as a significant victory for India and other developing countries:

> The extent to which developing country Parties will effectively implement their commitments under the Convention will depend on the effective implementation by developed country Parties of their commitments under the Convention related to financial resources and transfer of technology and will take fully into account that economic and social development and poverty eradication are the first and overriding priorities of the developing country Parties.

The above paragraph fully takes into account India's negotiating position and completely safeguards its national interests.

3.2.3 Right to Development

India's position in climate change negotiations has always put the right to development at the heart of its actions, since it faces monumental developmental challenges. It may be observed that the paragraph above (Article 4, paragraph 7 of the UNFCCC) fully acknowledges this. Both Principles 2 and 3 of the Rio Declaration ensure the right to development, but keeping in mind environmental considerations. Conversely, Principle 8 of the Rio Declaration specified that States should reduce and eliminate unsustainable patterns of production and consumption, and promote appropriate demographic policies.

The unsustainable consumption style of the Western countries was a major cause of their emissions. In literature, there is often a distinction made between 'lifestyle emissions' of those in the West and the 'survival emissions' of these in developing countries. This argument is important since the quality and nature of emissions are as critical as the quantitative aspect of emissions. It also goes to the heart of the issue of climate justice.

3.2.3.1 Per Capita Emissions

As we noted earlier, one of the arguments made by India was that while our cumulative GHG emissions may look big, the per capita emissions given the size of our country are miniscule. This too found its way only to the preamble of the UNFCCC and not to the body of the text. One of the reasons of course is that while this is accepted in principle by others, even some of our developing country brethren do not buy this argument in full. They simply shrug their shoulders as if to suggest that the population of India is not their problem, but ours. Nevertheless, we have continued to make this point, but with very little success.

3.2.4 UNFCCC: Annex I and Annex II

It has already been noted that one of the main achievements of the UNFCCC, from India's perspective, was that the onus was placed entirely on developed countries for taking on concrete commitments. The UNFCCC thus called on industrialized countries to take the lead by modifying their long-term emission trends and urged the richest among them to provide financial and technological resources to help developing countries tackle the problem and adapt to its adverse effects. More crucially, the UNFCCC acknowledged that the first and overriding priorities of developing countries were development and poverty alleviation.

These are no mean achievements. To put this plan into action, UNFCCC divided countries into three categories. Two of these are listed in Annex I and Annex II of the UNFCCC. Annex I (forty-one countries) comprises all OECD countries (wealthy and industrialized) plus countries with economies in transition (EITs) including the Russian Federation, the Baltic States and Central/East European States.

Annex II has just the twenty-four OECD countries listed (as in Annex I) but without the EITs. Then, of course, are countries which are not listed in either Annex, which were known as non-Annex I countries (145 in number), comprising the vast number of developing and least-developed countries. Annex I and Annex II countries had specific commitments under the UNFCCC, while non-Annex I countries had only general but no specific commitments. This followed a strict interpretation of the CBDR principle.

Annex I countries were subject to a specific commitment to adopt climate change policies and measures with the non-legally binding aim that they should have returned their GHG emissions to 1990 levels by the year 2000. The EITs had some flexibility in this regard.

Annex II countries are required to provide financial resources to enable developing countries to meet their obligations under the convention. In addition, Annex II countries must take 'all practicable steps' to promote development and transfer of environmentally-friendly technologies to developing countries. The UNFCCC has a financial mechanism for this purpose operated by the Global Environment Facility.

The role of Indian NGOs must be generally complimented in this whole exercise. In particular, the oldest and arguably the best in the business was the Centre for Science and Environment (CSE). As far back as 1991, in the run-up to the negotiations of the UNFCCC, two scholars from CSE wrote an article provocatively titled: 'Global Warming in an Unequal World: A Case of Environmental Colonialism'.[10] The article blew to smithereens a report by the World Resources Institute (WRI) in collaboration with the UN, which appeared to blame developing countries such as China and India, apparently to deflect attention from huge historical emitters such as the US, Japan and the EU.

The central contention of the two Indian authors was that compared to India's population (16.2 per cent of the world in 1990), its total production of carbon dioxide (CO_2) and methane (two of the most important gases contributing to global warming) amounted to only 6 per cent and 14.4 per cent. The US, they noted, had only 4.73 per cent of the world's population but emitted as much as 26 per cent CO_2 and 20 per cent methane. In fact, CSE adopted its own methodology, allocating natural sinks for CO_2 and methane to each country on a population basis. Using this methodology, it not only trashed the findings of the WRI report but also absolved developing countries such as India from any responsibility. It concluded by emphasizing the need for independent Third World research in climate change, and warned against the tendency to rely on Western research.

The expertise of the two authors from CSE served Indian negotiators very well in their need for marshalling evidence for their argumentation. It is also interesting to note that while in trade negotiations Indian NGOs would often accuse the government of a 'sell out', in the case of climate change they were broadly on the same page as the government.

Using the Integrated Assessment Framework developed earlier, given below is the evaluation of the UNFCCC negotiated by India:

UNFCCC

Gandhi Litmus Test: The poor in India suffered the most due to environmental degradation. Getting rich countries to take some action was the best India could have done.

Policy Space: Fully met, since no concrete commitments undertaken by India.

Domestic Politics: Environment yet to figure in domestic politics at the time, so very little focus.

Geopolitical Imperatives: India provided leadership to G77 group of developing countries, which China joined.

Commitment to Multilateralism and Principles: India pragmatic enough to realize that global action was required to deal with climate change.

Realpolitik and Material Gain: India pushed hard for technology transfer and financial assistance, but this did not materialize as expected.

The assessment is therefore that India ticked most of the boxes, when it came to negotiating the UNFCCC.

3.3 The Tortuous Road to Paris

It is worth reiterating that India took the most logical and tenable position it could in the negotiations leading up to the UNFCCC (1992) and well into the nineties when the famous Kyoto Protocol (1997) was adopted. Indeed, the Kyoto Protocol with its clear and legally binding emission targets for developed countries could be considered a high point for Indian negotiations. At that time, our emissions were so low and our development trajectory so much in its infancy (especially compared to China) that there was no imminent danger of our being asked to make specific commitments.

Then two things happened that should have raised alarm bells for India. First, developed countries steadfastly failed to meet GHG emission reduction targets and make substantial transfer of technology or financial assistance. The worst offender in this regard was the US. Eventually, it walked out of the Kyoto Protocol in 2001. Knowing the pattern of negotiations in other fora, it was simply a matter of time before the EU ganged up with the US and started putting pressure on countries like India. This is something we should have anticipated, but probably did not.

Second, could we have made conditional commitments to combat climate change, saying it depended entirely on the rich countries making concrete commitments and providing financial assistance to us? Could we, perhaps making use of our NGOs, have put more pressure on the US and others to undertake emission cuts, rather than exclusively focusing on our not taking on any commitments? Hindsight is always 20/20, but this approach may have been worth a try.

3.4 Strategic Shifts

If one is looking for strategic shifts in India's negotiating stand, then one need look no further than the infamous COP15 held in the Danish capital of Copenhagen. However, the pressure on India to shift had begun much earlier. The Kyoto Protocol adopted in 1997, was in many ways a crowning achievement for India's negotiating position, since it set binding targets for at least thirty-seven industrialized countries and the European Community for reducing GHG emissions. It may be construed as an agreement to effectively operationalize and fully implement the UNFCCC on a strict interpretation of CBDR.

Efforts to change the basic architecture of the UNFCCC began at the very first Conference of Parties, COP1 in 1995 in Berlin, when Germany proposed that the 'more advanced' among developing countries (an unmistakeable reference to China and India) also accept mitigation commitments. This was opposed strongly by India and its G77 supporters (excluding the OPEC group) and India succeeded in staving-off the challenge for the time being. But it was revived again in the form of a proposal at COP3 in Kyoto, 1997, when 'voluntary commitments' were sought from some developing countries. This too was successfully resisted by India and its partners. There were substantive reasons why this was sought to be done by developed countries. First, their domestic industry was unhappy to take on concrete commitments and lose competitiveness to countries like China and India. In this sense, their governments were under pressure to do something. Second, it was also an attempt to 'divide and rule' the vast G77 membership. Since India (and China to an extent) was providing leadership on the issue of climate change, it was a useful strategy for the developed countries to single out India and China.

The most important role in India's shift in climate change negotiations may be attributable to the US. The US position on climate change, right from the time of UNFCCC, was based on three propositions: First, they denied the notion of historical responsibility. Second, they loathed concrete emission reduction targets for themselves. Third, according to the US—since global warming was a global problem—all countries without exception must participate in the fight against climate change.

In July 1997, just months before the adoption of the Kyoto Protocol, the US senate adopted the Byrd-Hagel Resolution. This stated clearly that the US should not sign a climate agreement that included new, mandatory emission reduction commitments for the US, without such limits for developing countries within the same compliance period, or sign anything that would result in serious harm to the US economy.[11] While the operative part of the resolution referred to developing countries in general, the preamble made it clear that there was a particular concern with regard to China, Mexico, India, Brazil and South Korea.

It has been suggested that this concern for serious harm was not an independent concern, but one that flowed per se from the exclusion of developing country commitments. Anyway, the resolution was adopted unanimously in the Senate. The Clinton Administration did act on the Senate resolution by proposing an additional provision to be included in the Kyoto Protocol, which would have provided for developing countries voluntarily taking on binding commitments (an oxymoron if ever there was one!) with the added incentive of being able to engage in emissions trading with developed countries. But this proposal was not accepted. Nonetheless, the US kept pushing this line at every available opportunity. In 2001, the US formally pulled out of the Kyoto Protocol sounding the agreement's death knell.

It is fair to say that 2007 was probably the year in which India moved from a position of 'no commitments' to 'some commitment' in climate change negotiations. The first hint came at the G8 meeting in Germany in June 2007, when then PM, Manmohan Singh—after clarifying in detail all the usual points about India's climate change position—nevertheless stated unambiguously that 'India was determined that its per capita GHG emissions are not going to exceed those of developed countries even while pursuing policies of development and economic growth'.[12] In other words, for the very first time India set a ceiling for itself with regard to GHG emissions.

By the time COP13 took place in Bali in December 2007, a plan of action was adopted, which committed all countries (developed and developing) to some action. In fact, paragraph 1, sub para (b)(ii) says: 'Nationally appropriate mitigation actions by developing country Parties in the context of sustainable development, supported and enabled by technology, financing and capacity-building, in a measurable, reportable and verifiable manner'.

Considering that the Bali plan of action was to form the basis of future negotiations leading to a future climate change agreement, it was surprising that developing countries, including India, did not see a red flag. Nevertheless Bali had its moments of tension, with the leader of Papua New Guinea asking the US to get out of the way if it could not provide leadership. The US was finally forced to join the consensus.

The real and substantive shift in India's position in climate change negotiations happened in Copenhagen and this merits careful scrutiny.

3.5 Drama in Copenhagen

The run-up to the COP meeting in December 2009 at Copenhagen was already being billed as a game-changer. This was part of the hype by developed countries and other interested stakeholders to ensure the success of the conference. The US President Barack Obama launched the 'Major Economies Forum on Energy and Climate Change' (MEF) initiative in March 2009. It aimed to provide a platform for candid dialogue among developed and developing economies to enable political leadership to achieve a successful outcome in Copenhagen.

In May 2009 in India, Congress Party leader Jairam Ramesh was appointed Minister in charge of Environment and Forests. Ramesh was to play a crucial role in how India approached the negotiations at Copenhagen. In yet another sign that India could shift its stance in climate change negotiations at the MEF meeting in Italy in July 2009, it was represented by PM Manmohan Singh, who went along with the final leaders' declaration, which read thus:

Our countries will undertake transparent nationally appropriate mitigation actions, subject to applicable measurement, reporting, and verification, and prepare low-carbon growth plans. Developed countries among us will take the lead by promptly undertaking robust aggregate and individual reductions in the midterm consistent with our respective ambitious long-term objectives and will work together before Copenhagen to achieve a strong result in this regard. Developing countries among us will promptly undertake actions whose projected effects on emissions represent a meaningful deviation from business as usual in the midterm, in the context of sustainable development, supported by financing, technology, and capacity-building. The peaking of global and national emissions should take place as soon as possible, recognizing that the timeframe for peaking will be longer in developing countries, bearing in mind that social and economic development and poverty eradication are the first and overriding priorities in developing countries and that low-carbon development is indispensable to sustainable development. We recognize the scientific view that the increase in global average temperature above pre-industrial levels ought not to exceed 2 degrees C. In this regard and in the context of the ultimate objective of the Convention and the Bali Action Plan, we will work between now and Copenhagen, with each other and under the Convention, to identify a global goal for substantially reducing global emissions by 2050. Progress toward the global goal would be regularly reviewed, noting the importance of frequent, comprehensive, and accurate inventories.[13]

Taken along with the Bali Action Plan, this indicated a certain willingness by India to undertake mitigation action (albeit conditional), something it had not committed to earlier. The only other country in the forum in India's position was China. But then, China was in such a vastly different situation from India that it suited them to hide behind India and the G77.

It is quite difficult to be sure on why India made this shift. It could be that India felt its arguments on per capita emissions and on historical responsibility had run its course. The AOSIS was also beginning to change its perspective on China and India, saying advanced developing countries must also undertake concrete commitments. But there is no denying that the US was the major driver in India's shift. It is worth remembering that around this time Indo-US ties were going from strength to strength. After all, the NSG exemption for India in Vienna in 2008 was achieved entirely because of the diplomatic heft of the US, in the face of massive Chinese resistance. It would have been difficult for India to refuse American entreaties on climate change after what they had done for India at the NSG. Obama received Manmohan Singh in Washington in November 2009 and the relevant part of the Joint Statement read thus:

> The two leaders also affirmed that the Copenhagen outcome must be comprehensive and cover mitigation, adaptation, finance and technology, and in accordance with the principle of common but differentiated responsibilities and respective capabilities, it should reflect emission reduction targets of developed countries and nationally appropriate mitigation actions of developing countries. There should be full transparency through appropriate processes as to the implementation of aforesaid mitigation actions. The outcome should further reflect the need for substantially scaled-up financial resources to support mitigation and adaptation in developing countries, in particular, for the

poorest and most vulnerable. It should also include measures for promoting technology development, dissemination and transfer and capacity-building, including consideration of a center or a network of centers to support and stimulate climate innovation. India and the United States, consistent with their national circumstances, resolved to take significant national mitigation actions that will strengthen the world's ability to combat climate change. They resolved to stand by these commitments.

The above language is strong and in my view commits India and the US to taking 'significant national mitigation actions consistent with their national circumstances'. It is fair to say that India had never accepted such language in the UNFCCC. Again, the fact that this happened at the highest-level leads one to believe that it was done keeping the larger interests and quid pro quo that characterize Indo-US ties, in view. Climate change experts look to explain the shift in India's position as occurring due to pressure and the negotiating dynamics within the UNFCCC itself. It may be worthwhile to also look for explanations outside the UNFCCC and within the context of India's ties with its strategic partners, including the US.

Prime Minister Manmohan Singh had at least two people advising him in the run-up to the Copenhagen meeting on climate change. One was obviously his Minister for Environment and Forests, the young and dynamic Jairam Ramesh eager to make his mark in international negotiations. The second was Ambassador Shyam Saran, an outstanding IFS officer who, after retiring as Foreign Secretary, was now the PM's Special Envoy for Climate Change. It was perhaps inevitable that these two individuals should clash in the run-up to and at Copenhagen. Their views on India's domestic challenges and therefore its resultant role in the international climate change negotiations were hard to reconcile.

In many ways, they represented the two diametrically opposite points of view in India on the issue of climate change.

Jairam Ramesh sought to 'reposition India globally' in the context of the climate change negotiations. In fact, that is the title of a chapter in his book *Green Signals*.[15] Ramesh says in the very first sentence of the chapter that: 'Prime Minister Manmohan Singh's brief on our global engagement was simple: change the perception about India.' He goes on to add that with regard to climate change, while it was not a problem that India had created, India should nevertheless be part of the solution. He goes on to spell out the broad negotiating strategy: to reposition India, both in terms of style and substance, in international negotiations where India had acquired an image of being a naysayer; and for India to assume a pivotal role in shaping international agreements to ensure that India is best able to protect its core economic interests.

In practical terms, Ramesh wanted India to put forward concrete measures, such as domestic legislation—for instance specifying performance targets for mitigation actions in power, transport, industry etc. If these were to be done autonomously, then that would perhaps not have evoked any reaction. But Ramesh went one step further, suggesting a mechanism through which the international community could be kept informed of India's efforts. Ramesh argued what he had in mind was a Trade Policy Review kind of mechanism prevalent in the WTO, which was non-binding and consultative in character.[16] This may have been a tad naïve on his part since the US lawyers would have found a way to tie India to specific obligations. Ramesh also wished to deviate from the per capita emissions obsession of India and had asked Indian economist Arvind Subramanian to do a paper based on a 'per capita plus' approach. This had to be abandoned by him, since it was seen as a sharp deviation from India's long-held positions.

In a note to the PM on 13 October 2009, Ramesh suggested the nuancing of India's negotiating approach. The last paragraph attracted the maximum attention:

> India must listen more and speak less in negotiations or else we will be treated with disfavour and derision by developed countries and resented by small island states and other highly vulnerable countries, which will take away from India's standing as a global power and aspirant for permanent membership to the Security Council. This is also important so that we can retain maximum flexibility and we are not used by others and deserted at the last minute. (The President of Brazil has just said that Brazil could consider emission cuts and China has got a think tank to float the idea of a peaking year). India must not stick to G77 alone and must realize that it is now embedded in the G20. India's interests and India's interests alone should drive our negotiations. India must be seen as pragmatic and constructive, not argumentative, and polemical.[17]

The other thing Ramesh did under his watch, was that even before the Copenhagen meeting had begun, he announced India would voluntarily reduce the emissions intensity of its GDP by 20 to 25 per cent by 2020, compared to its 2005 levels, through domestic mitigation actions. This led to a raging debate in Parliament. Finally, to calm the Parliament, Ramesh was forced to announce three non-negotiables for India at Copenhagen: first, no legally binding emission reduction target; second, no acceptance of a peaking year for India; and finally all mitigation actions supported by international finance and technology to be subject to international scrutiny, but not other actions. Ramesh added, however, that the final view on this would be taken after consulting China, Brazil and South Africa, because the BASIC grouping, comprising Brazil, South Africa, India and China, was formed in November 2009 just ahead of the Copenhagen COP meeting on climate change. BASIC was to play an important role in climate change negotiations at least until the Paris accords of 2015.

Whichever way you look at it, Ramesh did ruffle feathers by shaking up quite a few things in India's negotiating strategy in climate change negotiations. First, India's customary negotiating strategy was and is to be maximalist, but not reveal any fallback position. Second, India loved (and loves) being noisy, a naysayer and stubborn, when defending its interests. Being constructive and flexible is not a preferred strategy that wins you any plaudits back home. Third, despite the many changes in India's foreign policy, the idea of strategic autonomy was still the basic mantra. Giving up policy space is not considered good negotiating tactics unless there are concrete benefits in return. Fourth, India still seeks the support of G77 and the developing countries and considers itself the voice of the Global South. On the idea of big power status and membership of the UNSC, India knows that these are not easily attained, nor can they be delivered on a platter by the US. These must be earned by India the hard way. Ramesh therefore had a baptism by fire even in the run-up to Copenhagen by questioning most, if not all, of the above points.

Ambassador Shyam Saran gives an evocative account of what happened in Copenhagen in his book, *How India sees the World*, with an entire chapter devoted to this issue.[18] The fact of the US putting pressure on India is brought out well by him when he says that during the preparations for PM Manmohan Singh's visit to Washington, the US had insisted that India align its negotiating position at Copenhagen with the US.[19] The idea was to get China to split the BASIC, which it eventually did in Paris. India demurred, but the Joint Statement it agreed to with the US was still more substantive than ever before, as we saw earlier.

The real negotiations as recounted by Saran give an indication of the two ends of the spectrum represented by himself and by Ramesh. For instance, there was an acrimonious discussion on an EU proposal for a target of reducing global GHG emissions by 50 per cent by 2050, with developed countries offering to reduce their own emissions by 80 per cent by the same date. The implicit assumption was that developing countries would have to undertake emission reduction targets of least 20 per cent, something that was unacceptable to BASIC countries. Saran says that Ramesh at one stage did suggest that the 50 per cent target (see above) would be fine so long as it was linked to the equity principle. This was rejected categorically by China, Saran adds.

The confusion on the dual negotiating role of Ramesh and Saran appears to have continued with the former at one stage handing over a draft to the latter telling him nothing was agreed to. Ambassadors Shyam Saran, and the late Chandrashekhar Dasgupta (our very first negotiator at the UNFCCC negotiations) then negotiated at an unpleasant session, with leaders like the French President Sarkozy questioning the plenipotentiary credentials of Saran and Dasgupta.

The most extraordinary thing to happen in Copenhagen was of course President Obama barging into a BASIC meeting of leaders and then negotiating the final deal, or a non-deal, if you like. The idea of the US President barging in uninvited was also a sign that the 'unipolar moment' of unquestioned hegemonic power of the US was over by this time and a multipolar world was clearly in the making. The final deal, if you can call it that, had no reference to 50 per cent, no reference to 80 per cent and no reference to a legally binding outcome. There was further drama in Copenhagen when the Chinese negotiator Xie ranted against his own PM.

Considering he has not been sacked since, one is inclined to think this was perhaps deliberate theatre.

The best assessment of the Copenhagen meeting is given by Ambassador Shyam Saran and then by the Chinese negotiator Xie Zhenhua. First, Saran at the beginning of the chapter says that at Copenhagen no country could set aside its selfish interests to come up with a robust framework for global collaboration to deal with the elemental threat staring humanity in the face. He boldly says, neither the developed countries nor countries like India were able to rise above their narrowly defined and near-term interests. Chinese negotiator Xie, who had ranted against his own PM earlier, had a much more sombre assessment when he told Saran at the end of it all: 'The UNFCCC and the Kyoto Protocol have been buried at this meeting and we (China and India) will learn to regret this day!'

Ramesh, perhaps being a conviction politician, went on to make yet another groundbreaking, impromptu, statement in Cancun in 2010: 'All countries must take binding commitments under appropriate legal form'. Ramesh in his book explains why he made the statement.[20] He says at Cancun, India's manoeuvring space for negotiation was fast vanishing and he made the statement to regain some negotiating space. He claims he was perceived as a hero abroad and a villain at home. Be that as it may, he believes he was right in doing all of what he did. It is his assessment that India after Cancun, moved away from active engagement with the world and relinquished the opportunity to actively fashion and shape an international climate agreement.

One simple inference from all this: regardless of which point of view you hold, the PM should have stepped in and expressed his preference for one of the two negotiators, so that the lines of command were clear and India's negotiating positions were coherent. That is perhaps the most important lesson for India from

Copenhagen. It weakens the negotiating stand of a country like India if different voices emerge on the same issue at a negotiating forum. Other countries will obviously take advantage of it.

On China though, Ramesh has a valid point when he says that it manages to straddle many groups all at once. For one thing, China, by joining with G77, weakens the position of countries like India. China's gross GHG emissions and even per capita emissions are up to four times higher than India's. China also consumes more coal than the entire world put together. More recently, China's GHG emissions exceeded that of the entire developed world put together.

One of the failures of Indian diplomacy, whether it is at WTO or the UNFCCC, is that we allowed the world to lump China and India together. For India, it may have been convenient to have had China's support at one time, but this expediency has come at a high cost. As we will see below, Paris pretty much sounded the death knell of the BASIC alliance and China was entirely responsible for this. The truth is that in climate change negotiations, China has been largely allowed to have its cake and eat it!

3.6 Hard-Earned Victory in Paris

The COP17 which took place in Durban in 2011, laid the foundation for what followed in Paris in 2015. India's the then minister for environment and forests, Jayanthi Natarajan, did wax eloquent at Durban about how the firewall of CBDR must not be broken. In effect, she tried to go back in time and recover lost ground. It must be said that India does this at times in negotiations, whether it is at WTO or on climate change. This has a huge impact on India's credibility and must be eschewed at all costs. Regardless of change of ministers or even governments, international negotiations represent a continuum, and it is both annoying and unreliable if we are going to flip-flop with our positions. In the event, Natarajan and India were just ignored and the Durban Platform for Enhanced Action neither made a reference to Common but Differentiated Responsibilities and Respective Capabilities nor took India's entreaties into account as far as the dual-track approach was concerned.

The Durban Platform came up with a single track for negotiations, pretty much doing away with the distinction between developed and developing countries. In effect, it decided:

> [...] to launch a process to develop a protocol, another legal instrument or an agreed outcome with legal force under the Convention applicable to all Parties, through a subsidiary body under the Convention hereby established and to be known as the Ad Hoc Working Group on the Durban Platform for Enhanced Action.[21]

As if this was not enough, it was also decided to launch a workplan on enhancing mitigation ambition to identify and to explore options for a range of actions that can close the ambition gap with a view to ensuring the highest possible mitigation efforts by all Parties.

In my view, it was Durban that proved to be the real turning point for India's stance in climate negotiations. Note that there was absolutely no mention of CBDR at all, which is extraordinary. Second, the AOSIS was co-opted by the EU. Note that there is no reference to 'right to development' insisted on by BASIC countries in the Durban decision. Apparently, Grenada's ambassador reportedly said at Durban, 'While the BASIC countries develop, we die!!!'[22]

Third, cracks appeared in the much-vaunted BASIC grouping. Brazil and South Africa were willing to accept binding commitments, with South Africa wanting the Durban conference to succeed at all costs. The EU used all the power it had to win over the small and vulnerable countries, by fair means and foul. Durban without doubt was where India may have lost the plot. As one US participant put it, 'There is no mention of historic responsibility or per capita emissions. There is no mention of economic development as the priority for developing countries. There is no mention of a difference between developed and developing country action.'[23]

One explanation of India's change of tack comes from Ajay Mathur, who was part of the climate negotiating team at Paris and is currently the Director General of the International Solar Alliance (ISA) secretariat based in Gurgaon, India. In an article titled 'India and Paris: A Pragmatic Way Forward' in the book edited by Navroz K. Dubash which was referred to earlier,[24] Ajay Mathur says:

> By the time Durban happened, India while publicly continuing to insist that the provision of technology and finance were key to its accelerated actions to address climate change, in private agreed that it was difficult to foresee a future in which these transfers would actually occur at scale. He therefore infers that the intellectual environment (pun perhaps intended) was ripe to absorb alternate approaches to the global issue.[25]

The negotiating track adopted in Durban also led subsequently to another paradigm shift towards a bottom-up architecture for climate governance where all countries would make pledges for climate action under a system of peer review. At COP19 in Warsaw in 2013, the idea of Nationally Determined Contributions was mooted, which then led to the Intended Nationally Determined Contributions (INDCs), which was adopted by countries in 2014 at the COP 20 meeting in Lima. Two points are worth noting.

One, this idea was, in fact, first mooted by the Japanese in the 1990s under their 'pledge and review' proposal, which was rejected out of hand at the first COP in Berlin (1995) as grossly inadequate, opting for legally binding commitments instead. The reason the INDCs were accepted was because the US and China were reluctant to take on legally binding cuts. After all, INDCs would not be legally binding and subject to revisions. The second point worthy of note before the COP at Lima, was the famous US-China Joint Announcement on Climate Change in November 2014, following the meeting between Presidents Obama and Xi Jinping. This was the first clear sign that China was now using BASIC for purely tactical purposes, and considered itself America's equal and preferred a G2 (US and China) system of climate governance. The US-China Joint Statement was notable for several things:

(a) China and US, the two biggest GHG emitters, committed themselves to an ambitious climate agreement in Paris in 2015. This may be construed as a political signal that no matter what, a successful and ambitious agreement would result in Paris. At a minimum, this put pressure on countries like India, which were already looking at tough negotiations to defend their interests.

(b) The statement modified the CBDR-RC found in the UNFCCC, to the following: 'CBDR and respective capabilities, in light of national circumstances.' The additional words 'in light of national circumstances' was unanimously interpreted by experts as diluting the concept of CBDR-RC further. It introduced another layer of differentiation to make the point that China (and presumably India) could not hide forever behind the façade of CBDR, to avoid making substantial commitments. Others may justifiably argue however that the words 'consistent with national circumstances' did figure even in the Joint Statement of PM Manmohan Singh and President Obama issued by the two leaders in November 2009.

(c)   The US undertook concrete emission reduction targets, which was to be expected. China, for the first time indicated a peaking year of around 2030, with best efforts to peak even earlier.

(d)   The two Presidents (US and China) said they would work closely in the run-up to the Paris meeting.

(e)   This first Joint Statement also got a lot of brownie points for the two big polluters from NGOs and other climate change activists.

If the first cracks appeared in BASIC at Durban, in Paris, China succeeded in sinking the grouping once and for all. As Ramesh correctly pointed out earlier, it is true that China was playing all sides, i.e., the G77, the US and of course BASIC, whenever it suited them. I have already stated earlier that one of the singular failures of India's diplomacy was not to insist on some kind of differentiation between China and India. Instead, we went along with the lumping of China and India, which actually suited not just China but also the US and EU.

A second Joint Statement between the US and China was issued in September 2015, recalling many of the points made in the previous Joint Statement and adding for good measure that 'differentiation should be reflected in relevant elements of the agreement in an appropriate manner'. Contrast this with PM Narendra Modi's trip to Washington in January 2015 and the Joint Statement issued, which has only a brief reference to climate change. It merely said the two leaders would work together and with other countries to conclude an ambitious climate agreement in Paris in 2015.

China, well before Paris, also tried its hand at establishing a grouping of Like-Minded Developing Countries (LMDC) on climate change, with a first meeting in Beijing in October 2012. It had the following countries as members: Bolivia, China, Ecuador, Egypt, India, Malaysia, Nicaragua, Pakistan, Philippines, Saudi Arabia, Thailand and Venezuela. This grouping claimed it was firmly anchored in the G77-plus-China, said it wished to strengthen the unity of G77-plus-China and play a meaningful role in negotiations.

In effect, this had the opposite impact with some G77 countries (especially the climate-vulnerable) feeling left out. Interestingly, LMDC did not comprise Brazil and South Africa, the other two BASIC participants, causing further fissures in the negotiating positions of developing countries. China lived with all this and still managed to do a 'G2-like' deal with the US on the eve of Paris. India, on the other hand, did suffer since it fell between two stools—the BASIC on the one hand and the G77 on the other. In terms of negotiating strategy, India should have been clear that relying on BASIC was a risky proposition because of China but also because of Brazil and South Africa, which were much more inclined to take on concrete commitments than India.

In the run-up to Paris, I, as India's ambassador to France, would often be asked whether India would block an agreement in Paris. It was a loaded question, of course. I would respond that India wanted to be part of a global solution on climate change, but I expressed the hope that our legitimate concerns would be taken into account. The US Secretary of State John Kerry, had added grist to the mill in this regard when he told the *Financial Times* of London that India could be a 'challenge' in the climate change negotiations. There were times in Paris when I thought India was being played or being lined up as a possible 'scapegoat', should efforts to conclude an agreement fail. I do not believe this affected our basic negotiating red lines and it is generally to our credit that we got the deal we did in Paris.

The French foreign minister at the time, Laurent Fabius, was as sharp a French diplomat as you could find. He would always say that no country was enthusiastic to host the COP21 (2015) climate conference and when he had innocently offered France as host, most people told him with a smirk: 'Wish you all the best!' He would also be asked by diplomats as to whether he had a Plan B under wraps. To which he would cleverly respond that there was no Plan B, because we do not have a Planet B! Fabius adopted a three-pronged strategy: one, when it came to the big players like the US, China, India and the EU, he would rely on the French President and on his own networks with his counterparts; two, all the French diplomatic missions would be instructed that this was the principal focus of activity for over one year; and lastly, he personally supervised the drafting and conducting of the negotiations himself, not delegating everything to the UN staff, as some of his predecessors had done. He was assisted ably by Laurence Tubiana, the climate change envoy of France in whom he had total trust. There is no question, in retrospect, that French diplomacy led by Laurent Fabius deserved a good deal of the credit for the success arrived at, at the COP21 meeting in Paris.

Fabius was acutely aware that India could not be brushed aside and had to be tackled with sensitivity. He made a trip to Delhi in November 2015, just before COP21 and assured PM Modi that our concerns would be taken on board. The fact that France was the COP President also helped matters. India considered France a trusted strategic partner and bilateral ties were rock solid. There was thus a certain degree of strategic comfort that India had in dealing with France. I also personally believe we did a better job of expressing our red lines to Fabius very early on. These were: retain some differentiation between developed and developing countries; CBDR-RC to permeate key parts of the Agreement; and developed countries to take the lead in finance and technology transfer.

For good measure, we also stressed our commitment to climate justice, a notion PM Modi was personally committed to. Fabius took careful note of our red lines, but obviously could make no overt commitment before the meeting began. In a surprising move, he made the procedure of the COP21 meeting in Paris stand on its head: instead of asking the heads of governments/States to come towards the end of the conference as had happened in previous conferences, he asked them to grace it in the beginning, make their speeches, grant their negotiators maximum flexibility and then get out of the way.

This was counterintuitive, but in retrospect turned out to be a masterstroke by Fabius. He wanted the leaders to publicly express their unconditional commitment for a successful agreement on climate change, thus tying their hands and making them buy-in in advance, into the success of these negotiations. This was the opposite of what had transpired in Copenhagen. Fabius certainly did not want a repeat of what happened there in Paris. In speech after speech at the opening ceremony of COP21 in Paris, leaders said that climate change was the main threat facing humanity and that it was important for the world to come together. France had just faced terrible terrorist attacks in November 2015 in Paris, which killed scores of people; this also garnered a lot of sympathy for the presidency. Arguments such as terrorists must not be allowed to win, were heard in the context of climate change negotiations. This bore an eerie similarity to the 9/11 attacks, which had an impact on the WTO Ministerial meeting in Doha in 2001.

Prime Minister Modi was still new to international negotiations when Paris took place in December 2015, having been sworn in as PM only in May 2014. But it is fair to say that he took to global diplomacy like a duck takes to water. I was fortunate to attend strategy meetings in Paris chaired by him. I was struck by his lucidity, more than anything else. When someone in the delegation gloated over the fact that the *Financial Times* in London had characterized India as a player that could play hardball and complicate the negotiations, the PM gently chided that person and said India did not need that kind of publicity. He then went on to make the following points:

(a) As a continuing victim of climate change, India needed the Paris agreement to be both successful and ambitious.

(b) India was happy to do its bit, keeping in mind its monumental developmental challenges, CBDR and subject to availability of climate finance and access to technology.

(c) He spoke about 'climate justice' and how poor people who had not at all contributed to this problem, were somehow the worst affected. This must be brought out by India, he stressed.

(d) The PM said India must be part of the solution to the global problem of climate change and in this context, outlined the proposal for the International Solar Alliance and how this could be a game-changer.

The PM's negotiating approach, conveyed above, was both pragmatic and shrewd. By the time all delegations gathered in Paris, it was looking more and more inevitable that an agreement would eventually be hammered out. Sure, we did not know exactly the contours of the global agreement, but the global mood was in favour of an agreement. China had already done a deal with the US by then, as we have seen, and it would have been naïve on our part to rely on China. Fissures in the G77 were also making their appearance. The AOSIS wanted a strong agreement quite badly, because they felt their very existence was at stake. Furthermore, for the very first time an alliance of states emerged calling themselves the 'High Ambition Coalition', which was expressly established (with The Marshall Islands playing a significant role) for the purpose of galvanizing a broad coalition in support of building momentum towards a strong climate change agreement at COP21 in Paris. The AOSIS and this High Ambition Coalition eventually ensured that the goal of limiting global warming to 1.5 degrees or less was kept alive in the Paris Agreement. In the light of all this, India had a delicate role to play even while strongly defending its vital interests.

I was tasked with the job of organizing the launch of the International Solar Alliance. Initially, the idea was that our PM alone would launch the ISA, since it was our idea after all. But when I approached the French authorities for a suitable venue on the margins of the main meeting, senior officials at Elysée (French President's Palace) said the French President would like to be present and if possible, jointly launch this with our PM. I promptly relayed this to Delhi, which asked for my view. I responded by saying that the French President was the Chair of COP21 and if he were to be present, it would lend our event even more prestige and gravitas. This was accepted by Delhi. A prime venue (of which there were not many available) was booked by me, but as often happens in these cases, one must expect the unexpected.

At the last minute, Bill Gates decided to announce his multi-billion dollar initiative 'Cleantech' with Barack Obama and PM Modi in tow. And he decided to do it just prior to our event. He wanted the best venue, which we had booked with great difficulty, and of course he got it, because what Bill Gates wants, he normally gets! It left me scrambling for another venue, which unfortunately did not have the same advantages as the other one. Fortunately, we were able to stitch together an event that was talked about, perhaps even more than the Bill Gates event itself. Several heads of government and heads of state attended the launch of the Solar Alliance. Secretary of State John Kerry represented the US at the launch.

The point I wish to make is that the political messaging from India was spot on at COP21 in Paris. Apart from the ISA initiative, India had also announced its INDC prior to the Paris conference. The INDC included reduction commitments of emissions intensity of its GDP by 33 to 35 per cent, apart from creating an additional carbon sink of 2.5 to 3 billion tonnes of CO_2-equivalent through additional forest cover by 2030. This was considered impressive by all, including climate activists and even India's critics.

As early as October 2015, American negotiator Todd Stern made it abundantly clear that the US was not looking for a legally binding agreement in Paris. The reason for this was that the Americans wanted the Paris climate deal to be an executive agreement, which could then be approved by their President, rather than an international 'treaty' which would then need Senate ratification. In fact, at a Senate hearing in October 2015, Todd Stern said the Paris deal would be in broad compliance with the Byrd-Hagel resolution of 1998, referred to earlier in the chapter. The US was fixated on two things in Paris: no legally binding deal, so Senate need not be involved in ratification; and all countries, including developing countries, to take on some commitments so that the broad conditionalities of the Byrd-Hagel resolution would be met. Fabius had said in response to a question that a deal without the US made no sense to him. So we should have guessed that the final deal from Paris would conform to the wishes of the US. The UNFCCC site does say that Paris is an international climate agreement that is legally binding. Other US commentators may disagree.

As a reflection of this problem there was a last-minute hiccup due to the US, which is worth recounting. In the draft circulated for final approval in Paris, Article 4, para 4 initially read as follows: 'Developed country Parties shall continue taking the lead by undertaking economy-wide absolute emission reduction targets.

Developing country Parties should continue enhancing their mitigation efforts and are encouraged to move over time towards economy-wide emission reduction or limitation targets in the light of different national circumstances.'

The draft caused a furore in the American delegation and US Secretary of State John Kerry became extremely agitated in his conversation with Laurent Fabius. The conference was held up for a while. The lawyers in the American delegation advised John Kerry that if the word 'shall' figured in the clause above, then the resulting agreement could be construed as legally binding and would have to be sent to the Senate. So the Americans wanted this word to be replaced by 'should'. This was done by Fabius under the guise of a typographical error by the Secretariat, and in so doing he was being economical with the truth.

The final version of the Paris Agreement has the word 'should' which casts serious aspersions on whether the agreement is really legally binding or not. The desire to conclude an agreement was so strong in Paris, that nothing could have prevented it from happening. Nicaragua desperately sought to object to the agreement even while it was being 'gavelled' by Fabius. But no one bothered about Nicaragua and the Paris Agreement went through.

The best characterization of the Paris Climate Change Agreement is by scholar Lavanya Rajamani in her article 'Understanding the 2015 Paris Agreement'.[26] She calls it a 'hybrid instrument', stating that the Paris Agreement's hybrid approach preserves state autonomy in the determination of NDCs but strengthens oversight of these contributions through a robust transparency system, a global stocktaking process and a compliance mechanism. In so doing, she says it limits the self-serving nature of self-determination (through NDCs) and generates normative expectations.[27]

The fact that Paris reaffirmed the bottom-up approach through NDCs is not at all a negative development from our point of view.

Yes, there is a five-year-review and ratchet mechanism, but that
too is something we need not necessarily fear. It is not the purpose
of this chapter to do a detailed assessment of the outcome in Paris
since this has been extensively covered in literature. The limited
purpose is to enquire whether there was anything in the deal
that should have invoked a veto from India. My honest answer,
keeping in mind all that had transpired in previous COPs, is a
categorical 'no'. I think India can live with this deal and India's
climate credentials stand burnished. India was successfully able to
meet its red lines and when compared to the Durban fiasco, was
able to retrieve some lost ground on the question of CBDR-RC!

Ajay Mathur, as noted earlier, was an important part of
the Indian negotiating team in Paris. He wrote about the
Paris Agreement as a paradigm change and mentioned India's
'diplomatic positioning'.[28] He argued that Paris provided India
an opportunity to showcase a new diplomatic configuration,
reflective of the new reality in which it was a stakeholder both
in the traditional developing world (the G77) and in the large
economies (the G20). He made the point that the ISA sought out
both developing and developed countries, and this reflected the
new geopolitical reality of India straddling the G77 and G20
blocs, as well as its stature in enabling the formation of a new
intergovernmental organization.[29]

This is probably true as far as it goes, but it is worth noting that
the BASIC grouping has perhaps run its course since Paris, not the
least because India and China now find it increasingly difficult to
cooperate in multilateral fora, thanks to their strained bilateral
ties emanating from Ladakh. The other thing worth noting is that
India will remain sui generis for the foreseeable future because of
its developmental challenges and because it appears to be the only
major economy that can potentially follow a low-carbon pathway
to development, something neither the West nor China has done.

It is noteworthy that India made an important declaration while ratifying the Paris Climate Change Agreement, which is worth quoting in full:

> The Government of India declares its understanding that, as per its national laws, keeping in view its development agenda, particularly the eradication of poverty and provision of basic needs for all its citizens, coupled with its commitment to follow the low-carbon path to progress, and on the assumption of unencumbered availability of cleaner sources of energy and technologies and financial resources from around the world, and based on a fair and ambitious assessment of global commitment to combating climate change, it is ratifying the Paris Agreement.[30]

It is interesting, from a legal perspective, that India has chosen to make this declaration. Article 27 of the Paris Agreement clearly states: 'No reservations may be made to this Agreement.' So, it is pertinent to ask what purpose this declaration serves. India's statement may be construed as an 'interpretative declaration' that presents its understanding and interpretation of provisions, reinforces the importance of certain provisions or provides a narrative context for the Paris Agreement. This is not unimportant in view of Article 15 of the agreement, which establishes a mechanism to facilitate implementation of and promote compliance with its provisions. Article 15 makes clear that this mechanism shall be facilitative in nature and function in a manner that is transparent, non-adversarial and non-punitive. This mechanism is expected to pay particular attention to the respective national capabilities and circumstances of the Parties. This provision, which is a pale shadow of the dispute settlement provision prevalent in most international agreements, demonstrates why the Paris Agreement is a hybrid instrument and not a classic, legally binding agreement. But it does demonstrate the importance of India's declaration, should there be questions raised about India's commitments in the future.

An evaluation of India and the Paris Agreement, using the Integrated Assessment Framework is given below:

PARIS AGREEEMENT

Gandhi Litmus Test: No commitments taken in a way that would adversely affect our fight against energy poverty.

Policy Space: Commitments such as peaking year or real reduction in emission targets were eschewed.

Domestic Politics: By and large laudatory of government action to ratify Paris. Some felt CBDR was given short shrift.

Geopolitical Imperatives: India cemented its relationship with US, France and burnished its climate credentials.

Commitment to Multilateralism and Principles: India pragmatic enough to realize that global action was required to deal with climate change.

Realpolitik and Material Gain: India pushed hard for technology transfer and financial assistance, but developed countries reneged on their commitments.

3.7 High Politics in Glasgow

The COP26 was held in Glasgow in October–November 2021. This was an important meeting since under the Paris Agreement and its 'ratchet' mechanism, countries were to submit updated NDCs, but it was also important because no COP could be held in 2020 because of Covid restrictions. The backdrop against which COP26 was being held may be described as follows:

- The Covid pandemic had taken its toll on the global economy and cut into the budgets of even rich countries. For poorer countries, the impact was much more severe, causing unemployment and widespread poverty.
- Article 9 of the Paris Agreement says developed countries 'shall' provide financial resources to developing countries for mitigation and adaptation. Copenhagen had earlier committed to a figure of $100 billion per year, which was reiterated at Paris. Glasgow was to see where things are in this regard.
- The sixth assessment report of the Intergovernmental Panel on Climate Change (IPCC) issued in August 2021 ahead of the COP26 meeting, noted with alarm that global temperatures would rise by 1.5 degrees Celsius within just two decades, adding that the world had already warmed by 1.1 degree Celsius. Therefore, it called for urgent and massive transformational action to fight climate change.
- Net Zero became the clarion call of climate activists and India was one of the few G20 countries not to set a net zero date in the run-up to the Glasgow meet.

In the event, the Glasgow Climate Pact was quite a significant achievement. The pact welcomed the IPCC special report on limiting global warming to 1.5 degree Celsius.[31] In other words, the dream of limiting global warming to 1.5 degrees Celsius was kept alive by the Glasgow pact, even while it reiterated that limiting global warming to 1.5 degrees Celsius required rapid, deep, and sustained emission cuts, with CO_2 emissions falling to 45 per cent below 2010 levels by 2030 and to net zero around mid-century. The Glasgow Climate Pact also deeply regretted that the $100 billion climate finance goal had not been met, and urged developed countries to fully deliver it through 2025.

India came under pressure on two issues, to come up with a revised NDC and to commit to a net-zero timeframe. Prime Minister Modi, as is his wont, defused the situation by his address to the Glasgow conference comprising 'Panchamrit' as he put it:

- India to reach 500 GW non-fossil energy capacity by 2030;
- 50 per cent of India's energy requirements from renewable energy by 2030;
- Reduction of India's total projected carbon emissions by one billion tonnes from now to 2030;
- Reduction of the carbon intensity of India's economy by 45 per cent by 2030, over 2005 levels; and
- India to achieve the target of net zero emissions by 2070.

Unsurprisingly, the bulk of the attention was on the last commitment—and it dragged India unfairly into controversy. While the usual India-baiters said 2070 was well beyond the target date of 2050, rational observers gave India a lot of credit. Even the BBC, not always used to praising India, said this was a bold and significant step and there was general welcome for the announcement. Other announcements (which have since become our NDC in submission to the UN) were also welcomed as being substantive. India's net zero date can only be reasonably compared to two other major emitters: the US and China. The US, which has historically been the biggest emitter and continues to be the second-biggest polluter in the world, announced 2050 as the year it would achieve net zero. Considering that President Trump had pulled out of the Paris accord altogether, activists cheered this announcement in 2021 from Biden.

Truth be told, 2050 is just way too late for the richest country (still in GDP terms) in the world. At a time when the Climate Crisis Advisory Group is saying 2050 is too late and that net zero must be replaced by 'net negative', to give US time till 2050 is grossly unfair. But after Trump, activists and critics were simply relieved to have the US on board. China's case was even more egregious. Given that China accounts for something like 27 per cent of global emissions and considering that its cumulative emissions exceeded that of the entire developed world for the first time in 2019, allowing it time till 2060 for the net-zero target is excessive, to put it mildly.

Figure 3.2 below gives an idea of how India compares vis-à-vis US and China. The point bears repetition that India has not been very successful in differentiating itself from China. Indeed, the popular website 'climate action tracker', very unfairly lumps both China and India in the same category and rates both as 'highly insufficient' in terms of country action to achieve the Paris goal of limiting global warming to below 2 degree Celsius. The MoEF would do well to commission some studies with reputed NGOs (both foreign and domestic) to set the record straight.

Figure 3.2: 2019 Net GHG Emissions from the World's Largest Emitters

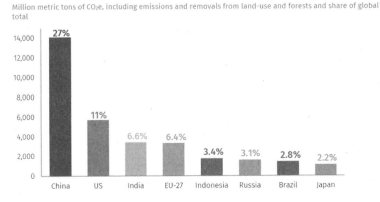

Million metric tons of CO₂e, including emissions and removals from land-use and forests and share of global total

Source: Rhodium Group

Source: Rhodium Group

This point about India being made the perennial scapegoat in climate negotiations is pertinent and came into sharp relief in the final stages of the Glasgow COP26 meeting. Coal, as is well known, is the typical bugbear of Western activists and NGOs. Unfortunately, India gets a lot more bad press than China does, despite the huge difference in coal consumption between the two countries. Indeed, the US consumes almost half as much coal as does India, despite the wide differences in population and levels of development. With 17 per cent of the global population, India contributes 5 per cent of GHG emissions and consumes 12.5 per cent of coal and gets pilloried for this with impunity. China, with the same population, accounts for a whopping 27 per cent of GHG emissions and a scandalous 53.8 per cent of coal consumption and gets lumped with India!

Table 3.1: Consumption of Coal (2021)

	Exajoules	Per cent
China	86.1	53.8
India	20.1	12.5
US	10.5	6.5

Source: Statistics for 2021, Statista

Table 3.1 above, illustrates clearly where the problem lies. Yet India never fails to get blamed for the problem. It is against this backdrop that a controversy erupted in Glasgow. When COP26 began its deliberations in Glasgow, the draft circulated for consideration by the members read thus: 'Calls upon Parties to accelerate the phasing-out of coal and subsidies for fossil fuels.'

Towards the final stages of the conference, the modified draft proposed was:

Calls upon Parties to accelerate the development, deployment and dissemination of technologies, and the adoption of policies, to transition towards low-emission energy systems, including by rapidly scaling up the deployment of clean power generation and energy efficiency measures, including accelerating efforts towards the phase-out of unabated coal power and inefficient fossil fuel subsidies, recognizing the need for support towards a just transition.[32]

The final agreed text in Glasgow was: 'Calls upon ... towards the phase down of unabated coal power and phase-out of inefficient fossil fuel subsidies, while providing targeted support to the poorest and most vulnerable in line with national circumstances and recognizing the need for support towards a just transition.'

These changes were proposed by the Indian environment minister, from the floor at the plenary, moments before the conference ended. After the Indian intervention, many countries did express disappointment at the change in language, with some calling it a bitter pill to swallow. Given this, the background as to how this came about is important. The term 'phase down' instead of 'phase-out' of unabated coal is not new. It figures in the US-China Joint Glasgow Declaration dated 10 November 2021.[33] Indeed, the declaration took everyone by surprise at the conference. China's preferred course is to conclude a bilateral with the US preceding a major conference which then it sees as the template for the conference outcome. The relevant portion of the US-China declaration read thus: 'China will phase down coal consumption during the 15th Five Year Plan and make best efforts to accelerate this work.'[34]

This language was reportedly negotiated between US, EU, China, India and the Conference Chair, the UK.

If the above is true, the question remains why the Indian minister chose (or was chosen?) to take the floor to bell the cat, as it were. Was he unaware of the implications of doing so? Officials later on said that the consensus was based on the US-China Joint declaration and that the Indian minister was merely following a request from the Chair. If so, the minister was probably misled and should have been advised by his officials not to do it. The Chair, Alok Sharma (from the UK), was later quoted as saying that the change of text by India and China had left him deeply frustrated and he went on to say that the two countries would have to explain to climate-vulnerable countries why they did what they did.

Again, one sees signs of how India is lumped with China despite the vast differences that we noted earlier. Also, Alok Sharma should have certainly known that the language emanated not from India and China (as he claims) but from the US and China.

Even US negotiator John Kerry did not admit the language came from the Sino-American Joint Declaration and said he did not appreciate the last-minute amendment but that he would take the outcome and take the fight into the next year.

Whatever the truth of the matter, India got a fair bit of criticism on being the country that somehow 'diluted' the formulation on coal. This completely overlooks the fact that China had already done a deal with the US on the word 'phase down' in its joint statement. Furthermore, India in the negotiations had also legitimately raised the point of why coal was being singled out and why other fossil fuels such as oil and gas were exempt from any 'phase down' or 'phase out'. India reportedly made a proposal to phase out all fossil fuels in developed countries and then for developing countries to do so after a certain transition period. The US apparently refused to even discuss this proposal. With politics trumping science and reason, the final declaration refers only to coal and in the process India became a convenient scapegoat.

Be that as it may, many reasonable experts have since said that even 'phase down' is a big deal for India, with millions still living in energy poverty. Indeed, that is why the words, 'while providing targeted support to the poorest and most vulnerable in line with national circumstances', were added to the final declaration by India. Also, it is hard to see how India's target of 500 GW of renewable energy by 2030 can be achieved without ceasing any substantial expansion of coal use in India. The fact of the matter is that it will be next to impossible, at least in the short term, for India to reduce the consumption of coal in absolute terms. What it can do, and is doing, is bring down the proportion of coal use in its overall energy mix even as renewables take the lion's share.

One of the most reputable climate change advocacy groups in India, the Centre for Science and Environment, may well be considered a bellwether for all NGOs on climate change in India. The interesting point to note is that there is general endorsement of the line taken by the Government of India in the climate change negotiations as well as appreciation for the NDC (of which India has made one in 2015 and another in 2022) India has made to the UNFCCC Secretariat. In this sense, the Government of India has behind it both public opinion and the intelligentsia in the way it conducts climate change negotiations. This is noteworthy, since in other areas like trade negotiations, opinions are far more contentious and divisive.

In a trenchant assessment of the Glasgow meet, CSE Director General Sunita Narain noted that the real problem at the Glasgow meet was the lack of understanding of 'climate justice'.[35] She noted that climate justice only figured in the preamble of the Glasgow Climate Pact and the formulation was so weak as to be meaningless: 'also noting the importance of some of the concepts of climate justice'. She went on to state that certain countries—the US, the twenty-seven EU nations, UK, Canada, Australia, Japan, Russia, and now China—had consumed roughly 70 per cent of the global carbon budget, the space that must not be exceeded if the goal of 1.5 degree Celsius is to be met. China alone will occupy one-third of the carbon space between now and 2030 and as of 2023 accounts for an astonishing 56 per cent of the world's consumption of coal, which in turn, largely explains its current dominance among the major carbon emitters.

According to the 2022 edition of the International Energy Agency's *World Energy Outlook*, China was responsible for 33 per cent of global CO2 emissions in 2021, compared with 15 per cent for the US, 11 per cent for the EU, and India a mere 8 per cent. Yet, 70 per cent of the people in the world belonging to South Asia and Sub-Saharan Africa are yet to have any claim on the global carbon budget. This factual argument lies at the core of climate justice. By brushing aside this issue, the Glasgow Climate Pact has done great injustice, according to CSE's Sunita Narain.

On climate finance, the other hot-button issue in climate negotiations, Narain's assessment is that only Germany, Sweden and Norway have met their share; no other country has. And the issue keeps getting postponed in every meeting of COP. Of all the issues, this is one that ranks as an abysmal failure of COP meetings and the UNFCCC process.

When Narain was asked about India's announcement, by PM Modi, of the five elixirs or Panchamrit, she said they were actually bold and ambitious. The fact of the matter is that given India's energy poverty, the massive number of people who live in poverty and the level of GDP (which is low at about $3 trillion), India's NDCs to date have been praiseworthy.

Evaluation of India's stand at Glasgow using the Integrated Assessment Framework, is given below:

GLASGOW CLIMATE PACT

Gandhi Litmus Test: Language on coal phase down and emphasis on vulnerable and weaker sections gaining access to energy.

Policy Space: Net zero in 2070 gives policy space. Still no peak year and no reduction of emissions per se, but reduction of emission intensity.

Domestic Politics: Serious think tanks and advocacy groups have generally lauded the government.

Geopolitical Imperatives: Still a tendency on the part of the UK, US and others to make a scapegoat of India and lump China and India together when it comes to coal.

Commitment to Multilateralism and Principles: India is committed to UNFCCC and realizes it is the only way out.

Realpolitik and Material Gain: India is still failing in its attempt to persuade developed countries to finance the fight against climate change in poor countries.

3.8 Sui Generis India

In a historic move in July 2022, the UNGA passed a resolution through a unanimous vote that affirmed a clean, healthy and sustainable environment as a human right, and more importantly as a human right for all, not just for a privileged few. This is significant because of its close link to the concept of climate justice referred to earlier. The UN Human Rights Council (UNHRC) had passed a resolution in October 2021 pretty much along similar lines.

If India does not get adequate space as part of the global carbon budget, then it is quite conceivable that a good part of its population may not have access to a clean, healthy, and sustainable environment. In other words, the poor people in India may find their 'human rights' violated. The question is, who is responsible for the violation of their human rights? Is it the Government of India or is it the international community, which has not allowed a reasonable carbon budget for a country the size of India? This issue becomes fraught, because of the issue of climate justice and the assertion of resolutions of both UNHRC and UNGA that a clean, healthy, and sustainable environment is a human right for all and not just for a few. In fact, there is a landmark judgement given by the International Court of Justice (ICJ) in 2018 in an environmental dispute involving Nicaragua and Costa Rica.[36] Leaving aside the details of the dispute, the main point to note is that, since 1993 the ICJ has established a seven-member Chamber for Environmental Matters. The Chamber reflects the ICJ's desire to demonstrate the particular interest that it attaches to environmental issues. Not too many cases have been brought to the ICJ, because States remain hesitant about referring international environmental disputes to international adjudication. But this may and should change.

There is a strong prima facie case to be brought before the ICJ regarding two issues. The first is the monumental failure of the developed countries to transfer financial resources to poorer countries. This is of course for the least-developed countries and others to consider, since they are the worst affected. The second issue is that for India, the real problem is whether there is enough space left in the global carbon budget for its vast millions, if China and the other developed countries continue to occupy and expand their carbon footprint. It is not too late for the Government of India to commission perhaps an agency like the CSE to prepare a case for India at the ICJ on the lines indicated above, arguing that developed countries and China must 'vacate' carbon space, not merely stop their emissions growth, in order for all Indians to have access to the human right of a safe, clean, healthy and sustainable environment. Climate justice demands this and the ICJ now arguably has the jurisdiction to deal with this.

All indications are that five countries will be the major drivers of global economic growth in the years to come: the US, China, Japan, Germany and India. The first four have followed a high-carbon pathway of development. This can be easily gauged in terms of not just historical emissions but also in terms of their being the largest producers of steel, cement and aluminium. Again, China is the worst culprit, because the gap between it and the next ranked country is at least a factor of 1:10. Given that China is the latest country to industrialize and has followed exactly the same high-carbon pathway, the key point is that India will be the only major economy asked to follow a low-carbon pathway in order to industrialize itself. The process of industrialization may be defined, admittedly somewhat arbitrarily, as reaching around a $10 trillion economy and arriving at a per capita income of around $10,000, which incidentally is also the World Bank definition of an upper-middle-income country.

The other four—the US, China, Japan, Germany—have arrived at this destination burning coal and by following a high carbon trajectory. This is particularly true of China. If India is now being told it has a 'responsibility' to follow a completely different and low-carbon pathway, then, the international community has a duty to help India achieve this goal by: vacating carbon space that can then be used by India; transferring massive financial resources to India, as grants, project assistance and investment; and by transferring the most relevant green technology without impediment and without delay. These are not unreasonable demands, since they are as much in the interest of the rich countries as they are in the interest of India and other climate-vulnerable countries. Unless a serious effort is made to meet these demands, it must be acknowledged that India by itself will not be able to undertake this monumental task.

According to the reputed New Delhi-based policy think-tank, Council on Energy, Environment and Water (CEEW), one estimate of the cumulative investments needed by India to achieve net zero by 2070 touches a whopping $10 trillion.[37] These investments would be necessary to decarbonize the power, industry, and transport sectors in India. The same report, however, cautions that there would be a significant shortfall of $3.5 trillion, which the developed countries would need to support India including concessional finance to the tune of $1.4 trillion. The bulk of this funding (about $8.4 trillion) would be needed for the power sector to shift from coal to renewable energy and for associated integration, distribution, and transmission infrastructure. The CEEW report also says that $1.5 trillion would be needed for investment in the industrial sector to set up Green Hydrogen production capacity to advance the sector's decarbonization.[38] It is clear, therefore, that nothing short of the establishment of a 'Green Marshall Fund' will be needed for India. If there is political will, this can and should be done by a coalition of countries led, of course, by the rich nations.

Another study in 2021 by CEEW on the 'Implications of a Net-zero Target for India's Sectoral Energy Transitions and Climate Policy',[39] has also estimated how five key sectors—power, transport, industry, building and refinery—need to evolve if India is to achieve net-zero by 2070. According to the study, India's total installed solar power capacity would need to increase to 5,630 GW (from the current 62 GW) by 2070. The usage of coal, especially for power generation, would need to peak by 2040 and drop by 99 per cent between 2040 and 2060. The sales of electric cars must reach 84 per cent by 2070. Further, crude oil consumption across sectors would need to peak by 2050 and fall substantially by 90 per cent between 2050 and 2070. Green Hydrogen would have to contribute 19 per cent of the total energy needs of the industrial sector. All this is to suggest that India will need massive investment to achieve the goal of net zero by 2070.

In a pathbreaking development, India raised $1 billion through the sale of its first-ever domestic sovereign 'green bonds' in January 2023.[40] The surprising feature is not just its ability to raise this kind of money for environmental projects, but that it has been done at lower borrowing cost (a 'greenium' if you like) than that of conventional bonds. This bodes very well for India's ability in the future to bankroll the big investments needed to achieve its ambitious climate targets. Most business analysts are of the view that India is poised to be one of the largest markets for renewable energy, and that green bonds of the kind mentioned above will attract the attention of asset managers. Meanwhile the Government of India has said it will use the proceeds for green bonds for projects such as clean transport, climate change adaptation, water, waste management, pollution prevention and biodiversity. If the Government of India can borrow at less than market rates, it can raise substantial resources to meet its decarbonization targets. While Indian companies and some government-backed entities have issued green bonds in the past, these have been in foreign currency. This green bond raised in January 2023 is the first sovereign green bond in Indian currency and will go a long way in the creation of the local green bond market.

On coal, where there was so much controversy at Glasgow, the Figure 3.2 reveals the situation as it pertains to India.

Figure 3.3: India's Energy Capacity, Past and Projected (2011–20 and 2030)

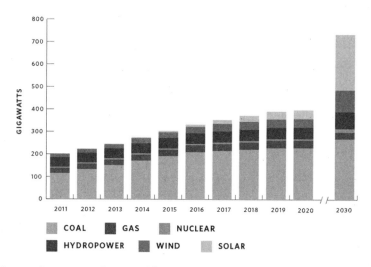

Source: International Renewable Energy Agency (2021), International Energy Agency (2021), Global Energy Monitor (2021), and Ministry of Statistics and Programme Implementation (2020)

The following points that emerge from the Figure 3.3 are noteworthy:

(a) There is no question of completely 'phasing out' coal as far as India is concerned.

(b) But coal as a proportion of our energy matrix is slowly but surely coming down. In 2030, it should be no more than 50 per cent, perhaps even less of our energy mix.

(c) Almost the entire additional capacity year-on-year is from renewable energy, with solar and wind playing a crucial role.

(d) But India will still add something like 56 GW of coal-fired generation capacity by 2030.

(e) The Gandhi Litmus Test obliges India to some use of coal even while increasing the share of renewable energy in the mix.

The story of what the Indian Railways is about to do is pathbreaking as well, in terms of its impact on climate change. Indian Railways is the country's lifeline. As one of the largest rail networks in the world, the Indian Railways network spans 123,236 km, with 13,452 passenger trains and 9,141 freight trains transporting 23,000,000 passengers and 3,000,000 tonnes of freight daily. India's railway network is the fourth-largest in the world and the second-largest in Asia.

The railways will play an important role in the achievement of India's NDC. The ambitious goal is that the Indian Railways hopes to become a net zero carbon emitter by 2030.[41] It will do so by taking the following measures:

• Setting up Dedicated Freight Corridors (DFCs) across the country. The first phase of the project alone is estimated to reduce emissions by about 457-million-ton CO_2 over a thirty year period;

- Increasing the share of renewable energy in its energy mix;
- Further improving its energy efficiency for both diesel and electric traction, thereby facilitating the reduction of GHG emissions for the country;
- Improving water-use efficiency by 20 per cent by 2030;
- Undertaking tree planting drives to increase Carbon sink;
- Undertaking waste management and pollution control;
- Adopting good practices on green buildings, industrial units and other establishments for the management of infrastructure to achieve environmental sustainability.

3.9 Postscript

India participated in the COP27 meeting held in Sharm El-Sheikh from 6–18 November 2022. It was billed as an 'Implementation Conference'. In the event, it did come up with a 'Sharm El-Sheikh Implementation Plan, which repeats language on 1.5 degree Celsius and on phasing down coal taken from the Glasgow Climate Pact.[42] It does mention food security risks, climate tipping points and the need for financial system reform. The main achievement of COP27 was the establishment of a 'loss and damage' fund. Targeting vulnerable developing countries, the fund will respond to loss and damage due to the adverse effects of climate change. A transitional committee is to make recommendations at COP28 in 2023 on operationalizing the fund, with an emphasis on finding new and innovative funding arrangements. COP27 also finalized a mitigation work programme focused on pooling ideas to accelerate action, with no binding elements. Calls to ensure a peak in emissions by 2025 and a phase-down of fossil fuels were not included in the final text.

Agreement on the establishment of the loss and damage fund is no mean achievement. For a long time, the advanced countries refused to entertain the very idea of the loss and damage fund, fearing that it would be tantamount to an admission of historic responsibility, culpability for climate change, and could even be a liability. Although the proof of the pudding is in the eating, the loss and damage fund, when established, will help the most climate-vulnerable countries deal with the devastation caused by climate change. It is to be hoped that the developed countries will provide finance for this fund, unlike the broken promise of the $100 billion, which is yet to materialize.

Despite very little chance of India benefitting from the loss and damage fund, India provided valuable diplomatic support to the poorer countries on this issue at Sharm El-Sheikh. Perhaps, India has realized that negotiating groups like the BASIC have run their course and that India will in the future rely on its developing and least-developed country partners in climate change negotiations. As of September 2023, India could also push for the financing of the loss and damage fund by the rich countries in the context of the presidency of the G20 that it has assumed from 1 December 2022 to 30 September 2023.

The other initiative that India took during the Sharm El-Sheikh meeting was to submit its 'Long-Term Low-Carbon Development Strategy' to the UNFCCC.[43] In the foreword, India's environment minister makes it clear that India's responsibility for the current global warming is minimal and India is making this long-term commitment in accordance with the principle of CBDR-RC. More importantly, the minister also invokes the principle of equity and climate justice, affirming that the key is equitable access to the global carbon budget.

Four key considerations underpin India's long-term low-carbon development strategy: one, it has contributed very little to global warming; two, it has significant energy needs for its development; three, India is committed to pursuing low-carbon strategies for development as per its national circumstances;

and four, India needs to build climate resilience. The salient features of the strategy are:

- National Hydrogen Mission launched in 2021 which aims to make India a Green Hydrogen Hub;
- Increased use of biofuels;
- Smart City initiatives;
- Enhancing forest and tree cover; and
- Transitioning to a low-carbon development pathway is contingent on climate finance from developed countries.

India is one of the sixty Parties to the UNFCCC that have submitted their long-term low-carbon strategy development strategy. Without indulging in hyperbole, it is fair to say that India's decision to stick to a low-carbon strategy for development may well turn out to be the most decisive factor in the global fight against climate change.

4

Taking a Stand: The Case of the War in Ukraine

4.1 Introduction

In what Russia has euphemistically described as a 'special military operation', its armed forces invaded parts of Ukraine on the morning of 24 February 2022 with about 200,000 troops. International relations experts rarely agree on anything, but they agreed that this Russian action in Ukraine constituted a 'black swan' event (an extremely rare and unexpected event with very significant consequences). Indeed, experts now agree that the war in Ukraine has upended both geopolitics and geoeconomics.

Why Ukraine, and why now?

It is important to understand the answers to both questions before we examine India's stand on this conflict. Ukraine, due to its strategic location, is of existential importance to Russia. Late US National Security Adviser Brzezinski had said as far back as 1994, in an article in *Foreign Affairs*: 'It cannot be stressed strongly enough that without Ukraine, Russia ceases to be an empire, but with Ukraine suborned and then subordinated, Russia automatically becomes an empire.' Such was the importance of Ukraine to Russia that President Putin penned a detailed article titled, 'On the historical Unity of Russians and Ukrainians', where he essentially made the case against the independent existence of Ukraine, while underlining that Kyiv was the mother of all Russian cities.[1] It was to Kyiv that Christianity was brought from Byzantium to the Slavic peoples in the eighth and ninth centuries, and it was Christianity that served as the anchor for Kievan Rus—the early Slavic state from which modern Russians, Ukrainians, and Belarussians draw their lineage.

Some eight million ethnic Russians were living in Ukraine, mainly in the east and south, at the start of this war in 2022. There was also the question of 'strategic depth' that Russia has always sought vis-à-vis the West. Put simply, this meant that Russia would not accept Ukraine in the EU and most certainly not in NATO. Indeed, the latter was the brightest of all the red lines for Putin and for Russia. By 2014, the pro-Russian President of Ukraine, Viktor Yanukovych had been overthrown through what was subsequently known as 'Maidan' protests. In response, Russia annexed Crimea in eastern Ukraine—primarily to protect the ethnic Russians there and to safeguard the military infrastructure present in Sevastopol, the major port in Crimea, which was also the seat of Russia's Black Sea Fleet. The Black Sea Fleet had been stationed in Ukraine's Crimea following an agreement between Russia and Ukraine in 2010.

The annexation of Crimea by Russia in 2014 should have alerted the West about the strategic importance of Ukraine to Russia, but the West did not react strongly at that time. In fact, it implicitly seemed to accept the Russian annexation of Crimea, although some token sanctions were imposed on Russia after the event. This, in retrospect, may have also played a role in Putin's decision to invade Ukraine in 2022.

Although the Russian President had massed thousands of troops at the border with Ukraine well ahead of February, no one believed Putin would really carry out an invasion. But invade he did. The official reasons given by Russia for the 'special military operation' of 24 February 2022, were:

- To protect Russians living in Ukraine's Donetsk and Luhansk regions;
- To 'denazify' and 'demilitarize' Ukraine; and
- To eliminate threats to Russian national security.

The most substantive reason appears to be the third point— perceived threats to Russian national security from the West. The most detailed line of reasoning comes from John Mearsheimer, the influential American political scientist and international relations scholar. Mearsheimer wrote as far back as 2014 (following the Russian annexation of Crimea) that the US and its European allies share most of the responsibility for the crisis in Ukraine.[2] According to him, the root of the trouble is NATO's enlargement, which is the central element of a larger strategy by the West to move Ukraine out of Russia's orbit and integrate it into the West. The EU's expansion eastward and the West's backing of the pro-democracy movement in Ukraine are also cited as critical elements in this. As Mearsheimer points out, the West's triple package of policies— NATO enlargement, EU expansion and democracy promotion (regime change from Russia's point of view)—had a huge negative impact on Russia's strategic calculus and it reacted when Ukraine's pro-Russian President Yanukovych was removed from power.[3] Presciently, Mearsheimer in 2014 suggested that the US and its allies should abandon their plan to westernize Ukraine and instead aim to make it a neutral buffer.[4]

George Kennan, the author of the 'Long Telegram' (written in 1946) and the architect of the policy of containment by the US vis-à-vis the erstwhile Soviet Union, wrote in 1997 that expanding NATO would be the most fateful error of American policy in the entire post-cold-war era.[5] He wrote, again presciently much like Mearsheimer, that NATO expansion:

[...] may be expected to inflame the nationalistic, anti-Western and militaristic tendencies in Russian opinion; to have an adverse effect on the development of Russian democracy; to restore the atmosphere of the Cold War to East-West relations; and to impel Russian foreign policy in directions decidedly not to the West's liking.[6]

Kennan went as far as to suggest that NATO expansion could be altered in ways that would mitigate the unhappy effects on Russian policy. Since this was said in February 1997, it is interesting to note the NATO expansion that has since occurred:

Table 4.1: NATO Expansion (1949–2022)

NATO Founding members
Belgium, Canada, Denmark, France, Iceland, Italy, Luxembourg, Netherlands, Norway, Portugal, United Kingdom, United States
1949: Cold War expansion
1952: Greece, Turkey
1955: West Germany
1982: Spain, Post–Cold War expansion
1990: Germany*
1999: Czech Republic, Hungary, Poland

2004: Bulgaria, Estonia, Latvia, Lithuania, Romania, Slovakia, Slovenia
2009: Albania, Croatia
2017: Montenegro
2020: North Macedonia, Pending ratification
2022: Finland, Sweden

In 1999, NATO moved substantially eastward with the addition of Czech, Hungary and Poland. NATO also bombed Yugoslavia in 1999, which was questionable, to put it mildly. So, for NATO to keep saying it is a purely defensive alliance does not cut much ice with Russia. In 2004, NATO moved to Russia's borders with Estonia and Latvia being admitted as members. Both nations were also admitted to the EU the same year. In retrospect, Russia's annexation of Crimea in 2014 was a dress rehearsal for what would happen later in 2022. Both Mearsheimer and Kennan were remarkable in their prediction of Ukraine becoming the battleground in a renewed US/West–Russia rivalry. This background is important in understanding why Russia did what it did in Ukraine.[7]

As for the timing of the invasion in February 2022, the explanation is a bit more complicated. Russia saw several provocative actions from the West in the run-up to its invasion of Ukraine. Ukraine had begun to develop close ties with NATO, for instance in the form of annual military exercises. In June 2020, Ukraine became an Enhanced Opportunity Partner (EOP) of NATO. This is a status offered to those participants in NATO's Partnership Interoperability Initiative who have made particularly significant contributions to NATO operations and other Alliance objectives. Ukraine was thus now one of six EOPs, alongside Australia, Finland, Georgia, Jordan and Sweden. Ukraine had also provided troops to Allied operations, including in Afghanistan and Kosovo, as well as to the NATO Response Force and NATO exercises. So, in all but name, Ukraine was essentially tying itself close to NATO.

The real trigger could have been in February 2021, when Ukraine's President Zelensky on a state visit to Washington sought to press President Joe Biden on Ukraine joining NATO. The US was non-committal, but there was no outright denial of the Ukrainian demand for NATO membership. In any case, from Russia's perspective, American credibility on promises with regard to NATO expansion was very low, given the latter's track record in the matter. Considering this as the red line of all red lines, in March/April 2021 the Russian Armed Forces began massing thousands of personnel and military equipment near Russia's border with Ukraine, and in Crimea (which Russia had annexed from Ukraine in 2014). This represented the largest mobilization since Russia's annexation of Crimea.

Despite this, the West refused to back down and on 14 June 2021, NATO issued the following communiqué at its annual Brussels summit:

> We reiterate the decision made at the 2008 Bucharest Summit that Ukraine will become a member of the Alliance with the Membership Action Plan (MAP) as an integral part of the process; we reaffirm all elements of that decision, as well as subsequent decisions, including that each partner will be judged on its own merits. We stand firm in our support for Ukraine's right to decide its own future and foreign policy course free from outside interference.[8]

In July 2021, Kyiv and Washington co-hosted Operation Sea Breeze, a naval exercise in the Black Sea that included navies from thirty-one countries and was directly aimed at Russia. In October

2021 a few months prior to the Russian invasion, Ukraine held joint military exercises with US and NATO troops. On 1 September 2021, Zelensky visited the White House, where Biden made it clear that the US was 'firmly committed' to 'Ukraine's Euro-Atlantic aspirations'. Then on 10 November 2021, Secretary of State Antony Blinken and his Ukrainian counterpart, Dmytro Kuleba, signed an important document, the 'US-Ukraine Charter on Strategic Partnership'. The aim of both parties, the document stated, was to underscore the commitment to Ukraine's implementation of the deep and comprehensive reforms necessary for full integration into European and Euro-Atlantic institutions.

To be fair to Russia, it made a set of detailed proposals in December 2021 to the US,[9] and NATO,[10] on what could be done to defuse the situation. The crux of the proposals may be summarized thus:

- No expansion of NATO, neither for Ukraine nor for any other State;
- US not to establish any military bases in former Soviet Republics which are not NATO members;
- No offensive weapons to be stationed near Russia's borders; and
- NATO troops and equipment moved into Eastern Europe since 1997 to be moved back to Western Europe.

The proposals were probably maximalist but if the West had wanted, it could have given an undertaking that Ukraine would not be allowed to join NATO and then sat down to negotiate with Russia on the other contentious points. In fact, no such thing happened, leaving Putin backed into a corner.

The situation was serious enough by December 2021 for American President Joe Biden and Russian President Putin to talk twice, once on a video call on 6 December and the second, a phone call lasting fifty minutes on 30 December 2021. In the first conversation, Biden stressed Ukraine's sovereignty and territorial integrity and asked Russia to de-escalate; in the second conversation Biden warned Putin if Russia were to invade, then US and its allies would 'respond decisively'. There was no substantive response from Biden to the detailed proposals submitted by Russia to the US and NATO on 17 December 2021.[11]

All this is not to justify the Russian invasion of Ukraine on 24 February 2022. At the end of the day no military invasion, regardless of the provocation, can be justified under the UN Charter except in self-defence when attacked. Nevertheless, it is important to understand why the simplistic argument that Russia just decided to invade Ukraine to further its revanchist or imperialist ambitions, does not provide either a full or a valid explanation. Equally, the facile point made by the West that this was 'unprovoked' aggression by Russia is simply not true. Russia was provoked plenty. The war in Ukraine is a complex event and a deep understanding of the underlying issues along with geopolitics is necessary to make an objective assessment of the situation.

4.2 Military Stalemate?

It is not the purpose of this book to go into the granular details of the 'special military operation' that Russia undertook on 24 February 2022. But a few comments are in order. A conventional, land war in the heart of Europe was inconceivable for Western scholars and thinkers. It could happen in Yemen or Iraq or even the Balkans, but Ukraine? Yet here we are, staring at a World War II kind of situation, with tanks rolling, missiles flying and people dying by the thousands.

Then there was the element of timing. Despite the massing of troops by Putin along the border from the spring of 2021, which was a dead giveaway, and despite the drip-drip leaks of intelligence information by the US, there was an overwhelming sentiment that Putin was bluffing and that he would not dare do the unthinkable.

In the event, Putin took a bold and arguably his last gambit and decided to invade Ukraine.

Once the war began, the big element of surprise was the state of the conventional Russian armed forces. There was every reason to believe that Russia banked on two things: one, its troops would be welcomed by most people in Ukraine; and two, the military operation would be relatively swift. As it turned out, both assumptions were completely off the mark. The troops received a hostile reception and the war has meandered, for more than a year now, with no obvious victor in sight. Two factors have played an important role. One, the unbelievable tenacity and spunk displayed by the people, not just the armed forces, of Ukraine. President Zelensky has led from the front, epitomized by his immortal response when offered asylum by the West: 'I need ammunition, not a ride!' However, there is no gainsaying the fact that Ukraine would have likely surrendered by now, if it was not for the massive Western aid, both money and armaments. Aid from the US to Ukraine in 2022 has totalled around $50 billion which is broadly divided into humanitarian aid ($10 billion), financial aid ($15 billion), security and military aid ($25 billion). The US has pledged $45 billion in aid through 2023. The EU had pledged 10 billion Euros for 2022 (not all of it has been disbursed) and another 18 billion Euros for 2023.

The type of weapons that the US and its allies have given to Ukraine so far, also deserves scrutiny. First, the US and individual NATO countries have scrambled to send artillery, ammunition and air-defence missiles. Basically, these were not considered essential after the Cold War and stocks were low in the US and Europe. Now there is a massive demand for it. As one military analyst put it, one day in Ukraine uses more ammunition than was used in one full month in Afghanistan. Second, the US and its allies were initially careful not to give long-range weapons to Ukraine for fear of provoking Russia. The US gave drones, High mobility artillery rocket systems (HIMARS), Javelin anti-tank and Stinger anti-aircraft weapons. None of these really have the capacity to hit Russia deep in its territory. But Ukraine has pushed for long-range drones and an Army Tactical Missile System which has a range of 300 km, to strike targets within Russia. Crucially, when Zelensky visited Washington on December 21, Secretary of State Blinken announced the supply, for the first time, of the Patriot surface-to-air missile system. This will inevitably have the effect of further escalating a conflict that has already resulted in enormous loss of life and property for both sides. At least 100,000 people have died on each side, according to some estimates.

In an important move to ratchet up pressure on Russia, both the US and Germany in January 2023 agreed to supply heavy battle tanks, Abrams by the US and Leopard 2 by Germany. This was a long-standing demand by Ukraine. Germany had been reluctant to deliver these tanks, mainly for fear of provoking Russia. For this reason, it said it would supply tanks to Ukraine only if the US also did the same. At the time of going to print ,there are reports that the US has okayed the delivery of F-16 fighter jets to Ukraine, from the Netherlands and Denmark.

Russia has described this as blatant provocation and talked of unspecified consequences. The fact of the matter is that Ukraine hopes to use these tanks and fighter jets to retake territory it lost to Russia earlier in the war. If so, Russia could consider this as NATO countries now fighting a proxy war in its territory. The West is operating on two premises, both dangerous. One, the tanks and fighter jets to Ukraine are necessary to help it conduct a massive counter-offensive. Second, the West believes the only way to drag Putin to the negotiating table is by defeating him first in the battlefield. The West appears to have crossed the Rubicon in

Ukraine in terms of weapon deliveries. The strategic nightmare is that a proxy war in Ukraine may soon turn into a direct NATO-Russia war!

At the time of writing, it is clear that neither side has won decisively and the best way to characterize this conflict is to dub it a stalemate. Sure, Russia's war aims have not been met and it has had to recalibrate its war goals constantly. Worse, Russia's own army has been shown in the worst possible light in this war. On the other hand, Russia does occupy something like 20 per cent of Ukrainian territory. Ukraine, on the other hand, has shown grit and determination and has managed to hurt Russia. But the longer this war goes on, it is hard to see an outright winner. It is difficult to see Ukraine winning this war, but Russia will also not lose this war easily, although it will suffer enormous strategic setbacks. The year 2023 may turn out to be significant for this war. There have been moments when the N-word (nuclear weapons) has been uttered, but should these actually be used, the international condemnation, including from countries like China and India, will be so severe that it is inconceivable that President Putin would use them.

4.3 Mediation

Despite the military stalemate, the situation is such that it is very hard to see a mediated end to this conflict at present. Both sides are well entrenched in their positions. The problem is the ebb and flow of the conflict. Just when you think one side has the upper hand, the other side lands a blow that is difficult to ignore. The result is that each side thinks it can win if only it persists long enough. For Ukraine, the initial negotiating position was to restore the borders to the pre-2014 positions, when Russia had annexed Crimea. For Russia, Crimea is non-negotiable, and its initial negotiating position was that the 'People's Republics of Donetsk and Luhansk' were independent territories. There are other important Russian demands as well, such as the neutrality of Ukraine. With current maximalist demands on both sides, any attempt at mediation in this conflict would amount to 'mission impossible'!

Past attempts do not inspire confidence either. Perhaps the best possible chance of resolving this were the two Minsk Agreements signed in September 2014 and March 2015, aimed at arriving at a permanent solution between Russia and Ukraine. In particular, the second Minsk Agreement that was signed between Russia, Ukraine, France and Germany (called the Normandy Four) provided for an immediate and comprehensive ceasefire in Donetsk and Luhansk regions, special status for the two regions, full control of the border for Ukraine after political settlement, and other confidence-building measures such as pardon, amnesty, etc. The real problem was the differing interpretations by both Russia and Ukraine of the Minsk Agreements themselves. Ukraine thought it was re-establishing its sovereignty over its territory; Russia, on the other hand, thought it was achieving semi-independent status for Donetsk and Luhansk and that Ukraine would have less than full sovereignty in this region. But there was bad faith, especially on the part of Ukraine, egged on by its western friends. Current testimony from past leaders such as Angela Merkel and Francois Hollande is proof of this bad faith.

Even before the Russian invasion in February 2022, French President Macron spent hours talking to Putin on the phone, urging him not to take military action. This failed spectacularly, with Putin doing exactly what he wanted to do, going against global opinion. Perhaps the most serious attempt at mediation was made by Turkish President Erdogan in March 2022. He convened delegations from Russia and Ukraine and after detailed talks, Ukraine reportedly gave Russia a series of written proposals.[12] These comprised, inter alia: Ukraine proclaiming itself a neutral state promising to remain non-aligned with any blocs and refrain from developing nuclear weapons in exchange for international legal guarantees; possible guarantor states include Russia, the UK, China, the US, France, Turkey, Germany, Canada, Italy, Poland, Israel and others who would be welcome; such guarantees would not extend to Crimea, Sevastopol or certain areas of Donbas, boundaries of these regions to be defined by the two Parties; Ukraine confirms not to join any military coalition (read NATO) but hopes to join EU; such guarantees to kick in when there is armed aggression against Ukraine; the treaty to kick in after it is approved by a national referendum and ratified in the parliaments of the guarantor States; and a possible meeting between the presidents of the two countries for the purpose of signing the treaty.

For a variety of reasons, the above proposals did not take off. Apparently, Putin, when handed this proposal, turned it down. Other reports say that some NATO countries saw an opportunity to punch and humiliate Russia and therefore vetoed the proposals. Whatever the reasons, hostilities resumed soon after, and both sides blamed each other of bad faith.

In a sign that Ukraine had considerably hardened its position, President Zelensky outlined another ten-point plan at the Bali G20 meeting in November 2022 via video link. It comprised the following:

- Radiation and nuclear safety, focusing on restoring security around Europe's largest nuclear power plant in Zaporizhzhia, Ukraine, which is now under Russian occupation.
- Food security, including protecting and ensuring Ukraine's grain exports to the world's poorest nations.
- Energy security, with a focus on price restrictions on Russian energy exports, as well as aiding Ukraine with restoring its power infrastructure, half of which has been damaged by Russian attacks.

- Release of all prisoners and deportees, including war prisoners and children deported to Russia.
- Restoring Ukraine's territorial integrity and Russia reaffirming it according to the UN Charter, which Zelenskyy said is 'not up for negotiation'.
- Withdrawal of Russian troops and the cessation of hostilities, the restoration of Ukraine's state borders with Russia.
- Justice, including the establishment of a special tribunal to prosecute Russian war crimes.
- The prevention of ecocide and the protection of the environment, with a focus on demining and restoring water treatment facilities.
- Prevention of an escalation of conflict and building security architecture in the Euro-Atlantic space, including guarantees for Ukraine.
- Confirmation of the war's end, including a document signed by the involved parties.

For good measure, Zelensky also suggested a peace summit. It may be noted that these proposals were considerably more hardline than the ones he made earlier. This may be a sign of confidence in the outcome of the war from Ukraine's point of view, or the proposals may have been made for Russia to reject them, which Russia did. Points like the restoration of Ukraine's territorial integrity, which was not up for negotiation, or setting up a tribunal for Russian war crimes really meant that the proposals were dead-on-arrival for Russia. Interestingly, none of Ukraine's Western allies were excited about these proposals either.

At the time of writing, while there is no dearth of mediators including China, the African Union and even Saudi Arabia, no mediation attempt looks likely to succeed. Sadly, the war in Ukraine appears set to drag on for an indefinite period.

4.4 Geopolitics

The war in Ukraine upended geopolitics. Prior to the Russian invasion, President Putin had paid a visit to Beijing on the eve of the Winter Olympics on 4 February 2022. The two leaders reportedly met for hours before agreeing on an epic Joint Statement.[13] Just short of an alliance, the Joint Statement, which is 5,000 words long, pronounces itself on every major issue in the world. Stating that their relationship is superior to political and military alliances of the Cold War era, the two leaders affirm solemnly that the bilateral relationship has 'no limits' and there are 'no forbidden areas' of cooperation. They seek genuine multipolarity, with the UN and the UNSC playing a central role. The new era, according to the two countries, has seen a trend towards the redistribution of power in the world. The US is obviously singled out for criticism. There is a general sense that this Joint Statement is an important development in international relations. Whether or not it creates a bloc, we will have to see. But there is no question that the two countries have laid out an alternative view of the liberal world order, which has been in existence since World War II.

For the purposes of this book, though, the key question is this: did Putin take Xi Jinping into confidence on 4 February about Russia's impending invasion of Ukraine on 24 February? You would think so, considering the 'no limits' friendship and all that followed a little later. While we may never know the full truth in the matter, there is now circumstantial evidence that Putin may not have taken Xi Jinping fully into confidence.

Providing proof of this is the former foreign minister of China (who has since been removed from office and whose whereabouts are unknown), Qin Gang, who, when he was still China's ambassador to the US, wrote in March 2022 in the *Washington Post* that if China had known of Russia's intentions in advance, it would have tried to stop the war in Ukraine. If this is true, it does cast some doubt on the nature and extent of the 'no limits' friendship between the two countries. There is no doubt that China has been increasingly discomfited by Russia's actions in Ukraine. Russia's actions in Ukraine have highlighted the following provisions of the Sino-Russian Joint Statement of 4 February 2022:

- The Joint Statement noted that the UN Charter and the Universal Declaration of Human Rights set noble goals in the area of universal human rights and set forth fundamental principles, which all the States must comply with and observe in deed. How does one reconcile this with Russia violating UN Law and the Charter by invading Ukraine?

- The Joint Statement opposed further enlargement of NATO and called on the North Atlantic Alliance to abandon its ideologized Cold War approaches, to respect the sovereignty, security and interests of other countries, the diversity of their civilizational, cultural and historical backgrounds and to exercise a fair and objective attitude towards the peaceful development of other States. This may be construed as clear support for Russia's core interests and this is juxtaposed with Russia's support for the 'one-China principle', a core interest of China's. Can this be construed as ex-ante justification for Russia's invasion of Ukraine?

- The Joint Statement says Russia and China stand against attempts by external forces to undermine security and stability in their common adjacent regions, intend to counter interference by outside forces in the internal affairs of sovereign countries under any pretext, oppose regime change, and will increase cooperation in the aforementioned areas. The fact that the words 'regime change' (colour revolutions) are used makes it clear that both countries are vitally interested in the security of their adjacent regions: Ukraine in Russia's case, but could it equally apply to Taiwan in China's case?

All indications at present are that China is doubling down on its relationship with Russia since the war in Ukraine has played out. It has been careful, and it does appear there are some limits to the Sino-Russian relationship after all. First, China has not provided any lethal military assistance to Russia so far, despite unconfirmed reports that Russia has sought security assistance. Second, China would have preferred a quick end to the war, preferably an outright Russian victory. After all, no one, least of all China, wants to back a loser. Third, China has expressed some concerns and raised some questions about Russia's actions in Ukraine. This was confirmed by Putin in a face-to-face meeting with Xi Jinping in Uzbekistan in September 2022 at the Shanghai Cooperation Organization (SCO) when he said, 'We understand China's questions and concerns on the war in Ukraine. We will explain this.' Last but not least, China appears to have warned Russia about the dangers of using nuclear weapons and dissuaded it from doing so.

China must be closely watching two outcomes that followed the Russian invasion of Ukraine. One, the strong international condemnation of Russia, including resolutions in the UNGA passed by an overwhelming majority of States. After all, the UNGA is the court of world opinion. Two, the sanctions that have been unleashed against Russia, beginning with its removal from the SWIFT payments system and the immediate freeze of the assets of its Central Bank, have been unprecedented in their harshness. Three, a lot of observers felt that after the initial rhetoric, Western solidarity would crumble. This has not happened, at least not yet. There may be 'Ukraine fatigue', but by and large, the West has remained solid and united.

There are important lessons for China in all of this. Should China decide to move on Taiwan, then it could also conceivably be the subject of harsh sanctions and global opinion ranged against it. In many ways, China will know what to expect if and when it moves against Taiwan.

The Russian invasion has put several countries in a strategic dilemma. Not all ASEAN countries, for instance, are comfortable with outright condemnation of Russia. Vietnam abstained, as did the Lao Peoples Democratic Republic (PDR). A number of African countries abstained as well. But there is no question that more than two-thirds of the UN membership (143, to be precise) voted to condemn Russia in the UNGA, and this is significant by any reckoning.

While China may not give up on Russia in the short term, there are now signs that the newly appointed foreign minister Wang Yi is under instructions from Xi Ping to mend bilateral ties with the US. China is being shrewd by holding out an olive branch to the US. For one thing, China had opened too many fronts by following the 'wolf warrior' brand of diplomacy. Thus, it had acted unilaterally in the East and South China Seas, to the consternation of Japan and some ASEAN countries. In the Himalayas, it literally crossed swords with India, leading to the most serious deterioration in ties since the two countries fought a war in 1962. With the US, relations had touched rock bottom by the end of 2022.

To complicate matters, China faces serious economic headwinds within the country, with the real estate sector in deep trouble and Xi Jinping implementing his mantra of 'common prosperity' by going after the private sector and business titans. However, the breaking point may have been the unprecedented anti-Covid protests in China in November, which forced Xi Jinping to do a volte face on the stringent Covid restrictions that were in place. In so doing, he was not merely bowing to the protesters but also allowing serious damage to his aura and reputation. All this has led to China seeking détente with the US in the new year. The question is how China will deal with other powers such as the EU, Japan, South Korea, Australia, and India. That will give us an idea of Xi Jinping's approach in the wake of his virtual coronation as China's emperor in October 2022.

Russia's invasion of Ukraine has occupied centre stage, thus relegating the Indo-Pacific to the background. Yet, the US, in its National Security Strategy released in October 2022, did call China the most consequential geopolitical challenge. So, does the US have the bandwidth and the wherewithal to tackle the challenge from China and Russia at the same time? The answer to this is important for all of America's allies and partners. The test could come before the end of 2023.

China, as a permanent member of the UNSC, had to take positions on the war in Ukraine and thus came under scrutiny. China (much like India, as we will see later) abstained from most of the resolutions at the UNSC and the UNGA, and of course refrained from condemning Russia by name.

In a meeting of the UNSC in September 2022, Chinese Foreign Minister Wang Yi, who is also the present foreign minister, said that China's position on the Ukraine issue was consistent and clear:

- The sovereignty and territorial integrity of all countries should be safeguarded;
- The purposes and principles of the UN Charter should be abided by;
- The legitimate security concerns of all parties should be taken seriously; and
- All efforts conducive to the peaceful settlement of the crisis should be supported.

China's position, as outlined in the points above, appears to be an attempt not merely to sit on the fence but also to say something that can be interpreted as being supportive of both Russia and Ukraine. The expression 'legitimate security concerns of all parties' can be interpreted to mean that Russia had legitimate security interests in Ukraine that needed to be safeguarded. On the other hand, references to the sovereignty and territorial integrity of countries as well as to the purposes and principles of the UN Charter cannot but be interpreted as being in support of Ukraine in the present case. Other things in the statement made by the Chinese foreign minister, such as dialogue, diplomacy, peace talks and alleviating the humanitarian situation may be considered the 'motherhood and apple pie' kind of expressions.

The Russian invasion of Ukraine is therefore a seminal event with geopolitical implications that are still playing out and therefore bear close watching.

4.5 India's Stand

Before we examine India's stand on the war in Ukraine, it would be useful to look at some similar geopolitical events in the past and see how India reacted to them. This will help put India's current stand on the war in Ukraine into historical context. The list is not exhaustive but indicative.

4.5.1 Suez Canal Crisis (1956)

The Suez Canal, a crucial waterway, was managed by a firm, the Suez Canal Company, in which the British and French governments held the majority stake. Egyptian President Nasser sought help from these countries to build a dam to tackle the problem of flooding but did not get it. For this and other reasons, President Nasser stunned the world by nationalizing the Suez Canal in late 1956. The Suez Canal was a strategic chokepoint, so a conflict between the UK and Egypt was in the offing. India's first PM, Nehru, foresaw this and in a letter to C. Rajagopalachari wrote, 'This is by far the most difficult and dangerous situation in international affairs that India has faced since independence.'[14]

India then took a position that was underpinned by two factors: one, India had a major stake in the security of West Asia; two, India should not automatically align itself with any power bloc and should thus take an independent stance on major international issues. The situation was also complicated by the fact that India had close ties with the UK, having obtained independence only nine years earlier. India did not automatically side with Egypt, even though both were key members of the non-aligned movement. Nehru in fact conceded to C. Rajagopalachari, 'Probably, we shall end by displeasing our friends on both sides.'[15]

India was taken by surprise by Nasser's decision to nationalize the Suez Canal. Nehru did not automatically support Nasser and this was illustrated by India sending a delegation to attend a British-convened conference aimed at a diplomatic solution. But this failed and the invasion by Britain, France and Israel happened in end October. Nehru was clear and stated that Israel had attacked Egypt and was therefore the aggressor. Nehru then asked the US to intervene, and the final solution was called the 'Eisenhower-Nehru formula'.[16] It is ironic that a non-aligned leader asked for intervention by a superpower. What is more, when it was decided to form the first UN peacekeeping force, India lent its soldiers, who were then deployed in the Sinai Peninsula. In fact, the UN force was led by an Indian Army officer, Lt. Gen. P.S. Gyani, from 1959 to 1964.

A few things emerge from the very first test faced by Indian diplomacy. There was an Indian strategic interest in the security of West Asia. Second, India adopted a position of neutrality or fence-sitting in the beginning. India condemned the Anglo-French invasion of the Suez Canal. It then sought a peaceful resolution of the issue. Finally, when the formation of the UN peacekeeping force was decided, India lent its heft to it.

4.5.2 Hungarian Revolution (1956)

The protests in Hungary were aimed at the Soviet Union and Hungarian Prime Minister Imre Nagy, a liberal, who talked about free elections and the withdrawal of Soviet troops from Hungary.

But the last straw was when he said Hungary would leave the Warsaw Pact. Soviet tanks simply rolled in, hundreds of protesters were killed, and a new PM, Janos Kador, was installed. Nagy was executed later. Whatever the details, the facts of the matter were straightforward.

India's response was interesting.

Initially, Nehru said very little on the subject. Considering the Suez Canal crisis was so close in time to the Soviet invasion of Hungary, it is remarkable how much Nehru gave the Soviet Union the benefit of the doubt. Indeed, there are questions as to why he spoke out quickly on one issue (Suez) and not on the other (Hungary).[17] Nehru certainly dilly-dallied for three weeks, before saying that Hungarians must have the right to self-determination and the Soviets ought to recognize Hungarian sovereignty. The only way India's stance can be justified is that there were geopolitical considerations that Nehru may have had—the US was beginning to cosy up to Pakistan, and India needed the Soviet Union for its own strategic balancing purposes. In the end, when it was clear that the Soviets were crushing dissent, Nehru could not keep quiet. But the initial reticence was there for all to see.

Geopolitical imperatives held sway before the Soviet invasion was criticized by India.

4.5.3 Vietnam War (1966)

The Vietnam War was a long, costly and divisive conflict that pitted the communist government of North Vietnam against South Vietnam and its principal ally, the US. The conflict was intensified by the ongoing Cold War between the US and the Soviet Union. China had become communist in 1949, and communists were in control of North Vietnam. The US believed in the 'domino theory' that communism would spread to South Vietnam and then the rest of Asia. It decided to send money, supplies and military advisers to help the South Vietnamese government. This was one of the longest wars and lasted from at least 1965 to 1975.

It is fair to say that India was strongly opposed to the American war in Vietnam. By 1964, India's first PM Jawaharlal Nehru passed away and by January 1966, his daughter Indira Gandhi became PM after a political power struggle. So, the American war in Vietnam was one of the first international issues on which she was expected to take a stand on behalf of India. In March 1966, she paid a visit to the US, met President Lyndon Johnson and discussed the issue of PL-480 food grains to India. The meetings apparently went well, with President Johnson willing to help India.

In May 1966, the American Air Force bombed the major North Vietnamese population centres of Hanoi and Haiphong for the first time, destroying oil depots located near the two cities. The US military hoped that by bombing Hanoi, the capital of North Vietnam, and Haiphong, North Vietnam's largest port, communist forces would be deprived of essential military supplies and thus the ability to wage war. For almost three months, India said nothing. Then, on 1 July, the Government of India issued a statement deploring the American bombing of Hanoi and Haiphong. Veteran journalist Inder Malhotra, in 2013, offered an interesting explanation of why Indira Gandhi did this. He argued that Indira Gandhi had made up her mind to pursue left-wing policies and she chose Vietnam as a test case.[18] He said that the timing may have partly been influenced by Indira Gandhi's forthcoming visits to Egypt, Yugoslavia and the Soviet Union.

In Moscow, she signed a joint statement with Soviet Premier Alexei Kosygin that not only called for an immediate and unconditional end to the bombings of Hanoi and Haiphong but also condemned the imperialist aggression in Vietnam. This caused the Americans to go ballistic. Lyndon Johnson was indignant and put a hold on the PL-480 wheat shipments. The American ambassador in Delhi, Chester Bowles, tried to point out to President Johnson that what the Indian PM Indira Gandhi said was not very different from what the UN Secretary General or the Pope were saying at the time. Lyndon Johnson is said to have shot back, 'But the UN Secretary General or the Pope do not want our wheat!'

Indira Gandhi kept up her criticism of American policy in Vietnam. Even towards the end of the war in 1973, when she was addressing the One-Asia Assembly sponsored by the Press Foundation of Asia,[19] she asked the delegates present, 'Would this sort of war or the savage bombing that has taken place in Vietnam have been tolerated for so long had the people been European?' Of course, this came after the liberation of Bangladesh in 1971, which also soured relations between India and the US. Indira Gandhi also clarified at the conference:

We have been non-aligned and what we meant by non-alignment is, firstly, that we did not belong to any military bloc and, secondly, that we reserve the right to judge an issue and to take action according to our own interests and what we consider to be the interests of world peace.[20]

The US officials termed her comments 'inadmissible' and the American ambassador-designate to India, Daniel Patrick Moynihan, had to defer his arrival in India.

What we see in India's position on the American War in Vietnam is that it faced barely any moral dilemma. In effect, India's geopolitical imperatives and commitment to principles made it a clear-cut decision. The only risk Indira Gandhi took was regarding American President Lyndon Johnson's reaction. His, perhaps not unexpected, anger led him to put on hold the wheat shipments that India desperately needed.

4.5.4 Soviet 'Intervention' in Afghanistan (1979)

At the end of December 1979, the Soviet Union sent thousands of troops into Afghanistan and immediately assumed complete military and political control of Kabul and large portions of the country. This event began a brutal, decade-long attempt by Moscow to subdue the Afghan civil war and maintain a friendly and socialist government on its border. It was a watershed event of the Cold War, marking the only time the Soviet Union invaded a country outside the Eastern Bloc—a strategic decision met by nearly worldwide condemnation. Undoubtedly, leaders in the Kremlin had hoped that a rapid and complete military takeover would secure Afghanistan's place as an exemplar of the Brezhnev Doctrine, which held that once a country became socialist, Moscow would never permit it to return to the capitalist camp. The US and its European allies, guided by their own doctrine of containment, sharply criticized the Soviet move into Afghanistan and devised numerous measures to compel Moscow to withdraw.

The Soviet intervention in Afghanistan put India in something of a quandary. On the one hand, India at this point had the strongest of ties with the Soviet Union, as evidenced by the Treaty of Peace, Friendship and Cooperation signed by both countries in 1971, which played a pivotal role in the war to liberate Bangladesh. On the other hand, there could not be two views to the matter, the Soviet Union had quite simply invaded a sovereign, independent country that happened to be in Asia and in India's neighbourhood. The idea of 'intervention' rather than 'invasion' was a fig leaf, no more or no less!

On 14 January 1980 the UNGA held an emergency special session to discuss the issue of the Soviet invasion of Afghanistan. In a speech that stretched credulity, the Indian Permanent Representative to the UN, Ambassador Brajesh Mishra, stated:

India cannot look with equanimity at the attempt by some outside powers to interfere in the internal affairs of Afghanistan by training, arming and encouraging subversive elements to create a disturbance inside Afghanistan.

Moscow has assured the new Indian government that Soviet troops entered Afghanistan at the request of the Hafizullah Amin government on Dec. 26, and of Amin's successors on Dec. 28.

We have been further assured that Soviet troops will be withdrawn when requested to do so by the Afghan government.

India has no reason to doubt these assurances, particularly by a friendly country such as the Soviet Union.

India hopes that the Soviets will not violate the independence of Afghanistan and that Soviet forces will not remain there a day longer than necessary.[21]

The US called it a 'great disappointment'.[22] It was all the more jarring since other non-aligned countries like Yugoslavia officially condemned the Soviet intervention and expressed 'astonishment' and 'deep concern' about developments in Afghanistan.

The statement by Ambassador Brajesh Mishra lays more emphasis on causal factors, namely, the training and arming of subversive elements in Afghanistan, rather than on the actual invasion, which is justified as Soviet forces being there at the invitation of Afghan President Amin and his successors (who were themselves installed by the Soviet Union). Further, India accepted the Soviet Union's assurance that it would quit Afghanistan when asked to do so. India went on to express the naive hope that the Soviets would not violate the independence of Afghanistan and not remain a day longer than necessary. India abstained from the UNGA resolution.

The best explanation of the process of making decisions at the time, and the dilemma faced by India, comes from none other than former PM I.K. Gujral, who was at the time the Indian ambassador to Russia. In a detailed oral history, which has been recorded in the *Indian Foreign Affairs Journal*,[23] I.K. Gujral recalls step-by-step how India responded to the intervention. He tries hard to dispel the impression that India endorsed the Soviet intervention in Afghanistan in 1979. He begins by saying that the diplomatic corps (of which he was a part of as the Indian ambassador) in Moscow was taken by surprise. One of the main driving factors for the Soviet intervention was the ousting of the Taraki regime in Afghanistan and the capturing of power in September 1979 by Hafizullah Amin. This caused 'immense distress' to the Soviets.

Gujral says that when he met Soviet Premier Kosygin during a flight to Delhi, the latter was not even aware of the ouster of the Taraki regime and the takeover by Hafizullah Amin. After hearing Gujral, Kosygin opined that Amin was an American agent whom the Soviets had never trusted. What is extraordinary is that years later when Gujral met Soviet leader Gorbachev in 2001 and told him that India had no idea about the Soviet intervention in Afghanistan—even though it had implications for us and we were a friendly country to the Soviet Union—Gorbachev reportedly told Gujral, 'I too read about it the next day in the newspapers'.[24]

It turned out later that the full Politbureau had not been consulted and that only a handful of powerful people—Andropov, Chernenko, Ustinov and Gromyko—had decided to intervene in Afghanistan. Gujral suggested that the Soviets had hugely underestimated the military challenge in Afghanistan!

Gujral gives a fascinating account of Soviet Foreign Minister Gromyko's visit to Delhi in February 1980 to brief Indira Gandhi on the Soviet action in Afghanistan.

In a meeting at which Gromyko and the Soviet ambassador to India were present and Indira Gandhi was accompanied by Foreign Minister Narasimha Rao and Gujral (still the Indian ambassador to Russia), Gromyko—who was very articulate in English—explained the Russian motives, including America's and Pakistan's subversive role in Afghanistan, which had huge security implications for India. Indira Gandhi listened even as she doodled without saying a word for over an hour. Gromyko then concluded and asked Indira Gandhi whether she appreciated the position. Indira Gandhi asked, 'You mean your entry in Afghanistan?' Upon hearing Gromyko say, 'Yes, madam.', Indira Gandhi said, 'I am sorry I can't appreciate it!'

Gujral says that this response left Gromyko stunned. Gujral goes on to say that Brezhnev asked the Soviet ambassador to India for another meeting between Indira Gandhi and Gromyko, which happened the next day. At the meeting, Gromyko began by saying that Brezhnev held Indira Gandhi in high regard and that as a special token of that, he was 'willing to extend the credit terms for the supply of a large quantity of arms from ten to thirteen years'. He made it a point to say that this was a special gesture of friendship, since such terms were not given even to fraternal socialist countries. Again, according to Gujral, Indira Gandhi kept quiet. Gromyko had to leave Delhi empty-handed. Indeed, the coverage in the Washington Post said that India urged the withdrawal of the Soviets from Afghanistan.[25]

Gujral says that Indira Gandhi, despite the above, could not afford public condemnation of Soviet intervention because of three factors:

• Pakistan was getting substantial arms supplies from the US in return for its anti-Soviet involvement in Afghanistan;

- Pakistan was deeply involved in the mobilization of jihadi elements in Afghanistan; and
- America also secured the support of China in this effort.

In the circumstances, there was no way we could have broken our ties with the Soviet Union, which would have left us high and dry in terms of weapon supplies and support. Gujral argues that while we could chide them privately and urge them to withdraw, we could not do more. He vehemently denies that we sided with the Soviet Union. On the contrary, he says we abstained at the UN every single time. He also claims that the Soviet Union did not put any undue pressure on India to change its position. Be that as it may, all statements by PM Indira Gandhi and the foreign minister, Narasimha Rao, linked the Soviet intervention in Afghanistan to American aid and arms to Pakistan.

The bottom line is that we did not condemn the Soviet intervention in Afghanistan, abstained from all resolutions in the UN and maintained our vital ties with the then Soviet Union on account of geopolitics and realpolitik.

4.5.5 Gulf War (1990)

On 2 August 1990, the Iraqi armed forces invaded Kuwait and within a few hours ran over the tiny Emirate; six days later, the Iraqi parliament annexed it and declared Kuwait to be the nineteenth province of the Republic of Iraq. The immediate reason for the Iraqi action was the economic crisis that Iraq faced due to its prolonged war with Iran and a substantial debt that its President Saddam Hussein wanted Kuwait to defer. Saddam Hussein also felt that he had fought a costly war with Iran on behalf of the Gulf Arab monarchies, hence the Iraqi debt should be annulled by the latter. Kuwait was obviously defiant. There was also a historical dimension to the Iraqi action. In the past, Iraq had laid claims to Kuwait on the plea that the tiny

Emirate was a part of the Wilayat-e-Basra (Basra Province) under the Ottoman Empire. Anyway, things came to a head, and Saddam Hussein made the specious accusation that Kuwait was stealing Iraqi oil and launched his fateful invasion on 2 August 1990.[26]

As Iraq invaded and annexed Kuwait, the ruling family of Kuwait fled the country and took refuge in neighbouring Saudi Arabia. Having the Iraqi army close to its borders unnerved Saudi Arabia and King Fahd decided to seek military help from Washington, leading to the deployment of large US forces in the Saudi Kingdom. Within days after the Iraqi invasion, 'Operation Desert Shield' was in place to secure the Saudi borders from a possible Iraqi invasion. Iraq not only disregarded international condemnation but also rejected a host of UNSC resolutions that called for an immediate and unconditional withdrawal from Kuwait. Eventually, on 17 January 1991, the UN-backed coalition forces, led by the US with the participation of thirty-four countries, launched 'Operation Desert Storm'. After a massive aerial campaign followed by a limited ground offensive in the later stages, in February 1991, Kuwait was liberated with the total withdrawal of the Iraqi forces and the return of the Emir back to Kuwait a few days later.

Between August 1990, when the crisis began and February 1991, when the status quo ante was restored in Kuwait, the Arab world was deeply divided. While no country explicitly endorsed or justified the Iraqi action, there were serious differences over the means of resolving it. The first Arab League statement on this issue, which called for an 'immediate and unconditional' withdrawal, was preceded by the unanimous condemnation of the Iraqi invasion by the UNSC.

Egypt's re-entry into the Arab League following the Camp David peace accords with Israel was completed in May 1990 with the return of the League headquarters from Tunis to Cairo. Egyptian President Hosni Mubarak took the lead in the Kuwait

crisis and convened an emergency meeting of the Arab League on
10 August. It adopted a resolution that called the Iraqi action a
violation of Kuwaiti sovereignty and demanded immediate and
unconditional withdrawal. The resolution also stated that the
members of the League would support Saudi Arabia and other
Gulf states by dispatching Arab forces 'to defend their territorial
and regional security against outside invasion'. The Cairo meeting
could not hide deep internal divisions over the handling of the
crisis, especially the wisdom of inviting the US to undo the Iraqi
invasion. Four Arab League members, namely Jordan, Sudan,
Yemen, and Palestine, were opposed to a 'military' solution and
therefore implicitly stood by Iraq.

Iraq's Saddam Hussein made huge miscalculations. First about
US intentions, then about the reactions of the Arab governments
(public reaction was somewhat in favour of him), and finally about
international condemnation. The swiftness with which the US put
together a UN-backed coalition and the rapidity with which the
status quo ante was restored in Kuwait were matters of much
appreciation. It must be noted, however, that this was the era when
the so-called 'unipolar moment' of the unbridled power of the US
came into full display.

The way India approached this issue had some interesting
dimensions. First and foremost, India was in the middle of the
'coalition era' of minority governments and had, during this
period, as many as two prime ministers and three foreign ministers.
That said, there is enough evidence to suggest that foreign policy
was essentially in the hands of the PM, I.K. Gujral. The concrete
interests of India in Iraq may be summarized thus:

• Traditionally friendly ties with the Iraqi leader Saddam Hussein,
who had gone out of his way to support India on the Kashmir

issue when the traditional Gulf monarchies were toeing the Pakistani line;

- As many as 180,000 Indian expatriates living and working in Iraq;

- Iraq and Kuwait provided 7 per cent of India's oil supplies. Iraq also supplied oil to India at concessional rates. So the impact on India was: reduced oil supply; increase in price per barrel from $15 to $30; reduction in remittances from Indians working in the region; and the cost of evacuating 180,000 people from Iraq.

So, India's position had to fully consider above factors.

India began by neither condemning nor condoning the Iraqi invasion of Kuwait. With V.P. Singh as PM, the foreign minister, I.K. Gujral, stated on 3 August that 'We are closely watching the changing situation and the Indians living in that region are safe.'[27] Days later a more measured statement was made, in which we expressed 'opposition to the use of force to settle inter-state differences even while calling for the withdrawal of Iraqi troops from Kuwait'.[28] India did not use the word 'condemnation', and this did not go well with Kuwait. India's assessment at the time seemed to be that an outright condemnation of Iraqi invasion could jeopardize the lives of the thousands of Indian citizens who resided in the region. Indeed, Foreign Minister Gujral visited Baghdad and met Saddam Hussein (gave him an infamous bear hug, which did not go well with Kuwait and other Gulf monarchies) and brought back a planeload of Indians with him. Between mid-August and mid-October 1990, India organized the largest-ever evacuation of over 150,000 of its citizens from Kuwait via Amman and Baghdad.

India, it is clear in hindsight, misread the situation in at least two ways. One, it strongly expected Saddam Hussein to prevail and did not expect the US to go the whole hog. Two, in anticipation of that, another disastrous move was to shift the Embassy from Kuwait to the Iraqi port city of Basra within days of the Iraqi invasion. It is, however, fair to say that the presence of thousands of Indian citizens played an outsized role in all of this.

There was a final twist in India's position in the Gulf War. India's relations with the US, which were not great at the beginning of the Iraqi invasion, improved when India decided to join the international consensus in support of UN economic sanctions against Saddam Hussein. Taking a step towards the US, the V.P. Singh government (December 1989 to November 1990) had taken a decision to allow US military aircraft to refuel at Indian airports. The US appreciated this move, which was later continued by PM Chandra Shekhar, who succeeded V.P. Singh in November 1990. Indian media released photographs of the US military transport refuelling in January 1991 and once the pictures were out, PM Chandra Shekhar received criticism from India's entire political spectrum except for the BJP. The late Congress leader, Rajiv Gandhi, even went as far as to threaten to withdraw his party's support from the minority government led by Chandra Shekhar. Finally, the Indian government was forced to withdraw the refuelling facility for US aircraft once the matter became public.

There are some parallels between this case and the present one related to the war in Ukraine, as we will see later. Not condemning the invasion outright, the interest of thousands of Indians working in the region, and oil supplies from the region were and are all characteristic features of India's stand.

4.5.6 American Invasion of Iraq (2003)

The American invasion of Iraq has now become a case study on how military interventions should not be carried out. It began with the US and the UK making extravagant claims about Iraq possessing weapons of mass destruction (WMD). This came up in the UNSC in January 2003 when countries like France and Germany (a non-permanent member at the time) expressed themselves against any hasty military action. France, supported by China and Russia (all permanent members of the UNSC), stated that UN Inspectors be given a mandate and time to verify claims that Iraq did possess WMD. The UN Monitoring, Verification and Inspection Commission (UNMOVIC), subsequently stated in unambiguous terms that no WMD was ever found in Iraq. By then it was too late, since the US and UK had decided to go ahead with the invasion of Iraq.

The US put together what came to be known as a 'coalition of the willing'. There were forty-eight countries on the list, though just four (the US, UK, Australia, and Poland) contributed troops or boots on the ground. Other countries provided limited troops to support military operations after the invasion was complete. So, going against its transatlantic allies such as France, and against fellow permanent members of the UNSC such as China and Russia, the US and its allies began the invasion on 20 March 2003 and once the air strikes failed to remove the Iraqi leadership, they began a ground invasion, and by 9 April 2003 the Iraqi troops were overwhelmed. By 1 May 2003, President Bush proudly announced 'mission accomplished'. Then, in a move that was to have lasting repercussions, the Americans not only disbanded the 'Baathists' (those loyal to Saddam Hussain) from their positions but also disbanded the Iraqi Army itself. This created such a massive vacuum that Iraq quickly descended into lawlessness, never to recover from it.

India's position on this conflict was noteworthy. At a meeting of the UNSC in March, one week after the American invasion, India termed the US-led military action against the Saddam Hussein regime 'unjustified' and called for all possible efforts to bring 'hostilities' to an early end. 'One can have differences over the necessity of war but one cannot have differences about the urgent need to restore peace,' said India's UN ambassador during the first UNSC debate on Iraq since the war began. He said the main focus of the UNSC should have been to secure Iraq's cooperation with the weapons inspection regime and its compliance with the UNSC resolution. Since that has not happened and India was now presented with a situation where some UNSC members have decided to proceed unilaterally, India stressed the need to work for 'ending hostilities and bringing peace'. For good measure, India also stressed the need for maintaining the sovereignty and integrity of Iraq, preserving its secular traditions and ensuring that its people exercised their right to determine their political future and exercised full control over their natural resources.

In an unprecedented move, however, the Indian parliament passed a unanimous resolution:

> Reflecting national sentiment, this House (Lok Sabha) deplores the military action by the coalition forces led by the USA against a sovereign Iraq. This military action, with a view to changing the Government of Iraq, is unacceptable. The resultant suffering of the innocent people of Iraq, especially women and children, is a matter of grave human dimension [sic]. This action without the specific sanction of the UN Security Council and is not in conformity with the UN Charter. The House, therefore, expresses profound anguish and deep sympathy for the people of Iraq.[29]

The Government of India had already gone through turbulence in the run-up to the Iraq invasion, with PM Atal Bihari Vajpayee sticking to the position that the UN framework was the only platform to meet the concerns of the international community about weapons of mass destructions (WMDs) under the Saddam Hussain regime. 'If unilateralism prevails, the UN would be deeply scarred, with disastrous consequences for the world order,' PM Vajpayee said in a statement to both houses of Parliament on

12 March 2003. By that date, it was clear that the US, UK and their allies would go ahead with the invasion of Iraq even without the UN's blessings.

The real twist in this story is what emerged later in terms of the US putting pressure on India for boots on the ground in Iraq (in the post-war phase) and India coming close to agreeing to it. The story about how this played out is told succinctly by Devirupa Mitra in her article in *The Wire*.[30]

The formal end of hostilities proclaimed by Bush was when the American heat on India began to mount. In New Delhi, Bush's close friend Robert Blackwill was ambassador but was nearing the end of his term. After his predecessor Richard Celeste had carefully steered ties in the post-Pokhran phase two years earlier, Blackwill had described his term as seeing a 'transformation' in the India-US relationship. And he made it his mission to get Indian troops to Iraq.

In an oral history interview two years after his retirement, US diplomat Albert Thibault Jr, who was the deputy chief of mission at the US embassy in India in 2003, recounted how Washington mounted a concerted campaign to keep New Delhi in the loop about the Iraq invasion. According to Thibault, Indian and American defence officials were in intense dialogue about putting a large Indian military contingent in Iraq.[31]

The long and short of it was this: voices within the government were leaning towards agreeing to the US demand of having Indian troops stationed in Iraq; there were strategic thinkers and journalists who were in favour of India sending troops to Iraq; the Rashtriya Swayamsevak Sangh was opposed to this; and most importantly, PM Vajpayee had made up his mind very early on that he would not agree to the American request. So, after going through the motions of consultation and discussion, which was quintessentially Vajpayee's style as well, the cabinet led by PM Vajpayee took the decision not to put Indian boots on the ground in Iraq. The cabinet meeting itself lasted only ten minutes. But such were the divisions at the highest levels in the Government of India that the decision did not directly turn down the US request. Instead, it stated that 'were there to be an explicit UN mandate for the purpose, the Government of India could consider the deployment of our troops in Iraq.'[32]

India's foreign minister, Yashwant Sinha, in a brief statement to journalists after the meeting, said, 'Our longer-term national interest, our concern for the people of Iraq, our long-standing ties with the Gulf region as a whole, as well as our growing dialogue and strengthened ties with the US, have been key elements in this consideration.'

In other words, India was able to pin the whole thing on the lack of a UN mandate. In effect, India was grappling with the following questions while the US was putting pressure on it for the troops:

1. Why are the Indian forces being asked for?
2. Would they be tasked with maintaining law and order, or in the event of any potential revolt, would they be required to use force?
3. How long will Indian troops be required to stay?
4. What is the roadmap for Iraq?
5. Under whose command would Indian troops function?

The answers to some of the questions above were neither clear nor palatable for India. In retrospect, the majority view in India was certainly that India was both prudent and right in not acceding to the American request to put boots on the ground in Iraq.

The curious thing about India's stand in this case is that it swung from condemnation of the American invasion of Iraq by the Indian Parliament to coming very close to putting Indian boots on the ground!

4.5.7 Libyan Civil War (2011)

In December 2010, a relatively minor incident in Tunisia, where a street vendor committed self-immolation in response to police harassment, set off a chain of protests in the Arab world. These protests, dubbed the Arab Spring, had far-reaching consequences in places like Egypt, where the long-time ruler Hosni Mubarak was overthrown. In Libya too, protests against the brutal rule of the leader Muammar Qaddafi were held in Benghazi in February 2011. The protesters called on Qaddafi to step down and demanded the release of all political prisoners. In response, Libyan security forces used water cannons and rubber bullets against the crowds, resulting in scores of injuries. To counter the demonstrations, a pro-government rally orchestrated by the Libyan authorities was organized and given wide publicity. But the protests failed to die down.

On the contrary, the protests intensified, with demonstrators taking control of Benghazi and unrest spreading to Tripoli. It was then that the Libyan authorities began using lethal force against demonstrators. Security forces and squads of mercenaries fired live ammunition into crowds of protesters, who were also attacked by tanks and artillery on the ground and by warplanes and helicopter gunships from the air. The Qaddafi regime restricted communications by blocking the internet and interrupting telephone services throughout the country. On 21 February 2011, one of Qaddafi's sons, Sayf al-Islam, gave a defiant address on state television, blaming outside agitators for the unrest and saying that further demonstrations could lead to civil war in the country. He vowed that the regime would fight 'to the last bullet'. By 25 February, most of eastern Libya was under the control of protesters and rebel forces, while Qaddafi controlled the main cities of Tripoli, Sirte and Sabha.

Even though Qaddafi had regained control of most of the cities by 15 March 2011, on 17 March the UNSC decided to pass Resolution no. 1973 (detailed below), which unleashed a chain of events in Libya. By way of background, it should be mentioned that the UN had in 2005 unanimously agreed on the concept of 'responsibility to protect' (R2P) that called on the international community to intervene in countries where governments failed to protect their populations against 'atrocity crimes' such as genocide, war crimes and crimes against humanity. Libya in 2011 thus became the laboratory for assessing the implementation of R2P by the UN.

India had joined the UNSC as a non-permanent member by January 2011. The Libyan case was the first on which India had to decide how to vote. On 26 February, the UNSC passed Resolution no. 1970, which expressed grave concern at the situation in the Libyan Arab Jamahiriya; condemned violence and use of force against civilians; deplored the gross and systematic violation of human rights (including the repression of peaceful demonstrators) and expressed deep concern at the deaths of civilians; rejected unequivocally, the incitement to hostility and violence against the civilian population made from the highest level of the Libyan government; welcomed the condemnation by the Arab League, the African Union and the Organization of Islamic Cooperation (OIC) regarding serious human rights violations in Libya and most importantly, referred the situation in Libya to the Prosecutor of the International Criminal Court asking him to report back to the UNSC in two months. Resolution no. 1970 was unanimously passed by the entire membership of the UNSC, including India.

This is interesting because in the normal course of things, one might have expected India to abstain and ask for more information on what was going on in Libya, especially since the resolution involved serious accusations of human rights violations, an arms embargo and referring the matter to the International Criminal Court. Furthermore, the resolution was being passed under Chapter VII of the UN Charter, which is always a red flag for India. A combination of reasons probably made India go along with the resolution:

- The Arab Spring had just broken out and was sweeping Arab countries one by one. India may have wanted to be on the right side of history.
- The fact that all regional organizations, such as the Arab League, African Union and OIC, condemned rights violations in Libya may have influenced India.
- The 18,000 Indian citizens who were present in Libya played a role.
- The Indian statement (explanation of vote) stated that 'while India was not a member of the International Criminal Court, and would have preferred a calibrated and gradual approach, it noted, however, that several members of the UNSC, including its colleagues from Africa and the Middle East, believed that such a referral to the International Criminal Court would have the effect of immediate cessation of violence and restoration of calm and stability. India was therefore going along with the consensus in the UNSC.'

The above vote to go along was even more significant because of what followed. In March 2011, the UNSC passed the famous Resolution no. 1973, which, inter alia, did the following:

- Deplored Libya for failing to comply with the above resolution no. 1970.
- Invoked the Libyan government's responsibility to protect its civilian population.
- Invoked Chapter VII of the UN Charter to demand a ceasefire, establish a no-fly zone over Libya and enforce the arms embargo.
- Authorized Member States to take all necessary measures to protect civilians and civilian-populated areas under threat of attack in the Libyan Arab Jamahiriya, including Benghazi.

The last-mentioned point, namely the expression 'to take all necessary measures' under Chapter VII was UN-speak for military intervention. So, India, along with China, Russia, Germany and Brazil abstained on this resolution. The relevant part of the explanation of the vote is given below:[33]

> The resolution that the Security Council has adopted today authorizes far-reaching measures under Chapter VII of the UN Charter with relatively little credible information on the situation on the ground in Libya. We also do not have clarity about details of enforcement measures, including who and with what assets will participate and how these measures will be exactly carried out. It is, of course, very important that there is full respect for sovereignty, unity, and territorial integrity of Libya.
>
> India has abstained on the resolution in view of the above. India continues to be gravely concerned about the deteriorating humanitarian situation in Libya and calls on the Libyan authorities to cease fire, protect the civilian population and address the legitimate demands of the Libyan people.

India's Permanent Representative to the UN at the time, was
Ambassador H.S. Puri. He wrote a book on the subject,[34] and it is
scathing when it comes to events surrounding Libya in the UNSC.
He says there was no evidence of mass atrocities or genocide, but
of deaths caused by a civil war. He also says that Western diplomats
pilloried anyone who was sceptical about the situation. He also
makes the point that the Arab League was eager to overthrow
Qaddafi. Also, one of the failures in this whole episode was that
the government of Qaddafi did not get an opportunity to defend
itself. Most importantly, Ambassador Puri makes the point that
the West had decided to act militarily even before Resolution no.
1973 was passed by the UNSC. He also makes the point that
R2P got a bad name, particularly because of Libya, since the West
eventually wished a regime change in Libya, which R2P did not
provide for.

The question remains as to why India went along with Resolution
no. 1970, but abstained in the case of Resolution no. 1973. Both
were, after all, under Chapter VII of the UN Charter, both held the
Qaddafi government guilty of human rights violations and both
talked of civilian casualties and the need for protecting civilians.
The only difference was that Resolution no. 1973 talked of taking
'all necessary measures'—this was a code-phrase for military
intervention which was anathema to India, especially before other
alternatives were fully exhausted.

4.6 India and the War in Ukraine

Russia's military invasion of Ukraine (euphemistically referred to by
Russia as a 'special military operation') has been described as a black
swan event, as noted earlier.[35] However, as a matter of fact, President
Putin was massing troops along the Russian-Ukrainian border in
the spring of 2021. At the time, it was thought that Putin was trying
to intimidate Ukraine and was not going to launch a full-fledged

invasion. Indeed, President Biden spoke to Putin and expressed his unwavering commitment to the sovereignty and territorial integrity of Ukraine and called on Russia to de-escalate. And for a while, it did seem as though Putin pulled his troops back from the borders. But by December 2021, it became clear that Putin had massed 90,000 troops at the border with Ukraine. It should have been clear to all concerned that he was certainly going to launch a military operation of some kind.

Yet the first ever UNSC meeting on Ukraine on 31 January 2022 (when Russia had already massed about 100,000 troops) talked down the possibility of invasion, with Russia denying it outright and even Ukraine rejecting the possibility of an invasion and asking people not to panic. The US alone noted with concern that this was the largest troop mobilization since 2014 by Russia. India, which was already a non-permanent member of the UNSC, made a statement along the following lines (It was the first in a long list of statements that India made on the issue at the UN in the first half of 2022).

India stated its interest in finding a solution that could provide 'immediate de-escalation of tensions, taking into account the legitimate security interests of all countries and aimed towards securing long-term peace and stability in the region and beyond'. India said it had been in touch with all concerned parties and added that the issue could only be resolved through diplomatic dialogue. In this context, it welcomed the efforts underway, including under the Minsk Agreements and the Normandy format.[36]

The statement above deserves careful scrutiny. First, it calls for diplomatic dialogue preceded by de-escalation of tensions, which is standard and boilerplate. Second, there is a reference to the Minsk Agreements and the Normandy format, which too is understandable—though, by then, it was all but buried with no prospect of revival. But the most important part of the statement was this: 'taking into account the legitimate security interests of all countries and aimed towards securing long-term peace and stability in the region and beyond'. This expression—'the legitimate security interests of all countries'—was a repeat from the statement made by India following the annexation of Crimea by Russia in 2014. It referred, first and foremost, to Russia's legitimate security concerns of possible NATO troops and missiles in Ukraine, barely 300 miles from Moscow and therefore its interest in keeping Ukraine free of any hostile presence. Second, it referred to the reciprocal and legitimate security interests of Germany, Poland, Austria, and others in light of Russia's military presence in Ukraine. Lastly, but not the least, it referred to the Ukrainian security interest in safeguarding its territorial integrity and sovereignty. The only way all the legitimate security interests above could have been reconciled was for Ukraine to be deemed 'neutral' by some international agreement. It is clear that in January 2022, India was still hoping against hope for a peaceful resolution and for things to not spin out of control.

On 17 February 2022, just a week before Russia's invasion of Ukraine, the UNSC was briefed about the status of the Minsk Agreements. Again, the Indian Permanent Representative at the UN made a statement, the operative part of which read as follows:

India has been in touch with all concerned parties. It is our considered view that the issue can only be resolved through diplomatic dialogue. India's interest is in finding a solution that can provide for immediate de-escalation of tensions taking into account the legitimate security interests of all countries and aimed towards securing long-term peace and stability in the region and beyond. More than twenty thousand Indian students and nationals live and study in different parts of Ukraine, including in its border areas. The well-being of Indian nationals is of priority to us.[37]

This statement broadly mirrors the earlier one, except that the legitimate well-being of 20,000 Indian students living and studying in different parts of Ukraine was highlighted.

On 21 February 2022, the UN Undersecretary for Political and Peacebuilding Affairs briefed the UNSC on the evolving situation in Ukraine. Again, the Indian Permanent Representative made a statement that repeated the above, including the 'legitimate security interests of all countries' as well as de-escalation, diplomacy and the well-being of 20,000 Indian students.[38] On 23 February, when the UN Secretary General briefed the UNSC, the Indian Representative said pretty much the same thing.

It was on 25 February (a day after the Russian military invasion of Ukraine), that the UNSC debated a resolution to call on Russia to stop all attacks and withdraw all its troops from Ukraine. Russia, a veto-wielding permanent member, obviously exercised its veto. India, interestingly, abstained from the resolution (along with China and the UAE) and gave the following explanation, which is reproduced in full:

Explanation of Vote

- India is deeply disturbed by the recent turn of developments in Ukraine.
- We urge that all efforts are made for the immediate cessation of violence and hostilities.
- No solution can ever be arrived at, at the cost of human lives.
- We are also deeply concerned about the welfare and security of the Indian community, including a large number of Indian students in Ukraine.

- The contemporary global order has been built on the UN Charter, international law, and respect for the sovereignty and territorial integrity of states.
- All member states need to honour these principles in finding a constructive way forward.
- Dialogue is the only answer to settling differences and disputes, however daunting that may appear at this moment.
- It is a matter of regret that the path of diplomacy was given up. We must return to it.
- For all these reasons, India has chosen to abstain on this resolution.[39]

On 27 February 2022, a second UNSC resolution was proposed along similar lines and our statement was also along similar lines.[40]

Explanation of Vote

- It is regrettable that the situation in Ukraine has worsened further since the Council last convened on this matter.
- We reiterate our call for immediate cessation of violence and an end to all hostilities.
- There is no other choice but to return to the path of diplomacy and dialogue.
- Our PM has advocated this strongly in his recent conversations with the leadership of the Russian Federation and Ukraine. In this regard, we welcome today's announcement by both sides to hold talks at the Belarus border.
- The global order is anchored on international law, UN Charter and respect for territorial integrity and sovereignty of all states. We are all agreed on these principles.

- We continue to be deeply concerned about the safety and security of Indian nationals, including a large number of Indian students, who are still stranded in Ukraine.
- Our evacuation efforts have been adversely impacted by the complex and uncertain situation at the border crossings. It is important to maintain an uninterrupted and predictable movement of people. It is an urgent humanitarian necessity that must be immediately addressed.
- Taking into consideration the totality of the circumstances, we have decided to abstain.

It bears mentioning that both the above statements were made after the Russian invasion of Ukraine on 24 February 2022. In any case, the resolution at the UNSC was doomed to fail, since Russia had a veto as a permanent member, which it used to block the resolution. It is worth examining the two Indian statements. First, our decision to abstain on this resolution. Second, the loaded expression 'legitimate security interests of all countries'—which characterized every single statement on Ukraine previously made by India—was dropped and does not figure in any of India's statements after the Russian invasion of Ukraine. Third, a reference to the 'UN Charter, international law and respect for the sovereignty and territorial integrity of states' makes its appearance for the first time.

The decision to abstain needs some explanation. There is no way India could have condoned Russia's actions (regardless of whether you consider it an invasion or not!) and voted against the resolution. Voting in favour of the resolution and condemning Russia for its invasion was potentially an option. That option could not be exercised for the following reasons:

- The erstwhile Soviet Union and present-day Russia were/are both longstanding strategic partners of India and have stood by

India on numerous occasions. They did so at a time when the West basically spurned India for their own strategic reasons. The occasions most cited are the 1971 war to liberate Bangladesh, and the numerous times that the Soviet Union and later Russia cast its veto at the UNSC on behalf of India to protect India's core interests including Kashmir. This is a legacy relationship that India still finds very difficult to ignore.

- India has deep defence ties with Russia, bordering on extreme dependence.[41] It is believed by some at the Washington-based Stimson Center, that 70 to 85 per cent of India's military platforms are of Russian origin.[42] Jaffrelot assesses that something like 90 per cent of equipment in the Indian Army, 70 per cent of the equipment in the Indian Air Force and 40 per cent of the equipment in the Indian Navy is of Russian origin.[43] Although India has been trying hard to diversify its defence purchases from France, US and Israel to name a few, these matters take time and effort, not to mention resources—all this at a time when India faces a two-front security challenge posed by China and Pakistan.

- India also has a longstanding economic and energy relationship with Russia.[44] Trade ties are not substantial and barely amount to $10 billion. However, in the field of energy, the former Soviet Union played a major role in building India's energy sector by building tens of hydropower stations, developing India's coal industry, finding oil on Indian soil and helping in setting up India's energy major, the Oil and Natural Gas Corporation (ONGC).

- Indo-Russian energy cooperation acquired new dimensions in the post-Soviet period, particularly in the hydrocarbon and nuclear sector. India has invested $2.8 billion in the Sakhalin energy project. In the post-Soviet era, oil imports actually dipped and it is true that just prior to the Russian invasion of Ukraine, hardly any oil was being imported by India from

Russia. In FY22 (April 2021 to March 2022), purchases of Russian oil comprised 0.2 per cent of all oil imported by India. But by November 2022, India was buying 23 per cent of its oil requirements from Russia on the discounted market. This came in for criticism from the West, to which Indian ministers had a ready response—India was still buying in a month what Europe was buying in an afternoon. And if Europe, which had a per capita income of $60,000, was allowed to buy discounted Russian oil, India with a per capita of $2,000 certainly had a more moral case to buy Russian oil. In any case, India was not violating the sanctions regime put in place by the West. Moreover, in the last five years, India's import of energy from the US rose thirteen-fold to something like $20 billion!

- The coming together of China and Russia in the form of a 'no limits' partnership through a joint statement issued on 4 February 2022 posed the biggest strategic challenge since India's Independence. Condemning Russia will likely force it into a tighter embrace with China (perhaps as a junior partner), with all the negative repercussions for India's national security. While it is not certain that India can prevent this in the medium term, it can gain valuable time by not forcing this choice on Russia in the near term.

- Since Russia would have anyway vetoed resolutions emanating from the UNSC by virtue of a veto-wielding permanent member, there was nothing to be lost for the West by India abstaining from the issue. In that sense, the issue was an academic one. India was not hurting the West in any way by its abstention.

- From the beginning of the conflict in Ukraine, India kept in touch with both leaders, namely, President Putin of Russia and President Zelensky of Ukraine. Maintaining channels of communication with both leaders was thought to be in the fundamental interest, as was keeping open the possibilities of mediation, should the occasion present itself and the means be available for the same. This also came in handy when India wanted to repatriate its citizens from Ukraine. Condemning Russia would have cut off communication links with at least one of the leaders, namely, President Putin.

For all of the above reasons, India, very early on, chose to abstain from resolutions condemning Russia's invasion and itself chose not to explicitly name and shame Russia.

In an interesting article in *Times of India*, former Indian Permanent Representative, Ambassador T.S. Tirumurti, says that soon after our decision to abstain, UN Secretary General Guterres came to him and said that India as a democracy and a strong leadership was in a unique position to talk to both sides.[45] He reportedly urged our leadership to do so, underlining the need for a ceasefire and negotiations. Indeed, soon thereafter, PM Modi spoke to both Russian leader Putin and Ukrainian leader Zelensky. Abstention came to India naturally. After all, on many of the geopolitical events mentioned before, India had refrained from taking sides. In this case, there were substantive reasons for India to abstain on a UN resolution seeking to condemn Russia.

The more intriguing question, from a diplomatic perspective, is why India chose to drop the expression 'legitimate security interests of all countries' from its statement after the Russian invasion, when it had served it so well in the past. Well, for one thing, the military invasion by Russia changed everything. There are those who believe that annexation of Crimea was one thing, but invading Ukraine is something different altogether. In the case of Crimea, Russia's Black Sea fleet was based in Sevastopol, and it may be argued that this was under threat. But in the case of Ukraine, there was no imminent threat that Russia faced. So, India too saw this differently than the annexation of Crimea. Once Russia had decided to take matters into its own hands by invading Ukraine, it would have been futile for India to talk of Russia's legitimate security interests. India also came under pressure from its Western partners who argued that it was the only major democracy that was on the wrong side. Ambassador Tirumurti in the article mentioned above refers to 'considerable pressure' on India in both Delhi and New York and even 'pushback from our friends'.[46]

In as much as the reference to 'legitimate security interests of all countries' in India's statement would have implied support for Russia, this may not have gone down well with India's friends and partners in the West. The more general point is also that Russia lost a lot of sympathy and goodwill, as evidenced by the vote in the UNGA in March 2022 where as many as 141 out of 193 member states voted asking Russia to put an end to its military operations in Ukraine. Predictably, India abstained at the UNGA as well. It was abundantly clear that the world's sympathies lay with Ukraine, not Russia.

Finally, a word on the reference in India's statement to the global order anchored in international law, the UN Charter and respect for territorial integrity and sovereignty of all states. Although for reasons explained above India did not condemn Russia by name, it is quite clear that the reference to international law, the UN Charter, and territorial integrity and sovereignty essentially supported Ukraine after what it had to endure because of the Russian invasion. We thus not only gave strong, unconditional support to the principle of territorial integrity and sovereignty but also stated unambiguously that the global order was anchored in international law and the UN Charter.

In every single statement thereafter, India repeated this formulation like a mantra.

Purely in terms of foreign policy analysis, India had a realpolitik and material interest in Ukraine in the form of approximately 20,000 plus Indian nationals, mostly students, who were stuck there at the time of the war. It had a strategic interest too—its long-standing ties with Russia, especially in the field of defence. It had a point of principle, which was the UN Charter and International Law. And there were geopolitical imperatives at work, since we had close relations with the US and the West. All these came into play when India formulated its stand on the war in Ukraine.

India's first and foremost task, as often happens in such crises, was how to evacuate the 20,000-plus Indian nationals, mostly students who could not leave their universities before the outbreak of war. Indians now live almost in every part of the world without exception. Increasingly, they also live in conflict-prone zones. For many, if not all of them, going abroad is a dream that they have fulfilled at considerable cost to their families. So, it is not easy for them to make the decision to return home. Advisories by the Embassy, which tend to be issued at the last minute, are often taken with a pinch of salt. So, when war breaks out, as it did in Ukraine, it falls on the government of the day to do everything in its power to evacuate all its citizens. Any failure to do so, and worse if there are fatalities, inflicts huge political costs on the government of the day.

The Government of India, realizing the difficult task on its hands, launched an evacuation plan called 'Operation Ganga' on 26 February 2022, barely two days after the Russian invasion began. It was conducted by the MEA and the Indian armed forces and lasted till 11 March 2022. Two crucial decisions were key to ensuring the success of the Mission. One, the PM made it a point to talk not just to the leaders of Russia and Ukraine, but also to his counterparts in Romania, the Slovak Republic, Poland and Hungary. This was to ensure that our students could get out of Ukraine by using the land route to transit via the countries mentioned above. This was the only viable way out, since all flights in and out of Ukraine were practically impossible once the hostilities began. Second, the OpGanga Helpline was launched on social media with control centres, 24/7 helplines and WhatsApp/e-mails in. Prime Minister Modi also decided to send ministers H.S. Puri, V.K. Singh, J. Scindia and K. Rijiju to these four countries to oversee the evacuation. Aircraft were then sent to their capitals to bring back the students safely. By 11 March as many as ninety flights, including fourteen Indian Air Force flights, had been organized. Between 1 February and 11 March 2022, about 22,500 Indian nationals returned from Ukraine to India.

Evacuation of Indian students from Sumy in Ukraine was extremely complex and needed a credible ceasefire which finally materialized due to the personal intervention of PM Narendra Modi and the Presidents of Ukraine and Russia. Making a statement on the 'Situation in Ukraine' in both Houses of Parliament in March 2022, External Affairs Minister (EAM) S. Jaishankar said, 'The Prime Minister took up the issue of safe evacuation of Indians, especially from Kharkiv and Sumy.' The PM had spoken to both the leaders on 7 March and earlier also, following which the evacuation mission got the support it needed.

All things considered, this was a hugely successful mission by the Modi government. This is obvious when you compare it with what the Chinese struggled to do in Ukraine with a far smaller number, just 6,000 students, in Ukraine. Chinese advisories were not issued in time and their students came in for some rough treatment when they travelled in vehicles with Chinese flags. Even the Americans had problems evacuating their nationals. So whichever way one looks at it, Operation Ganga was a tremendously well-executed evacuation in extremely difficult circumstances from a war zone.

Western pressure on India could be gauged from a statement by no less a person than US President Joe Biden. On 21 March, in a press conference, Biden had this to say:

> In response to Putin's aggression, we presented a united front throughout NATO and in the Pacific. The Quad is—with the possible exception of India being somewhat shaky on some of this... but Japan has been extremely strong, so has Australia, in terms of dealing with Putin's aggression. We presented a united front throughout NATO and the Pacific.[47]

By late March, there was a report of alleged Russian massacre of innocent civilians in Bucha (Ukraine) where 458 bodies, including those of children, were recovered. With furore in the Western media, India's position on the war in Ukraine came under the scanner once again. The UNSC addressed the issue of the Bucha killing on 5 April where the main gist of the Indian statement is given below:

> The situation in Ukraine has not shown any significant improvement since the Council last discussed the issue. The security situation has only deteriorated, as well as its humanitarian consequences. Recent reports of civilian killings in Bucha are deeply disturbing. We unequivocally condemn these killings and support the call for an independent investigation.
>
> We hope the international community will continue to respond positively to the humanitarian needs. We support calls urging guarantees of safe passage to deliver essential humanitarian and medical supplies.
>
> Keeping in view the dire humanitarian situation in Ukraine, India has been sending humanitarian supplies to Ukraine and its neighbours, which include medicines and

other essential relief material. We stand ready to provide more medical supplies to Ukraine in the coming days.

India continues to remain deeply concerned at the worsening situation and reiterates its call for immediate cessation of violence and end to hostilities. We have emphasized right from the beginning of the conflict the need to pursue the path of diplomacy and dialogue. When innocent human lives are at stake, diplomacy must prevail as the only viable option. In this context, we take note of the ongoing efforts, including the meetings held recently between the Parties.

The impact of the crisis is being felt beyond the region with increasing food and energy costs, especially for many developing countries. It is in our collective interest to work constructively, both inside the United Nations and outside, towards seeking an early resolution to the conflict.

Allow me to reiterate the importance of UN Guiding Principles of Humanitarian Assistance. Humanitarian action must always be guided by the principles of humanitarian assistance, i.e., humanity, neutrality, impartiality, and independence. These measures should never be politicized.

We continue to emphasize to all member states of the UN that the global order is anchored on international law, UN Charter and respect for territorial integrity and sovereignty of states.

This was a moment when the Indian policy on Ukraine was criticized not just abroad, but also within India. External Affairs Minister S. Jaishankar therefore had to make a statement in the Indian Parliament on 6 April 2022: 'India was "deeply disturbed" by the Bucha killings and strongly condemns the killings that have taken place there. This is an extremely serious matter and India supports the call for an independent investigation.'

This was probably the strongest statement made by India on the conflict in Ukraine. India did not condemn the perpetrator but it did condemn the actions of the perpetrator. And because Russia denied it was responsible for the deaths, India called for an independent investigation. On 11 April, PM Modi had a virtual meeting with American President Biden in which he conveyed the following:

- Recent news of the killing of innocent citizens in Bucha city was very concerning. We immediately condemned it and also demanded an impartial probe. We hope that through the talks between Russia and Ukraine, a path for peace would come out.
- I have spoken with Presidents of both Ukraine and Russia over telephone, several times. I not only appealed to them for peace but also suggested President Putin to hold direct talks with the Ukrainian President. Detailed discussions were held over Ukraine, in our Parliament.

In response, President Biden said:

- The United States and India are going to continue our close consultation and how to manage the negative effects of this Russian war. Our continued consultation and dialogue are key to ensuring US-Indian relationship continues to grow deep and stronger.
- I want to welcome India's humanitarian support for the people of Ukraine.

This was an attempt by both countries to assuage each other's sentiments and ensure their differing perceptions did not imperil their larger bilateral strategic partnership. In effect, this was arguably the most important achievement from an Indian diplomatic perspective. It was important to keep the relationship with the US on an even keel and this was achieved in full measure. This has involved detailed conversations between Indian and American interlocutors at multiple levels. Of all these, perhaps the most important have been the conversations between EAM S. Jaishankar and his American counterpart Secretary Anthony Blinken.

India has explained its ties with Russia at present, by drawing parallels with the American relationship with Pakistan in the eighties and nineties. Just as the Americans had developed dependencies vis-à-vis Pakistan, so has India vis-à-vis Russia over time. And India's dependency on Russia is a forced one, with the US and others in a way responsible because of their refusal to deal with India for a long period of time, especially in areas such as defence. Every indication is that our friends in the US have understood India's stand on Ukraine. Most importantly, everything that India has said from the beginning—namely that there is no military solution to the conflict in Ukraine and the only options are dialogue and diplomacy—is turning out to be prophetic.

As for the EU, the best analysis of its view towards India's stand is captured by an article by Frederic Grare.[48] He concludes after consideration of all factors that while EU officials may be frustrated over India's apparent 'fence-sitting' on the invasion of Ukraine, there are weighty reasons for India doing so and that Europeans should be aware of how India defines its strategic positioning and should support India where possible. Frederic Grare is a respected French commentator and his views carry weight in the European strategic community.

By September 2022, India was frustrated that Russia, a trusted strategic partner, was not paying heed to India's repeated calls for it to return to the path of dialogue and diplomacy. Against this backdrop, when PM Modi met President Putin on 16 September at the Shanghai Cooperation Summit meeting, he told Putin in unambiguous language that today's era is not one of war. This was picked up the world over, particularly in the Western media, and was construed as a 'reprimand' of Putin, which it was. For India, it was a way of telling Russia that it could not endorse its continued war against Ukraine with terrible consequences all around.

Following up on the PM's 'reprimand' of Putin, the EAM made an important statement in the UNSC on 22 September on the war in Ukraine. The main excerpts are given below:

- The trajectory of the Ukraine conflict is a matter of profound concern for the entire international community. The future outlook appears even more disturbing. The nuclear issue is a particular anxiety. In a globalized world, the impact of the conflict is being felt even in distant regions. We have all experienced its consequences in terms of surging costs and actual shortages of food grains, fertilizers and fuel. On this score too, there are good grounds to be worried about what awaits us. The global south, especially, is feeling the pain acutely. We must therefore not initiate measures that further complicate the struggling global economy. That is why India strongly reiterates the need for an immediate cessation of all hostilities and a return to dialogue and diplomacy. Clearly, as Prime Minister Narendra Modi has emphasized, this cannot be an era of war. On our part, we are providing both humanitarian assistance to Ukraine and economic support to our neighbours under economic distress.
- Turning to the specific topic before the Council today, let me emphasize that even in conflict situations, there

can be no justification for violation of human rights
or of international law. Where any such acts occur, it
is imperative that they are investigated in an objective
and independent manner. This was the position that we
took with regard to the killings in Bucha. This is the
position we take even today. The Council will also recall
that we had then supported calls for an independent
investigation into that incident.

- Once again, let me emphasize Madam President, that
the need of the hour is to end this conflict and return
to the negotiating table. This Council is the most
powerful contemporary symbol of diplomacy. It must
continue to live up to its purpose. The global order
that we all subscribe to, is based on international law,
the UN Charter and respect for territorial integrity
and sovereignty of all States. These principles must be
upheld, without exception.

Two points are noteworthy. One, India continued to provide
whatever modest humanitarian assistance it could to Ukraine, even
while buying oil from Russia for its energy needs. There is some
criticism of the UNSC, which is urged to live up to its purpose.
This is implicit criticism of Russia, since it has been using its veto.
Last, but certainly not the least, is while repeating the mantra of the
UN Charter and respect for territorial integrity and sovereignty of
all States, the EAM states categorically that these principles must
be upheld without exception. This again is criticism of Russia and
its continued military aggression against Ukraine, even while not
naming the aggressor.

For purposes of comparison, it is interesting to see what
China said at the UNSC and whether its stance was different

from India's. The Sino-Russian Joint Statement of 4 February 2022 was issued barely three weeks before the Russian invasion of Ukraine. The fact that China had difficulty in evacuating its citizens and other evidence leads us to believe that Putin did not take Xi Jinping into confidence on Ukraine. This may have also been a reason why Putin acknowledged in September 2022 at the Shanghai Cooperation Organization summit meeting, that China had concerns and questions on Ukraine, which he understood. China, unlike India, is also a veto-wielding permanent member of the UNSC and to that extent its words and actions are under greater scrutiny. The Chinese foreign minister made a statement at the UNSC on 22 September 2022. This was reported as:

Wang Yi said that China's position on the Ukraine issue is consistent and clear. The sovereignty and territorial integrity of all countries should be safeguarded, the purposes and principles of the UN Charter should be abided by, the legitimate security concerns of all parties should be taken seriously, and all efforts conducive to the peaceful settlement of the crisis should be supported.

Not very different from India's, except for the 'legitimate security concerns of all parties should be taken seriously', which can only mean that of Russia, in the present case. This may also be seen against the backdrop of the famous 4 February Joint Statement by China and Russia, which, inter alia, stated the following:

Both sides oppose further enlargement of NATO and call on the North Atlantic Alliance to abandon its ideologized cold war approaches, respect the sovereignty, security and interests of other countries, the diversity of their

civilizational, cultural and historical backgrounds and
exercise a fair and objective attitude towards the peaceful
development of other States.

Given the above common position on NATO expansion, China
appears more aligned with Russia's position than any other major
power. China has, so far, refrained from either lethal weapon supplies
to Russia or taking any action to bust the Western sanctions. There
are reasons to believe that China may be recalibrating its 'alliance'
with Russia, but broadly, Xi Jinping has doubled down on China's ties
with Russia and course correction appears unlikely in the near term.

4.6.1 Assessment of India's Stand

India's stand on the war in Ukraine was explained succinctly by its
EAM S. Jaishankar through the following principles on which it was
based. Speaking in the Rajya Sabha (Upper House) on 23 March
2022, he listed them as follows:

- Immediate cessation of violence and hostilities;
- No way other than to return to the path of dialogue and
  diplomacy;
- Global order anchored in international law, UN Charter and
  respect for territorial integrity and sovereignty of all states;
- Humanitarian access to a conflict situation;
- India has given 90 tonnes of humanitarian assistance. Wish to
  do more; and
- We are in touch with the leadership of both Russia and Ukraine
  at the highest levels and PM Modi is in touch with both leaders,
  President Putin and President Zelensky.

At one level, these propositions are unexceptionable. But it is
the way in which they have been implemented by the Indian

PM/EAM duo that is remarkably praiseworthy. They have done so by protecting India's vital national interests and by achieving its strategic objectives.

It may be appropriate now to examine India's stand on the war in Ukraine in depth, using each of the benchmarks in the Integrated Assessment Framework (Gandhi Litmus Test; Policy Space; Domestic Politics; Geopolitical Imperatives; Commitment to Multilateralism and Principles; Realpolitik and Material Gain).

4.6.2 Integrated Assessment Framework applied to India's Stand

Gandhi Litmus Test: When the Russian invasion of Ukraine happened in February 2022, not many people focused on the economic repercussions of the conflict. Initial focus was on the geopolitics and the loss of lives on both sides. But as the war progressed, it became apparent that it would affect what has since come to be known as the 3Fs, namely, Food, Fertilizer and Fuel. The impact on food was perhaps the most obvious, since between Russia and Ukraine, these two countries were responsible for as much as 25 per cent of global wheat exports in 2019. Ukraine mainly grew and exported wheat, corn and barley. Also, with more than 50 per cent of world trade, Ukraine was also the main player on the sunflower oil market, something of interest to India.

Grain deliveries were initially suspended in February 2022 as a result of the war in Ukraine, fuelling fears of shortages worldwide and price hikes. By mid-May, export prices for wheat and corn had skyrocketed to unprecedented heights. According to the UN, this hike in export prices had far-reaching consequences, particularly in Africa, the Middle East and Asia—where the coronavirus pandemic and its fallout had already exacerbated the food situation.

In the case of fertilizers, Russia was the world's largest exporter when it invaded Ukraine on 24 February 2022. This exacerbated already tight conditions for global fertilizer supply, pushing fertilizer prices to hit all-time highs within days. Fertilizer is among the farmer's largest expenses. Despite measures to ease price pressures, a recent survey showed that higher input costs in the production of fertilizers were a top concern. Natural gas is a key resource for producing fertilizer, and as per the IEA, Russia was the world's largest exporter of natural gas in 2021.[49] Volatility in the natural gas market will likely keep global and US fertilizer prices high for some time.

In the case of fuel or oil, before the hostilities in Ukraine, India imported barely 0.2 per cent of its oil requirements from Russia. Bear in mind that India imports 80 per cent of its oil requirements. By the end of 2022, India was importing as much as 21 per cent of its oil requirements from Russia. This has come in for some criticism from Western commentators, but Indian ministers and others have pushed back against this criticism, precisely by using the argument that the Government of India had an obligation towards its poor people.

Oil is a critical commodity since it has multiplier effects on the cost of living in India. So, the government has basically met the Gandhi Litmus Test by buying large quantities of discounted Russian oil in the market. Russian oil also became more discounted because of the EU policy to put caps and reduce dependence on Russian oil. As EAM S. Jaishankar said in a trenchant comment, 'India needs energy security and probably buys as much Russian oil in a month, that EU buys in one single afternoon.'

He also stated in an interview that if the EU, a 60,000 Euro per capita economy, cared about energy security, then India, which is a $2,000 per capita economy should care even more about its energy security.

As for food, India is fortunately self-sufficient, so it was merely a question of making sure the supply of fertilizers continued uninterrupted for Indian farmers with imports from Russia surging by 666.24 per cent to $1,236.96 million in April–August 2022, up from $161.43 million during the same period last year. Fertilizers and fuel together account for over 91 per cent of the total imports from Russia for the year 2022.

India's stand of not condemning Russia for its invasion of Ukraine, may be seen against this background. If Russian oil and fertilizer were not available for India during 2022, it is a fair guess that the poor and common man in India would have been hit very badly indeed.

Policy Space: Even as India was buying discounted oil from Russia, it was also ramping up its energy imports from its main strategic partner, the US. In recent years, new countries have emerged as the source of crude oil imports, with the US being a prominent one. The period of its emergence among the top countries for crude oil imports coincides with the reduction of India's crude oil imports from Iran. In 2021–22, the US was the fourth-largest exporter of crude oil to India. Along with the top-three—Iraq, Saudi Arabia and the UAE—the US makes up 63 per cent of the total value of crude oil imports to India. The year 2021–22 also saw the emergence of Russia and Brazil among the top ten countries from which India now imports crude oil. All in all, India has followed a strategy of diversifying its oil supplies and acquiring valuable policy space and flexibility for itself in the process.

In any case, as the following table shows, India is not alone and is indeed the only poor country at $2,000 per capita to buy oil from Russia. The rich countries do just the same.

Table 4.1: Value of Fossil Fuel Exports from Russia (24.2.2022–6.1. 2023), by Country (Billion Euros)

China:	57.92
Germany:	24.99
Turkey:	21.62
India:	20.59
The Netherlands:	16.92
Italy:	13.62
Poland:	11.18
France:	9.2
Hungary:	8.21
Belgium:	8.03

Source: @ https://www.statista.com

The same goes for the defence purchases that India makes from Russia. It is true that India depends heavily on Russian military platforms, as we saw earlier, but again, India has been making serious efforts to diversify its weapons purchases. For instance, defence purchases by India from the US were virtually zero in 2001. In a span of just over twenty years, they now stand at a whopping $20 billion. In a similar vein, India has also augmented defence purchases from France and Israel, both of whom supply substantial quantities of armaments to India. Indeed, whichever way one looks at it, India has been making efforts to reduce dependence on Russia and acquire more policy space when it comes to purchase of arms and equipment.

The other way in which India is enhancing policy space is by following a policy of 'aatmanirbharta' or broadly speaking, self-reliance. This has meant that especially in the wake of the war in Ukraine, a policy of manufacturing weapons and equipment in India, rather than buying them off the shelf for a high price, is being put in place. French Company Safran has a tie-up with Hindustan Aeronautics Limited (HAL) for making engines for helicopters at a plant in India. The Naval group (earlier known as DCNS) is making six Scorpène-class submarines at Mazagon Docks Limited, Mumbai.

Again for arms imports, it may be seen from Figure 4.2, taken from the Stockholm International Peace Research Institute (SIPRI) website that India's arms imports from Russia using Trend Indicator Values (TIVs) hit a peak in 2013 and since then have shown a steady downward trend. France, on the other hand, has emerged as a big supplier to India for weapons and equipment.

[SIPRI] Figure 4.2: Indian Arms Imports From Top Five Suppliers (1992–2021)

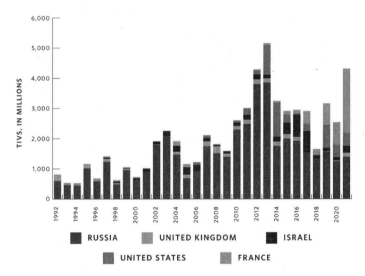

SOURCE: SIPRI Arms Transfer Database, accessed July 27, 2022.

NOTE: TIVs, or trend indicator values, are based on the known unit production costs of a core set of weapons. SIPRI intends to capture all military resources rather than a transfer's financial value.

The stand taken by India on the war in Ukraine essentially enhances the policy space available by keeping open options of defence purchases from Russia and not foreclosing them, while not precluding purchases from other partners such as the US, France and Israel. Indeed, these other partners have committed themselves to helping India reduce its dependence on Russia.

As a country that still depends a fair bit on Russian military platforms, there are two developments of concern that India must factor in, with regard to its medium- to long-range defence plans. The first is that the performance of Russian-made military equipment in the war in Ukraine so far, cannot possibly inspire much confidence in the Indian armed forces who still use Russian equipment. Second, it is anyone's guess as to what the state of Russia will be when the war ends.

Domestic Politics: Although India's stand on the war in Ukraine was along predictable lines, it did lead to debate and discussion amongst opposition political parties. In the early days of the war, the debate centred almost exclusively on whether the Government of India can successfully evacuate the 20,000-plus Indian nationals (mainly students) who were stuck in the war zone. Questions ranged from why travel advisories were not issued well in advance, to why the government was delaying matters. The main opposition party, the Congress, in fact issued a statement on 7 March 2022 saying it was alarmed and distressed over the escalation of military conflict in Ukraine and earnestly appealed for an end to all hostilities and the creation of geographically defined humanitarian corridors for safe evacuation. Putting pressure on the government it went on to say:

> It is the duty of Government of India to make all efforts to bring back our citizens and it is important to remember and recall that India has in the past undertaken successful large-scale operations by its Air Force and Navy to evacuate

Indians during Gulf War, Lebanon, Libya and Iraq without indulging in partisan propaganda.[50]

In effect, domestic politics surrounding the evacuation of Indian citizens in war-ridden zones has always been a major factor in India. Indeed, it even extends to the states, which tend to view things parochially. For instance, Tamil Nadu Chief Minister M.K. Stalin wrote to EAM S. Jaishankar just after hostilities broke out in Ukraine, requesting that Tamils (about 5,000), be evacuated from Ukraine 'immediately'.[51] He also requested the Government of India to arrange for special mission flights to evacuate Tamils from various parts of Ukraine. It is worth noting that to some extent, political parties were anticipating that they would face pressure to do 'something', and so they went ahead and put out these statements.

India now has millions of citizens living abroad—by some accounts thirteen million Indian citizens and about eighteen million persons of Indian origin (PIOs). Despite these figures, which are growing, Indian Embassies and High Commissions abroad are notoriously small and do not have the manpower and resources to evacuate thousands at short notice. So, the government in Delhi has to step in and use all means at its disposal to evacuate its citizens. Any failure to do so, will result in a huge political price to be paid by the government of the day.

The other problem pertains to travel advisories. No matter how serious the advisory, Indian citizens abroad tend to hedge their bets till the last minute and are disinclined to leave. This may have to do with two reasons: one, they have spent huge monetary resources to go abroad and would therefore not be inclined to leave in a hurry, even if push comes to shove; two, they probably know from past experience that the government of the day will step-in and evacuate them free of cost.

In the case of Ukraine, there were other complications as well. Universities in Ukraine discouraged students from leaving and said online education was not guaranteed. Exams were not postponed despite the imminent war, students were afraid of losing out on an year and their degree, for which they had spent time, money and effort.

In March 2022 opposition parties slammed the Government of India in Parliament, over delays in evacuation of students. External Affairs Minister S. Jaishankar had to make a statement on March 15 in the Rajya Sabha explaining that the delay was attributable to confusing statements by the Ukrainian government.[52] Despite all of the above, it is by now well recognized that the Indian government deserves praise for the manner in which they managed to evacuate all Indian citizens by 11 March 2022 through Operation Ganga.

The other issue that came to the fore, albeit briefly, was why India did not condemn Russia by name in this whole matter. This criticism, admittedly a minority view in India, was best expressed by charismatic Indian politician Shashi Tharoor who was from the Opposition Congress party. He wrote in *Mathrubhumi* that in the UN, the Indian Permanent Representative did not mention Russia by name, nor criticize or deplore, let alone condemn the invasion and Russia's violation of international law in undertaking it.[53] Tharoor went on to suggest that 'India had placed itself on the wrong side of history'.[54] In the same publication a day earlier, Tharoor had said that India's decision to abstain at the UNSC showed lack of conviction and courage by refraining from condemning the blatant violation of international law by Russia.

Former minister P. Chidambaram, an Indian parliamentarian also from the opposition Congress party, tweeted: 'The Government of India should stop its verbal balancing act and sternly demand that Russia stop immediately the bombing of key cities in Ukraine.'

What was interesting was the reaction of the Congress Party (to which Tharoor belonged) to Tharoor's statement and indirectly, to Chidambaram's statement above. In effect, the Congress Party distanced itself from Tharoor's statement. Senior leader Anand Sharma was authorized by the Congress Party to say the following: 'Shashi Tharoor's views were personal and strong words must not be used.'[55] Indeed, another Congress leader Manish Tiwari stated sarcastically while endorsing the Government of India on its stand on Ukraine: 'I would like to recommend to the government that strategic autonomy, the Nehruvian principles of non-alignment that held us in good stead, are worth going back to. Those principles have stood the test of time.'[56]

Whatever the West and other friends may have thought about India's stand on the war in Ukraine and regardless of the merits of the matter, it is a fact that India's stand was supported not just by political parties and the Parliament, but also by the population at large. Tharoor may have been right in what he said, but he was clearly in a minority. The reasons are not far to seek. One, the erstwhile Soviet Union and Russia are indeed well regarded by an overwhelming majority of people in India. Second, most Indians are aware of the extreme dependence of the Indian armed forces on arms and equipment from Russia. Third, most people also know that this dependence on Russia was forced on India because of Western (mainly American) sanctions and resultant lack of choice for India. Fourth, the same Western countries had no problem cultivating Pakistan and arming that country to the hilt, thereby negatively impacting India's security. Finally, a lot of Indians, while extremely uneasy with the invasion of Ukraine by Russia, nevertheless believe that Russia was 'done for' by the West with its eastward expansion of NATO and other injurious acts of regime change in Russia's neighbourhood. Despite all of this, there is a view among the intelligentsia in India that two wrongs do not make a right and therefore Russia was just plain wrong to invade Ukraine. But this viewpoint was overwhelmed by sheer realpolitik in the end.

Geopolitical Imperatives: The relationship with the US has turned out to be critical for India over the last couple of decades. China is the principal security threat that India faces in addition to Pakistan. Given the power differential between India and China in the foreseeable future, India has had no choice but to resort to external balancing to counter the security threats. In this scheme of things, the US assumes fundamental importance for India. Therefore, in assessing India's stand on the war in Ukraine, the one question that needs to be posed is whether it had any negative impact on bilateral ties with the US. To begin with, the positions taken by the US and India were far apart. There are reasons to believe that the US was initially unhappy with the position taken by India and that pressure was brought to bear on India to condemn Russia for its invasion of Ukraine. At the Senate hearing on US policy towards India on 2 March 2022, just days after the Russian invasion, in response to points by some senators expressing disappointment at the Indian vote to abstain in the UN, American Assistant Secretary of State Donald Lu had this to say:

The President and other senior officials in the State Department, have been relentlessly conducting very serious, high-level dialogue with their Indian counterparts over Ukraine over the course of months now, but culminating in this past week.

We can already see an evolution in some of India's public position. I will describe that, but maybe first I will say I had several conversations with Indian officials in the last 24 hours.

You may know, yesterday an Indian student was killed in the Russian bombing in Kharkiv, and what we can see already very quickly is that action has begun to turn public opinion in India against a country they perceived as a partner.[57]

Undeniably, that partner has just killed an Indian young person, who is an innocent victim in Ukraine.

Let me say that all of us have been working to urge India to take a clearer position, a position opposed to Russia's actions, but what have we seen so far? We have seen a number of abstentions. We have seen this interesting evolution just in the past couple of days. So you may have seen yesterday the Indian Government said it would send a humanitarian airlift of supplies from India to Ukraine. That is important. That is a request that is coming from Ukraine's leadership.

Second, it said in a UN session that it called for all states to abide by the UN Charter, to respect sovereignty and the territorial integrity of other states. That was not criticism of Russia, but a very clear reference to Russia's violation of the UN Charter and a violation of Ukraine's sovereignty.

Senator Shaheen: Thank you. I appreciate the entire State Department and diplomatic efforts in this regard and, again, it seems to me that India should be on notice that this is a time when it should stand up for its values and that an important value in a democracy is that you do not wage war on other sovereign nations.

Donald Lu: So we are making small steps, Senator Shaheen. I assure you we are on this and working every day to make sure that we are trying to close the gap between where we are and where our Indian partners are.[58]

The above is a clear indication that there was indeed pressure on India from the US to change its position of abstention on the war in Ukraine and there was enough nudging to make India condemn Russia.

The reaction at the highest level was from Biden (as we saw earlier) on March 21, when he described India's position as 'somewhat shaky' on the Russian invasion of Ukraine as it tried to balance its ties with Russia and the West. Indeed, India's stand was summarized by senior White House official Mira Rapp-Hooper, who is the Director for the Indo-Pacific in the White House National Security Council, who stated towards the end of March (just after President Biden's remarks):

> I think we would certainly all acknowledge and agree that when it comes to votes at the UN, India's position on the current crisis has been unsatisfactory, to say the least. But it's also been totally unsurprising. I think our perspective would be that the way forward involves keeping India close, thinking hard about how to present it with options, so that it can continue to provide for its strategic autonomy. We have a number of partners that have chosen to keep their chips in with Russia, in terms of their defence procurement, in part as a hedge against China, but who are now in a place of reconsidering the wisdom of those decisions. Not only will they need to make long-term decisions about how to potentially replace Russian systems in the immediate term, but they will also need to be able to get supplies and spare parts to be able to maintain their own militaries.[59]

This statement was remarkable for several reasons. Early in March, it was clear that the Americans were not exactly happy with the Indian stand on Ukraine in the UN. But by end of March, India may have succeeded in softening the American position a little. Thus, while calling India's stand 'unsatisfactory', the White House official also adds it was 'unsurprising'. More importantly, the official displays great understanding about India's defence dependency on

Russia in terms of supplies and spare parts. Finally, the official also suggests the way forward, namely, 'keeping India close and thinking hard about how to present it with options, so that it can continue to provide for its strategic autonomy'. This was a remarkably wise statement about India's stand on Ukraine.

Whatever American pressure was brought to bear on India in this regard, appears to have been done in private and that is an excellent sign of maturity in bilateral ties. The two factors that may have helped in tackling initial American disappointment were: one, our statement about adherence to the UN Charter, international law and territorial integrity and sovereignty (of Ukraine) and two, the fact that we sent humanitarian assistance to Ukraine. The other thing that became clear over time was the fundamental validity of the Indian position, namely, that there was no military solution to this conflict. And then of course PM Modi's remarks to Putin in September saying 'today's era is not one of war', really changed the way in which India was perceived by its Western partners in this matter. This led American Secretary of State Blinken to say after his meeting with Indian EAM S. Jaishankar in September 2022, that he entirely agreed with PM Modi in his message to Putin that today's era was not that of war.[60] Secretary Blinken also went on to add, 'it is very important that voices as consequential as India's make themselves heard and that's why I thought the Prime Minister's comments were so significant, as well as his clear support to the UN charter.'

This meeting between Jaishankar and Blinken appears to have been important in removing any wrinkles in the relationship, as it pertained to India's stand on Ukraine. EAM Jaishankar also publicly acknowledged the behind-the-scenes role played by India and said, 'During the grain shipment discussions in the Black Sea, we were approached to weigh in with Russia at a very delicate moment in the negotiations, which we did.' He added that he had also 'met the Ukrainian Prime Minister, who mentioned some specific issues where he thought we could be of some use'; he also met, on a different set of issues, 'with the UN Secretary General, who too had been active on specific issues pertaining to the conflict to see what could be resolved and mitigated even in the current circumstances. The minister said it would not be appropriate for him to go into more specifics than that.' In December 2022, the CIA Chief William Burns also commended India (and China) for passing on a message to Putin advising him against the use of nuclear weapons.[61]

One of the most important achievements of India's stand on the Ukraine imbroglio was that the relationship with the US was maintained intact and not allowed to worsen, for which there was ample risk. Yes, there were a few wrinkles, but they were sorted out quickly and admirably. Quite simply, there was too much at stake for India in its relationship with the US for it to become hostage to its stand on the war in Ukraine.

The EU reacted a little bit differently from the US on the issue of the Indian stand on Ukraine. The EU Mission in Delhi in February, soon after the Russian invasion, sought to make a demarche to senior officials of the Indian Ministry of External Affairs in order to request India to take a strong position against Russia.[62] The EU envoy to India also tried to draw a parallel with the Indo-Pacific, saying that the Russia-Ukraine war had set a risky precedence for the Indo-Pacific, and argued that the Russia-Ukraine issue therefore should not be seen as merely an European issue.[63]

The Indian EAM, during an interactive meeting in the Slovak capital Bratislava in June 2022, directly addressed this issue of the link between Ukraine and the Indo-Pacific in somewhat harsh terms: ' The Chinese do not need a precedent somewhere else on how to engage us or not engage us or be difficult with us or not be difficult with us.' He added that Europe had to grow out of the mindset that its problems are the world's problems, but the world's problems are not Europe's problems.[64] Again, when asked about India buying lots of oil from Russia, he said that EU probably bought in half a day the amount of Russian oil that India bought in a full month.

The visit of the EU President Ursula von der Leyen to Delhi in the last week of April 2022 and her meeting with PM Modi convinced the EU that India's stand on Ukraine was not going to change in the medium term. Indeed, the visit led to the establishment of the Indo-EU Trade and Technology Council.[65] In fact, this was a first for India and was just the second such institutional mechanism that EU had, other than the one it had with the US. So, with EU, India pretty much agreed to disagree on the issue of Ukraine. Again, it was important that relations with EU were not allowed to spin out of control, since the EU was emerging as a hugely important strategic partner in several areas. The Indian stand achieved precisely that.

Japan has emerged as the most trusted strategic partner of India in Asia and is of course part of the Quad. It was therefore important that India keep Japan fully informed on its stand on the war in Ukraine. A perfect opportunity presented itself when the new Japanese PM Fumio Kishida, visited Delhi for the Indo-Japan Summit in the last week of March 2022. Japan had, understandably, taken a very strong line on the Russian invasion of Ukraine and condemned it in no uncertain terms. Japan also felt that the Russian action could serve as a precedent for China to take unilateral action in the Indo-Pacific, a position that was not shared a priori by India. The Indo-Japan Joint Statement issued after the summit meeting between the leaders Modi and Kishida pertaining to Ukraine read thus:

The Prime Ministers expressed their serious concern about the ongoing conflict and humanitarian crisis in Ukraine and assessed its broader implications, particularly to the Indo-Pacific region. They emphasized that the contemporary global order has been built on the UN Charter, international law and respect for sovereignty and territorial integrity of states. They underscored the importance of safety and security of nuclear facilities in Ukraine and acknowledged active efforts of the IAEA towards it. They reiterated their call for an immediate cessation of violence and noted that there was no other choice but the path of dialogue and diplomacy for resolution of the conflict. The Leaders affirmed that they would undertake appropriate steps to address the humanitarian crisis in Ukraine.[66]

Two points are worthy of note. One, both leaders affirmed their call for an immediate cessation of violence and noted that there was no other choice but the path of dialogue and diplomacy for resolution of the conflict, a point India had been making relentlessly. Two, India seemed to have accepted at least implicitly the point of Japan (and others such as the EU) that there were implications of the Ukraine conflict for the broader Indo-Pacific region. This was perhaps necessary to get Japan on board and make it appreciate India's position. Indeed, the Japanese Press Secretary declared to the press on 20 March that 'Japan and India are on the same page on Ukraine'.[67]

Russia perhaps was the most critical for India, for reasons of military dependence etc., that have been mentioned before. The biggest favour India could have done Russia, was not to call it out for condemnation of its actions in Ukraine. What is more, Indian authorities steadfastly refrained from calling it an 'invasion', though it was precisely that. For these two reasons alone, Russians were obliged to India. That, however, did not prevent India from doing the following:

- Severe condemnation of the killing of civilians in Bucha and calling for an independent investigation;
- PM Modi telling off Putin that today's era was not one of war in September, when India found that its calls for cessation of hostilities were falling on deaf ears;
- PM making it clear that the 'nuclear option' was simply inconceivable and must not be an option for Russia; and
- Making it clear that the international order was anchored in the UN Charter, international law, sovereignty and territorial integrity of all states and there could be no exception to this.

In all of this, India maintained links with both Russian leader Putin and Ukraine's leader Zelensky. Not many countries pulled off this feat and credit must therefore go to Indian political leadership and its diplomacy for this.

As part of its G20 presidency, India launched an initiative of a summit of the global south to get views from something like 120 countries, which could then feed into the Delhi G20 Summit scheduled for September 2023. This was a diplomatic masterstroke and not just in the context of the G20 Summit. It may be recalled that when the Ukraine issue came up in the UNGA on 2 March 2022, UNGA adopted—by an overwhelming majority of 141 against 5—a resolution demanding that Russia immediately withdraw its forces and abide by international law.

India had abstained, even while most countries of the global South had voted in favour of the resolution. Yet, India had always stressed that the impact of the Russian war in Ukraine was brutally felt by the countries of the global South. By now launching an initiative with regard to the voice of the global South, India was making sure that its G20 presidency would focus on the disastrous effects of the war on poorer countries that had no role in causing the war. It was therefore an excellent move by India to connect with its 'natural constituency' so as to represent their priorities in the G20 Summit in September 2023. India, in all its statements on the Ukraine issue, had been focusing on how food security, energy security and humanitarian assistance to Ukraine of medicines and other relief material was vitally important in this conflict. It is good that India has found a way to channel this into the G20 discussions.

Commitment to Multilateralism and Principles: The Budapest Memorandum, a key instrument assuring Ukraine's sovereignty and territorial integrity, was agreed to in 1994, following lengthy and complicated negotiations involving then Russian President Boris Yeltsin, Ukrainian President Leonid Kuchma, US President Bill Clinton and British Prime Minister John Major. Under the terms of the memorandum, Ukraine agreed to relinquish its nuclear arsenal—the world's third largest, inherited from the erstwhile Soviet Union—and transfer all nuclear warheads to Russia for decommissioning. The Budapest Memorandum consists of a series of political assurances whereby the signatory states commit to respect the independence and sovereignty and the existing borders of Ukraine.

There was also a 1997 treaty between Russia and Ukraine. Under Article 2 of the treaty, which came into force in 1999, both sides agreed to respect their mutual territorial integrity and existing borders. From Kyiv's point of view, Russia grossly violated the treaty with the annexation of Crimea in 2014. When this treaty expired in 2019, Ukraine did not renew it because of what Russia did in Crimea. Additionally, another treaty was signed on 28 January 2003 between the Russian Federation and

Ukraine on the Russian-Ukrainian State Border, by then President Kuchma of Ukraine and President Putin of the Russian Federation. The treaty states that the Russian-Ukrainian state border will be the line and the vertical surface (a virtual vertical line that divides subsoil, waters, and airspace between two countries) following that line. The line and the vertical surface divide the state territories of the parties to the Treaty—from the point where the state borders of Ukraine, Russia, and Belarus meet, to a point located on the coast of the Taganrog Gulf. In addition to all of this, Crimea was also a member of the UN from 1945 onwards.

In the case of Crimea, Russia arguably had serious cause for concern. Its Sevastopol Naval Base was located in Crimea and could have faced a threat when the pro-Russia Ukrainian President, Viktor Yanukovych, was overthrown. The Russian invasion of parts of Ukraine in February 2022 was a completely different case. There can be little doubt that it was a blatant violation of the sovereignty and territorial integrity of Ukraine, an independent country recognized within its existing borders by not just the international community, but also by Russia as cited in the above agreements. True, Russia rescinded some of the agreements and Ukraine withdrew from at least one, but it still does not alter the fact that international law, the UN Charter and the territorial integrity and sovereignty of Ukraine was blatantly violated by Russia.

Right after the Russian invasion of February 2022, India stopped referring to 'legitimate security interests of all countries' in its statements and instead focused on violation of the UN Charter, international law etc. In the case of Russia's annexation of Crimea, India had fallen back on the expression 'legitimate security interests of all countries', but in the present case, India felt no need to say this at all. Instead, the focus was on how Russian actions were violative of the UN Charter, international law and the territorial integrity and sovereignty of Ukraine, though Indian statements named neither Russia nor Ukraine.

India's stand was based on the principle of the UN Charter, international law, sovereignty, and territorial integrity of states and this provided, in some ways, the perfect foil for our non-condemnation of Russia for its invasion of Ukraine.

Realpolitik and Material Gain: There is no question that, far from any material gain, the war in Ukraine has had a profoundly adverse impact on India's economic growth and its prospects. With around 500 million Indians living in poverty and the Covid pandemic having already taken its toll, the war in Ukraine could not have come at a worse time for India. As we noted earlier, India imports an overwhelming proportion of its crude oil, fertilizer and sunflower oil needs. These three items alone had the effect of pushing up our import bill substantially. This also contributed to global inflation, prompting Indian policymakers to raise interest rates in tandem with the rise in global rates. The net result for India has been higher inflation and lower economic growth. This is one of the main reasons why the Indian government has decided to extend the Pradhan Mantri Garib Kalyan Yojana for another year till the end of 2023. This programme comprised free rations of 5 kilograms of food grains and 1 kilogram of lentils for some 800 million people living in poverty.

Crude oil prices rose from $80 to $110 per barrel in the six months following the start Ukraine war in February 2022. Although Russian crude was available at a discount, India's oil import bill nevertheless rose 76 per cent in the first six months of FY2022/23 to $90.3 billion.

For fertilizers, the subsidy bill was expected to double according to the Fertilizer Association of India. While this is likely to moderate by 25 per cent in FY2024/25 on account of falling potash prices, the bill was still, on average, twice that of the last five fiscal years. While the government hiked petrol and diesel prices, it shied away from raising fertilizer prices and merely raised the subsidy, avoiding placing the burden on farmers. A rising import bill, coupled with supply-side disruptions, has meant that Indian consumer price inflation, which in the last fiscal year averaged between 4.5 and 5.5 per cent, is likely to be 5.2 per cent for the year ending March 2024, according to the Reserve Bank of India. The story is the same the world over, the only difference being that the pandemic-era stimulus in the Western economies also contributed to inflation. The result is that central banks the world over have had to hike rates to keep inflation in check and India's RBI has had to do the same. After a series of hikes, the repo rate in India stands at 6.25 per cent. With no social safety net at all for the poor, it is the free rations of food grains and lentils that act as a cushion against extreme poverty.

There are some silver linings though. Some reports indicate that export demand for Indian wheat, corn, and spices may have seen a significant rise after Russia invaded Ukraine. International trade may be shifting its sourcing to India since supplies from the two counties have come to a halt. Russia holds sway in the world metals supply. According to CRISIL Research, Russia and Europe together account for nearly 10 per cent of global primary aluminium supply. As far as the steel trade is concerned, Russia is the second-largest exporter with a 13 per cent share. As worsening tensions threaten supply, exporting countries including India may step in to plug any gap in steel or aluminium.

All things considered, the war in Ukraine has set India back in terms of its progress in accomplishing the Sustainable Development Goals in areas such as poverty abolition, zero hunger, health, education, decent work and gender equality. Goals for which the deadline was 2030 may have to be pushed back, because of the double whammy of first the Covid and now the war in Ukraine.

It is therefore clear that the war in Ukraine had caused material harm to India and the longer it lasts, the more harmful the effects will be for India.

We saw earlier that even the political parties in the Opposition had come around to appreciating the stand taken by India on the war in Ukraine. Among the intellectuals too, there was broad approval of the position taken by the Indian government. Thus, the widely respected former National Security Adviser, Ambassador Shivshankar Menon (who worked closely with the government of PM Manmohan Singh) stated in a TV interview with the anchor Karan Thapar in March 2022 that the Modi government had handled the Ukraine crisis 'very well', but added that in his view it should have called Russia's action an 'invasion'.[68] He suggested the Modi government should play an active role in finding a political solution acceptable to all sides.[69]

It is also fair to say that even among the general population, the government's stand on the war in Ukraine found acceptance and endorsement. A survey done by 'Local Circles' (described as a comprehensive social network) in March, just after the Russian invasion of Ukraine, gathered 29,000 responses from Indian citizens (62 per cent men and 38 per cent women) from 351 districts (India has 766 districts). It revealed that six in ten Indians, or 62 per cent of the country's citizens, supported India's decision of not voting on the resolution against Russia.[70] At the same time, one in two Indians also supported the sanctions placed on Russia and felt Russia should stop all violence in Ukraine and solve the problem through dialogue and peaceful negotiations.

It is hard to assess what the world thinks of India's stand on the war in Ukraine. There is a feeling in many quarters that as the world's largest democracy, India should have condemned Russia for its invasion of Ukraine. Perhaps that would have been the case in an ideal world. In the real world however, there are constraints. As we noted earlier India had more than its share of constraints in this case, for it to take a purely moral view of things. The best that can be said of the international community is that while not everyone may have appreciated India's stand, there was certainly great understanding of why India did what it did at the UN. The best article that one can cite in this regard is the one by Roger Cohen in *New York Times*.[71] He argues that the Russian invasion of Ukraine, compounding the effects of the pandemic, had contributed to the ascent of a giant that defies easy alignment and adds that India could be the decisive force in a changing global system. He quotes the cerebral Indian EAM S. Jaishankar as saying that the world order, which is still very deeply Western, is being hurried out of existence by the impact of the war in Ukraine, to be replaced by a world of 'multi-alignment', where countries will choose their own particular policies, preferences and interests.[72]And there is no better way of saying what India has practiced since the war in Ukraine in February 2022.

Cohen argues cogently that India has rejected American and European pressure at the UN to condemn the Russian invasion, turned Moscow into its largest oil supplier and dismissed the perceived hypocrisy of the West. Far from being apologetic, its tone has been unabashed and its self-interest broadly naked.[73] As the EAM S. Jaishankar said:

> Since February, Europe has imported six times the fossil fuel energy from Russia that India has done. So, if a $60,000 per capita society feels it needs to look after itself and I accept that as legitimate, they should not expect a $2000 per capita society to take a hit.[74]

In sum, India appears to have taken a calculated bet that its decision to abstain at the UN and not to condemn Russia, may not be appreciated by all but will be understood by its close friends and strategic partners. Certainly, that bet seems to have paid off.

Interestingly, India has assumed the rotating presidency of the G20 from December 2022 for a period of one year. Some in India are urging the PM and his team to see whether they can make a difference to the raging conflict in Ukraine. This view has gained prominence especially after the role played by India and its PM in forging a consensus at the G20 summit meeting in Bali in November 2022. The US Deputy National Security Adviser Jonathan Finer spoke about this when he lauded the role played by PM Modi at the G20 summit meeting in Bali by helping the Heads of State arrive at a consensus around the Joint Statement that was issued.[75] It is well known that there were serious differences between the major G20 delegations about the war in Ukraine. In the event, the consensus paragraph relating to Ukraine from the G20 Bali Leaders' Declaration reads thus:

> This year, we have also witnessed the war in Ukraine further adversely impact the global economy. There was a discussion on the issue. We reiterated our national positions as expressed in other fora, including the UN Security Council and the UN General Assembly, which, in Resolution No. ES-11/1 dated 2 March 2022, as adopted by majority vote (141 votes for, 5 against, 35 abstentions, 12 absent) deplores in the strongest terms the aggression by the Russian Federation against Ukraine and demands its complete and unconditional withdrawal from the territory of Ukraine. Most members strongly condemned the war in Ukraine and stressed it is causing immense human suffering and exacerbating existing fragilities in the global economy—constraining growth, increasing inflation, disrupting supply chains, heightening energy and food insecurity, and elevating financial stability

risks. There were other views and different assessments of the situation and sanctions. Recognizing that the G20 is not the forum to resolve security issues, we acknowledge that security issues can have significant consequences for the global economy. It is essential to uphold international law and the multilateral system that safeguards peace and stability. This includes defending all the Purposes and Principles enshrined in the Charter of the United Nations and adhering to international humanitarian law, including the protection of civilians and infrastructure in armed conflicts. The use or threat of use of nuclear weapons is inadmissible. The peaceful resolution of conflicts, efforts to address crises, as well as diplomacy and dialogue, are vital. Today's era must not be of war.[76]

The above statement is remarkable, given the presence of Russia in the G20 grouping and its willingness to go along with the final Leaders' Declaration above. This is all the more significant since there is another paragraph (33) in the same declaration, where the leaders reiterate their commitment to step up efforts to implement the Common Framework for Debt Treatment beyond the Debt Service Suspension Initiative (DSSI) in a predictable, timely, orderly, and coordinated manner. But there it is noted (as a footnote) that one member (China) had divergent views on debt issues and emphasized the importance of debt treatment by multilateral creditors. It would have therefore been perfectly possible to have a paragraph on Ukraine and then have a footnote saying that one member (in this case Russia) had divergent views in the matter. The fact that this did not happen is attributed to the role played by India at the summit meeting, to which the US Deputy NSA made a reference earlier.

The reference to the UNGA resolution—which was passed overwhelmingly and deplored in the strongest terms the aggression by Russia against Ukraine, demanding its unconditional withdrawal from the territory of Ukraine—is remarkable, considering Russia is part of the G20, and given the fact that both China and India had abstained on this UN resolution. For good measure, the G20 Leaders' Declaration also makes references to UN Charter, the inadmissibility of the use or threat to use nuclear weapons, emphasis on diplomacy and dialogue, and finally, PM Modi's own words: 'Today's era must not be of war.' All this bears the imprint of Indian negotiators.

Sir Robin Niblett, a Distinguished Fellow of the Europe programme at Chatham House, wrote an interesting comment, noting that G20 members such as Argentina, Brazil, India, Indonesia, Mexico, Saudi Arabia, South Africa and Turkey played an important role in Bali.[77] Instead of sitting on the fence, they actually backed those who wanted the use of the UN language: territorial integrity and sovereignty. He singles out India by saying, 'But it was Modi's phrase "today's era must not be of war" (which he had used earlier to admonish Putin) that concluded the Bali summit's statement on Ukraine'.[78]

The big question is what India, with its G20 presidency, can do to make a difference to the ongoing conflict in Ukraine. At the time of writing, the situation on the ground in Ukraine is dire. The Western countries, led by the US, have crossed the Rubicon by deciding to supply battle tanks to Ukraine. The thinking seems to be that tanks are necessary for two reasons: to pre-empt a massive Russian operation in the Spring and to help Ukraine retake territory from Russia. There is a widely held view among NATO allies that Russia must be defeated on the battlefield so that it can then be dragged to the negotiating table. Long-range missiles and combat aircraft are not on the cards yet, but if that were to happen, the war will be taken to a whole new level. Russia cannot be expected to take all this lying down. Indeed, the Deputy Chairman of Russia's

National Security Council former President, Medvedev, stated bluntly on 19 January 2023, that the defeat of a nuclear power in a conventional war may trigger a nuclear war.[79] All of this indicates that the war has only reached a temporary stalemate and is all set to rage, come spring time. Latest reports indicate that neither side is making significant gains.

Given this, and considering that the G20 is not the forum to resolve security issues, what can India possibly bring to the table? It would not be wise to raise expectations since India's own agency in the matter is neither vast nor unlimited. The maximum that can be attempted is perhaps a ceasefire for a limited duration. What the Bali Leaders' Declaration has done though, is provide a template for India to follow.

Beyond that, India has its own border problems with China to contend with. The first step for India would be to ensure the presence of all leaders at the G20 summit in September 2023 in Delhi. Second, it will have to see if bilateral meetings can take place between Biden and Putin, Biden and Xi, not to mention a meeting between Modi and Xi. So there are a lot of imponderables between now and September and it would be foolhardy to guess where the world will be at that time.

Given below is a summary of India's stand on the war in Ukraine, using the Integrated Assessment Framework

INDIA'S STAND ON THE WAR IN UKRAINE

Gandhi Litmus Test: Oil and fertilizer supplies ensured from all sources. Food grains and lentils were distributed to the poor.

Policy Space: Preserved defence ties with Russia while trying to reduce dependence on it through diversification of imports.

Domestic Politics: Quick and effective evacuation of Indian citizens silenced critics. Non-condemnation of Russia was in line with domestic political and public opinion.

Geopolitical Imperatives: Relations with the US intact despite causing annoyance. Gained the understanding, if not appreciation, of strategic partners like Japan, EU, Australia and others.

Commitment to Multilateralism and Principles: India's quick abandonment of the expression of legitimate security interests and stressing UN Charter, Int Law, territorial integrity and sovereignty of all states without exception.

Realpolitik and Material Gain: Despite buying large quantities of discounted Russian oil, no significant material gain to the Indian economy, it took a big hit like many other emerging economies. Realpolitik played a role in the non-condemnation of Russia because of defence dependence.

5

From a Balancing Power to a Leading Power?

It may therefore be seen that there is a method to India's negotiating strategy. Several commentators have observed that India should improve its method and become a proper stakeholder in international negotiations. The point to be noted is that the method is not at fault here. So, if there is to be a change in India's negotiating method, then, there must be a change in the fundamental factors undergirding India's national interests. In this concluding chapter, we will look at how this might happen.

5.1 The Poverty Veto

The very first criterion in our framework, namely, the Gandhi Litmus Test is very hard for any elected government in India to ignore. After all, 500 million citizens living in poverty is not a trifling matter. I had earlier coined the expression 'poverty veto' to explain how this factor constrains India's negotiating space. Whether it is the

WTO negotiations, the climate negotiations or even the discussions surrounding the war in Ukraine, it is hard for any government in India to get around this issue. The only way, then, to mitigate the poverty veto in the future is for India to bring down this figure of 500 million to something like 100 to 150 million. That is a manageable figure for any government in India and would bestow on it enough margin for manoeuvre in international negotiations.

There is no magic wand to achieve this except for the Indian economy to grow to something in the range of $10 trillion and for the growth to be both inclusive and resilient. Two specific challenges must be overcome by India in this regard. First, the share of manufacturing in India's GDP must hit at least 25 per cent, while at present it hovers around the 15 per cent mark. It is only manufacturing that can absorb the massive labour force that is currently dependent on agriculture, and which must be relocated as quickly as possible. Second, as a corollary, agriculture in India must be reformed, and reformed expeditiously. It was unfortunate that the eminently sensible farm bills proposed by the government in 2020 had to be withdrawn in 2021 in the face of unprecedented protests. The fact that there were protests does not make the farm bills any less relevant; nor did the fact that the protests mainly happened in Punjab and Haryana make it representative of the whole country. But it raises a larger issue: are Indians reformers by compulsion rather than by conviction?

If every reform, like the GST reform, is going to be part of partisan politics and thus take years to carry out, it is the country that ends up being a loser. This issue is dealt with later under the rubric 'domestic politics' but for now, India has to find a way to reform, to increase the share of manufacturing to something like 25 per cent of GDP and last but not least, to grow to a $10 trillion economy so that the pie is large enough for the figure of 500 million to be drastically reduced so that the poverty veto is rendered less potent than it is at present. Until then, it would be unconscionable for India to ignore this aspect in any international negotiations.

5.2 Too Much Policy Space?

The issue of policy space is more complex to resolve. In any negotiation, India seeks to preserve the maximum policy space for itself so that if (and this is a big 'if') the times are bad and crises erupt, the government can resort to emergency measures without falling foul of its international obligations flowing out of treaties. The key questions to ask in this regard are: one, is it possible that India acquires more policy space than is necessary in international negotiations? Two, is India putting to effective use the negotiating space that was acquired in past negotiations? It is hard to come up with definitive answers, but going by past track record it is likely that India is inclined to acquire more policy space than is absolutely necessary and there is enough evidence to suggest that the policy space that was painstakingly acquired in international negotiations has not been put to effective use by Indian stakeholders.

The best example of more policy space than necessary is the case of plurilateral negotiations on investment facilitation at the WTO, which India has steadfastly refused to be part of. The kind of agreement being negotiated at the WTO is something India could shape and eventually live with. Instead, we have taken the position that we will simply not accept an international investment agreement since it constrains us. But that has not prevented us from entering into bilateral investment negotiations of a far-reaching nature with the EU. This is particularly so at a time when India is seeking massive investment for its 'Make in India' programmes.

The second example of how we do not effectively use the policy space acquired by our negotiators comes from the sector of textiles and clothing in the WTO. In effect, it was only India, backed by Pakistan, that pushed for a 'quota-less' world in textiles and clothing in the Uruguay Round trade negotiations by arguing that this sector must be fully integrated into the GATT system and free trade must reign supreme. Having achieved this negotiating objective at great cost (by accepting in return onerous IPR obligations), India had a full ten-year-long transition period to put its house in order so that our products in textiles and clothing can be competitive in the global market. Alas, it is now accepted that this time was not put to good use by successive governments, for instance, by failing to reform the sector. The result is that today India finds it hard to compete with Vietnam, Sri Lanka and Bangladesh in textiles and clothing. This is clearly a case of policy space obtained at great cost by our negotiators not being put to effective use by our stakeholders, whether the government or indeed the private sector.

5.2.1 The Politics behind Domestic Politics

The fact that India is a rough-and-tumble democracy has meant that the executive at any given point can freely enter into international agreements/treaties as a consequence of the international negotiations without prior permission from the Parliament. However, it has to seek the ex post facto endorsement of the Parliament if the agreement has to be implemented and/or if any law has to be amended in Parliament. Either way, the track record of opposition parties, regardless of which party it is, is not stellar in this regard. It would seem as though the job of the opposition party in India is to oppose at all costs, without considering whether it is in the national interest or not.

The conclusion of the Uruguay Round of trade negotiations is a case in point. It led to the establishment of the WTO, and it was inconceivable that India would stay out of the newly formed international organization. The ruling party knew this, as did the

Opposition. Despite that, the Opposition did not help matters by attacking the government, knowing full well the latter was doing the best it could. Similarly, when the government was doing its utmost to evacuate the students from Ukraine, all the Opposition did was criticize the government for its delay in evacuating the students. This was bizarre because more powerful countries like China were unable to carry out the evacuation of their nationals as expeditiously as we did. The same thing happened with climate change negotiations at various points in time, when the Opposition accused the government of giving up on Common But Differentiated Responsibilities when India was doing its best as part of a coalition with like-minded countries or under the BASIC (Brazil, South Africa, India and China) alliance to defend its interests.

Perhaps the time has come for a code of conduct agreed upon amongst all political parties that when it comes to national interest in a small number of previously identified areas, there cannot be needless politicization. Take the case of agriculture reforms. Every political party in India has admitted the need for it and most of them have it as part of their election manifesto. Why then oppose reforms when they are proposed by another party in power? It should not be beyond the genius of Indian democracy to find a permanent solution to this perennial problem of politicizing every issue under the sun. This can have a bearing on India's negotiating strategy and the method adopted by it.

I remember interacting with the late Commerce Minister Murasoli Maran at the Doha WTO Ministerial Conference and it is fair to say that he was acutely conscious of how his negotiating performance would be perceived and assessed by the Opposition in Parliament. This did play a role in the negotiating strategies adopted by him at the WTO Doha Ministerial Conference, particularly in the way we approached the so-called 'Singapore Issues'. It is time for India to put an end to the needless politicization and devise a code of conduct to be followed by all political parties so that in the matter of international negotiations concerning matters of national interest, the country will be united behind its negotiators.

5.3 The Geopolitics of Multi-Alignment

India's negotiating method, like that of most other powers, is based on threat perceptions and national security assessments. One central feature of India's national security assessment is a wide consensus that China today is the main security challenge confronting India. Assuming this is true, the other fact acknowledged by most serious observers is that the power differential between India and China is so tilted in favour of the latter that India is left with no choice but to resort to external balancing. And it is now evident that India's partners of choice in this regard are the US, Japan and the West, for a variety of reasons that are beyond the scope of this book.

This too affects India's negotiating stand on a range of subjects. For instance, in the Uruguay Round of trade negotiations, it was clear that the US did exert pressure on India when it came to IPRs. In climate change negotiations, it is true that American negotiators did nudge us on things like coal, CBDR and adaptation. On the war in Ukraine, we saw that the US and EU would have very much liked India to condemn Russia for the latter's invasion of Ukraine, something India successfully resisted.

India may, of course, be expected to resort to external balancing through a policy of multi-alignment, if it is not able to deal with its security threats all by itself. The fact that India is not a treaty ally of any major power makes this even more critical. The policy of multi-alignment implies that India will have to deal with various like-minded powers, depending on the subject matter of negotiations. In the case of the war in Ukraine, not only did India have to deal with the US, but also had to convince its Quad partners, i.e. Japan and Australia, about the stand it took. India also has a wide-ranging partnership with the EU with big stakes, and wrinkles that appeared in the relationship in the context of Ukraine had to be ironed out. In other words, India has managed to do precisely what the mantra prescribed by EAM S. Jaishankar in his book *The India Way*: 'This is a time to *engage America*, manage China, cultivate Europe, reassure Russia, bring Japan into play.' India has successfully managed to do all of this in the case of the complex war in Ukraine.

By and large, there is grudging appreciation and unanimous understanding of India's stand on the war in Ukraine. This includes not just our strategic partners like the US, Japan, etc., but also countries of the ASEAN region and in India's neighbourhood. Going forward, India needs to take a strategic view of where this conflict is heading and whether there may be episodes and events when adjustments may need to be made to our stand in this conflict. This will come into sharp focus if the war drags on further and/or intensifies in a way not foreseeable. Until then, India could play a behind-the-scenes role in nudging the two adversaries towards a pause in the war, or better still, towards a ceasefire. India's agency in this regard is limited, but there is no harm in trying. The prognosis at present is dire, with all indications that it will likely be a 'frozen conflict' of indefinite duration. India's main objective will be to ensure that the negative repercussions of the war in Ukraine are alleviated both for itself and for the countries of the global south. India's presidency of the G20 will be all about building guardrails, which can protect poorer countries from the negative consequences of the war in Ukraine.

5.4 Commitment to Multilateralism and Principles

As we saw throughout this book, India had something akin to an unwavering commitment to multilateralism in general and the UN in particular. That plus the idealism that the first PM, Jawaharlal Nehru, harboured resulted in the Kashmir issue being taken to the UN. The UN did not treat the Kashmir issue fairly, to put it very mildly. Despite this initial setback, India persisted with its commitment to the UN in terms of contribution to peacekeeping forces, paying its dues unfailingly on time and supporting the UN agencies in their work. India has also actively participated in the substantive work of the committees and other organs of the UN. Despite all of this, India's legitimate aspiration to be a permanent member of the UNSC has hit a brick wall. The reasons for this are manifold and complex.

India's views were best put by its EAM S. Jaishankar, who, while speaking at the Australian think-tank Lowy Institute in October 2022, stated bluntly that while the UNSC reforms were a hard nut to crack, hard nuts can be cracked. He went on to caution that the world body runs the risk of becoming irrelevant without much-delayed reforms.[1] He also noted that US President Joe Biden had explicitly recognized the need for UN reform in an address in September 2022 at UNGA, where he had said: 'The time has come for the UN to be more inclusive so that it can better respond to the needs of today's world. The US is committed to this vital work'.[2] Despite this commitment by the US, a consensus on the issue is elusive both in the UNSC and in the UNGA. While a two-thirds vote in the General Assembly may be possible, a consensus in the UNSC appears difficult, with China all set to block it. It will be interesting to see what India does with the G20 presidency in this area. After all, reformed multilateralism fit for the twenty-first century is one of India's priorities.

It is this disillusionment with the UN system and multilateralism that has prompted India to now achieve its strategic objectives through a number of plurilateral groupings or what are now being called 'mini-laterals'. Because India is deprived of the possibility of acting in unison at the UNSC, it has had no choice but to work in tandem with major powers on what can be described as 'issue-based multi-alignment'. There are also many in India who believe that the G20 is certainly more representative of contemporary power realities than the UNSC. This may also explain the euphoria surrounding the presidency of the G20 in India.

What about India's commitment to principles when it comes to negotiations and policy positions? Well, in the multilateral trading system embodied first by GATT and then subsequently by the WTO, India often took principled positions when it came to Special and Differential Treatment, balanced interpretation of the Trade Related Intellectual Property Rights Agreement, as well as issues like public stockholding for food security purposes in agriculture. Indeed, India's opposition to the ongoing plurilateral negotiations at the WTO itself is based on a principled position that WTO should only negotiate multilateral agreements. Similarly, in climate negotiations, India argued steadfastly in favour of CBDR and in favour of climate finance obligations by developed countries towards developing and least-developed countries. And as we saw in the case of the war in Ukraine, India emphasized right from the beginning the adherence by all countries to the UN Charter, international law and the territorial integrity and sovereignty of all states.

It is possible to argue that India failed to condemn Russia for its invasion of Ukraine and was therefore acting against the principle enshrined in the UN Charter. But as we saw earlier, India did not really condone Russian actions in Ukraine. It is true that realpolitik prevented India from condemning Russia by name, although it did not hesitate in condemning the actions when they led to either civilian killings in Bucha or when the threat to use nuclear weapons was held out by Russia. Above all, India did state categorically in every single statement it made on the subject that the global order is based on international law, the UN Charter and respect for territorial integrity and sovereignty of all States and that these principles must be upheld without exception.

5.5 Realpolitik and Material Gain

All countries negotiate based on realpolitik and with a view to gaining material advantage. India is no exception to this rule. In the earliest period of the GATT India had negotiated hard for a waiver for the so-called Generalized System of Preferences from Article I relating to the MFN Clause. GSP entailed tariff concessions for beneficiaries and therefore there was material gain, without doubt. Similarly, India's position in the Uruguay Round on textiles and clothing aimed at fully integrating this sector into GATT rules, was also motivated by India's desire to export more of its products to the developed markets of the US and the EU. Again, at the Doha WTO Ministerial meeting, where India fought hard for the declaration on TRIPS and Public Health, it was also to help its generic pharmaceutical industry, among other things.

In climate negotiations, India has always pushed for climate finance not just for itself but also for its developing-country brethren and least-developed country partners. This was, of course, material gain at one level, but it was also based on the moralistic principle that developed countries owed it to developing and least-developed countries since there was the issue of historic responsibility for GHG emissions and the issue of climate justice. So, climate finance was very much a central pillar of India's negotiating position. It is another matter that India is yet to see the fruits of its labour!

As for the war in Ukraine, as noted earlier, it has really had a terribly negative impact on India's economy and pushed more people into poverty because of the three Fs, as it were: Food, Fuel and Fertilizer. India buying up discounted Russian oil hardly made up for the losses suffered across the board as a result of the war in Ukraine.

What we have seen in this book is that India's negotiating positions and methods are based on concrete, identifiable benchmarks rooted in the national circumstances and interests of the country. The negotiating method can change only when the basic circumstances and interests of India change. For that to happen, India needs to become a much bigger economy than it is at present. This is a necessary condition and a prerequisite for India's negotiating stand: to become confident and forward-looking. Internal cohesion and a political consensus on carrying out difficult reforms are the next two requirements. The political parties have less than a stellar record in this regard and must pull themselves up to act in the national interest. It cannot always be about politics.

If India can become, say, a $10 trillion economy, then the geopolitical considerations will automatically become more favourable, since the need for external balancing will diminish accordingly. Additionally, the number of people living in poverty must be brought down significantly and inequalities in income and wealth need to be tackled. Last but not least, India must stay faithful to some perennial principles in its foreign policy. Principles laid down in the UN Charter; a rules-based order, especially in the Indo-Pacific; opposition to unilateral measures by powers to change the status quo on land or maritime borders; and finally, respect for the territorial integrity and sovereignty of states, without any exception—are all principles that must continue to guide India in its negotiations with the world.

India's successful evolution as a country is not just important to itself but also to the world. As we saw in the chapter on climate change, whether or not India follows a low-carbon pathway to development will fundamentally determine whether the world's battle against climate change is successful or not. In a similar vein, if India succeeds in transforming itself into a prosperous country in the foreseeable future, then it will have demonstrated two things to the world. First, it would prove that it is perfectly possible for a country to be a democracy and achieve economic prosperity. Other countries have no doubt achieved this feat earlier, but the sheer size and diversity of India would make this achievement unique, and there will be obvious comparisons made with China in this context. Second, the size of India would also mean that it may be able to bring about big changes to the global economy.

A research report by Morgan Stanley in November 2022 titled 'India's Impending Boom' boldly predicts that India is on track to become the world's third-largest economy by 2027, surpassing Japan and Germany.[3] The report also expects India to become a $7.5 trillion economy by 2031, in addition to having the third largest stock market by then. If this promise is kept, then India's method of negotiating in international fora will also undergo a paradigm shift. India can then achieve its strategic objective of transitioning from a balancing power to a leading power.

Epilogue

A s this book was going to press, India held a hugely successful G20 summit in New Delhi on 9 and 10 September 2023, which concluded with a Leaders' Declaration[1] agreed to by all the G20 members. This consensus was neither expected nor easy for a variety of reasons. One, the world is a much more fragmented place than it was before. Two, the language reflecting the war in Ukraine had become a bone of contention among the G7/Western countries on the one hand and Russia/China on the other. The language of the Bali G20 Leaders' Declaration of 2022 was no longer acceptable to either Russia or China. Lastly, both China and Russia were without their paramount leaders, namely President Xi Jinping and President Vladimir Putin, both of whom decided to give the New Delhi G20 summit a miss for different reasons.

At the event India pulled off a miracle, with Prime Minister Narendra Modi announcing that a consensus had been reached on the Leaders' Declaration well before the conclusion of the summit. This was met with disbelief by people outside the conference venue. During the entire Indian presidency lasting nearly a year, there was violent disagreement among the G20 members on the language pertaining to Ukraine. So how did India pull it off?

For one thing, India used its influence with the G7/Western countries to convince them that the Bali G20 Leaders' Declaration, which strongly condemned Russian aggression in Ukraine, would simply not fly this time around. Secondly, Indian diplomats, who are nothing if not brilliant wordsmiths, eventually came up with a language that allowed all sides, namely, G7, Russia and the Global South, to claim that their concerns have been met. In so doing, India acted as an honest broker between the G7/Western countries and Russia/China. India played a deft hand and its foreign policy based on multi-alignment came in handy. The meetings held by Prime Minister Modi with US President Joe Biden before the summit commenced, and his telephonic conversation with Russian President Putin were crucial in this regard.

The Ukraine issue was also dealt with satisfactorily in the New Delhi Leaders' Declaration because the G7/Western countries knew that if they did not show flexibility, the G20 as a forum might have suffered irreparable damage. Therefore, they took a political decision to preserve the G20 as a premier forum for global economic cooperation, fearing that, otherwise, rival forums such as BRICS would steal a march. China, too, played a part as the dragon in the room. China's President Xi Jinping is said to prefer forums such as the BRICS and Shanghai Cooperation Organisation (SCO), where he can call the shots. The G7/Western countries did not want to hand China an advantage. Finally, the G7/Western countries also felt it necessary to court the Global South in the G20, aware that it was gaining prominence.

India, early on in its G20 presidency, had set itself a goal—to try and be the voice of the Global South. In January, soon after it assumed the G20 presidency, it held a virtual summit of some

125 countries, most of whom belonged to the Global South. It sought their inputs, interests and concerns, so that these could be reflected in the final Leaders' Declaration. All through its presidency, India made every effort to carry out this mandate, be it Sustainable Development Goals (SDGs), climate change or debt. The G20 New Delhi Leaders' Declaration, therefore, fully reflects the concerns of the Global South.

The tremendously successful hosting of the G20 summit by India is a pointer to the following:

(1) India showcased itself in all its glory and diversity by making the G20 'people-centric' and taking it to the far corners of this vast land.

(2) India succeeded in being the voice of the Global South. Facilitating the admission of the African Union as a member of the G20 by India was a masterstroke in this regard.

(3) India also succeeded in being an honest broker between the G7/ Western countries on the one hand and Russia/China on the other, especially on issues such as the war in Ukraine.

(4) India, perhaps for the first time, tried to be a rule-shaper rather than a rule-taker. This was evident in areas such as digital public infrastructure, Global Biofuel Alliance, Green Hydrogen Innovation Centre and Deccan High-Level Principles on Food Security and Nutrition, to name a few.

(5) On the sidelines of the summit, India launched initiatives such as the IMEC (India-Middle East-Europe-Economic Corridor), by far the most ambitious global infrastructure project undertaken by India involving the US, the EU, France, Germany, Italy, the UAE and Saudi Arabia.

(6) It is worth noting that India's own stock has been on the rise. This made it possible for it to be an able arbiter on some contentious issues at the G20.

It is fair to conclude that India's geopolitical clout may increase after the successful hosting of the G20 summit. The tell-tale signs are there for all to see. India's transition from a balancing power to a leading power may well be under way.[2]

Acknowledgements

The idea of writing a book on the method employed by India to negotiate with the world has always fascinated me. As someone who has represented India at many multilateral fora in an Indian Foreign Service (IFS) career spanning thirty-six years, it was always flattering to receive compliments about the quality of India's diplomats. Invariably, I was told that Indian negotiators were among the best in the business. And yet, several of my interlocutors would ask in the same breath why India was such a difficult customer when it came to international negotiations. Indeed, it was hard to escape the view held by our negotiating partners that India was somehow more of a visceral naysayer than a key stakeholder in international parleys.

This book, then, is a sincere attempt to set the record straight.

At one level, India is not very different from other countries since it seeks to protect where necessary and advance where possible, what it perceives as its vital national interests. That said, there are several unique aspects to India and the way it approaches negotiations with the world. This book dwells on some of those fundamental factors that undergird India's negotiating approach. It should also be clear to the average reader that India's negotiating positions are not static and have evolved over time. The book traces this evolution, highlighting that some of it is much more marked than others.

It is the central contention of this book that India has certainly moved, slowly but surely, from being a passive onlooker to becoming a strategic partner for the world in some key negotiations. More broadly, this reflects India's growing political, economic, and strategic clout in the world today. This transformation has only just begun. It is only when this transformation is fuller and more substantial that India will be able to fulfil its manifest destiny of becoming a leading power capable of shaping global rules through negotiations.

I owe a debt of gratitude to my employers, O.P. Jindal Global University, for having encouraged me in every possible way to write this book. I must also thank my publishers HarperCollins India, in particular its associate publisher, Ms Swati Chopra, who made valuable suggestions with regard to the book's content.

Notes

Scan this QR code to access the detailed notes

Index

About the Author

Ambassador **Dr Mohan Kumar** is Dean, Strategic and International Initiatives, as well as Professor of Diplomatic Practice at O.P. Jindal Global University, Sonipat, India.

Ambassador Kumar received his bachelor's degree in business administration (BBA) from the University of Madurai (India) and his master's degree in business administration (MBA) from the Faculty of Management Studies, University of Delhi, India. He then went on to complete his doctorate (PhD) from the prestigious institution, Sciences Po, in Paris, France.

Ambassador Kumar was a member of the Indian Foreign Service for thirty-six years until he retired in July 2017 as India's Ambassador to France, based in Paris.

Kumar cut his diplomatic teeth in 1982 in Geneva at the then United Nations Human Rights Commission. Thus began Kumar's journey in diplomatic negotiations, which was to take him back to Geneva again and again in the Nineties. His first close involvement with the General Agreement on Tariffs and Trade (GATT) was in

1992 and continued until the establishment of the World Trade Organization (WTO) in 1995. From 1995 to 2005, he was again associated with the WTO in one way or another. Finally, as India's Ambassador to France, Kumar was actively associated with the climate change negotiations that culminated in the Paris Accords of 2015.

Ambassador Kumar is married with two grown children. He is immensely fond of travel, reading and writing. He follows cricket and tennis and is an avowed music buff.

HarperCollins *Publishers* India

At HarperCollins India, we believe in telling the best stories and finding the widest readership for our books in every format possible. We started publishing in 1992; a great deal has changed since then, but what has remained constant is the passion with which our authors write their books, the love with which readers receive them, and the sheer joy and excitement that we as publishers feel in being a part of the publishing process.

Over the years, we've had the pleasure of publishing some of the finest writing from the subcontinent and around the world, including several award-winning titles and some of the biggest bestsellers in India's publishing history. But nothing has meant more to us than the fact that millions of people have read the books we published, and that somewhere, a book of ours might have made a difference.

As we look to the future, we go back to that one word— a word which has been a driving force for us all these years.

Read.

Harper
Collins

HARPER
PERENNIAL

HARPER
BUSINESS

HARPER
BLACK

हार्पर
हिन्दी

HarperCollins
Children'sBooks

HARPER
DESIGN

HARPER
VANTAGE

Harper
Sport